Data Analytics for Business

T0179044

Data analytics underpin our modern data-driven economy. This textbook explains the relevance of data analytics at the firm and industry levels, tracing the evolution and key components of the field, and showing how data analytics insights can be leveraged for business results.

The first section of the text covers key topics such as data analytics tools, data mining, business intelligence, customer relationship management, and cybersecurity. The chapters then take an industry focus, exploring how data analytics can be used in particular settings to strengthen business decision-making. A range of sectors are examined, including financial services, accounting, marketing, sport, health care, retail, transport, and education. With industry case studies, clear definitions of terminology, and no background knowledge required, this text supports students in gaining a solid understanding of data analytics and its practical applications. PowerPoint slides, a test bank of questions, and an instructor manual are also provided as online supplements.

This will be a valuable text for undergraduate level courses in data analytics, data mining, business intelligence, and related areas.

Fenio Annansingh is currently an Associate Professor at York College, City University of New York, where she teaches Information Systems, Project and Operations Management classes. Her main area of research is Information Systems in two key areas, namely Information Management and Knowledge Management. Her research interest includes knowledge leakage, Information System Risk Management, Smart and Mobile technologies, and Cybersecurity education organisations. Dr. Annansingh has several publications and professional papers with several affiliates.

Joseph Bon Sesay is a Certified Public Accountant (CPA) and a Chartered Global Management Accountant (CGMA). He teaches at York College, City University of New York (CUNY), and has over 20 years of experience in senior and management positions with Multinational Corporations such as Viacom/CBS, Interpublic Group (IPG)/Mediabrands, and Publicis/Mediavest Worldwide. Dr. Sesay holds a doctorate and an MBA in Finance from Pace University, New York City, New York, and Master of Liberal Arts in Extension Studies in Government from Harvard University, Cambridge, Massachusetts.

Data Analytics for Business

Foundations and Industry Applications

Fenio Annansingh and
Joseph Bon Sesay

Routledge
Taylor & Francis Group

LONDON AND NEW YORK

Cover image: © shulz / Getty Images

First published 2022
by Routledge
4 Park Square, Milton Park, Abingdon, Oxon OX14 4RN

and by Routledge
605 Third Avenue, New York, NY 10158

Routledge is an imprint of the Taylor & Francis Group, an informa business

© 2022 Fenio Annansingh and Joseph Bon Sesay

All rights reserved. No part of this book may be reprinted or
reproduced or utilised in any form or by any electronic, mechanical,
or other means, now known or hereafter invented, including
photocopying and recording, or in any information storage or
retrieval system, without permission in writing from the publishers.

Trademark notice: Product or corporate names may be trademarks
or registered trademarks, and are used only for identification and
explanation without intent to infringe.

British Library Cataloguing-in-Publication Data
A catalogue record for this book is available from the British Library

Library of Congress Cataloging-in-Publication Data
A catalog record has been requested for this book

ISBN: 978-0-367-65421-4 (hbk)
ISBN: 978-0-367-65419-1 (pbk)
ISBN: 978-1-003-12935-6 (ebk)

DOI: 10.4324/9781003129356

Typeset in Bembo
by codeMantra

Access the Support Material: www.routledge.com/9780367654191

Contents

Figures

Tables

Acknowledgements

Fenio Annansingh Jamieson

I want to thank my longsuffering husband, Joshua, whose patience and support of my dreams never cease to amaze me. Taslim Yakub, for his creativity and support during this process.

Joseph Sesay

I want to thank my wife, Zina, and my daughters, Josephine and Alice, for the love, understanding, and encouragement I received from them during the writing process.

1 History and Evolution of Data Analytics

Data analytics is statistically based. However, traditionally this was limited to the kinds of data available and solutions accessible to process it. This chapter introduces data analytics, history, and its development. Consequently, the types of roles for people working with data became highly specialised. However, the catalysts for change in this area started in the late 1960s, with the increased use of computers for decision support. As a result, data analytics has evolved significantly, as data is everywhere and exists in many forms. Since business, analytics, and technology have improved exponentially and will likely continue in this trajectory, it is crucial to track the development and growth of technology and just how meaningful it has been for business growth over time.

LEARNING OBJECTIVES:

At the end of this chapter, you should be able to:

- Understand the history and evolution of data analytics
- Identify the difference between data, information, knowledge, intelligence, and wisdom
- Define the different types of knowledge
- Identify the different categories of data
- Explain data science and its components
- Discuss the phases of data science

History and Evolution of Data Analytics

Data analytics emerged as a separate discipline from statistics in the 1950s with analytics 1.0. Associated with this period are the developing tools capable of capturing data and identifying patterns and trends faster than the human mind. Internal data sources were small and structured. Consequently, batch-processing operations took months and few detailed reports. The focus then was on data collection and preparation rather than data analysis. At this

DOI: 10.4324/9781003129356-1

time, most companies started experiencing a steady increase in their data volumes, leading to the growth in demand for software that could assist with data analysis.

In the mid-2000s, analytics 2.0 appeared, which created a difference in quality and quantity of data. The increasing popularity of social networking sites like Facebook and Google initiated discovering, collecting, and analysing new information. Companies' internal operations generated data from various sources such as the Internet, projects, and public data. The advancement and consideration of data quality led to the change to analytics 2.0. With analytics 2.0 came the increased ability of companies to analyse the data and gain greater insight into business processes and increase profit margins. This era saw the development of novel processing structures that include the use of software for productivity tracking such as No-SQL and Hadoop.

The third period of data analytics was from 2010, which led to the creation of analytics 3.0. Here, customers received a personalised user experience. The advent of new disciplines such as prescriptive and predictive analytics complements using descriptive-analytical, which existed in analytics 2.0. The evolution of business analytics continued as enterprises grew and became more resourceful, using the information to make competitive decisions.

Traditionally, data generation and usage were paper-based. However, the recent advances in technology relating to how data is processed, stored, and transmitted and advances in intelligent computer software, reducing costs and increasing capacity, have resulted in companies moving from paper to technologically driven data. With the growth and acceptance of the Internet of Things, larger quantities of data are generated and consumed. The increased connectivity among machines and data from financial transactions and sensors such as security cameras allows businesses to gather data from very diverse and widespread sources. These data provide a rich source of information transformed into new, valuable, valid, and human-understandable knowledge. Therefore, there is a growing interest in exploring data to extract knowledge and business intelligence used to support decision-making in a wide variety of fields: cybersecurity, accounting, education, environment, finance, government, industry, medicine, transport, and social care.

Data

Data is everywhere. It is considered the new oil and is fundamental to business decisions. Data is raw or unprocessed facts. It lacks meaning and is generally unorganised. Data exists and has no significance beyond its existence (in and of itself). It can exist in any form, usable or not. It has no meaning in itself. Some examples of data include a sequence of bits, numbers, characters on a page, and sound recordings. The ability to gather the correct data, analyse, interpret, and act accordingly is crucial for the company's success. But the quantity of data accessible to companies is ever increasing, as are the different types of data available.

When Does Data Become Information?

Data

Table 1.1 Provides Examples of Data

Example .
Looking at the examples given for data:

- 4,8,12,16, and 20
- lion, tiger, elephant, snakes, monkey
- 161.2, 175.3, 166.4, 164.7, 169.3

Information results from processing or analysing data into meaningful conclusions that can be used in various ways. The process of mining information from raw data is called data analysis. The purpose of data analysis is to extract information (Table 1.1).

Information

Information is data that has been cleaned of errors, analysed, and processed to give meaning. Once processed, it becomes easier to measure, visualise, and explore for a specific purpose. By asking relevant questions about "who," "what," "when," "where," and "how," companies can derive valuable information from the data, thus making it more useful. The purpose of processing data and transforming it into information is to help organisations make better and more informed decisions leading to successful outcomes and competitive advantage. The tool used for collecting and processing data for organisations is Information Systems (IS), a combination of technologies, procedures, and tools that assemble and distribute information needed to make decisions.

The diagram below shows the relationship between data, information, knowledge, and wisdom (Figure 1.1).

Knowledge

Knowledge resides or is contained within the brain and is generally a result of one's experience applied to the organisation. Knowledge is closely connected to doing and implies the capacity to act (know-how), cognition or recognition (know-what), and understanding (know-why). There are different types of knowledge: tacit, implicit, and explicit.

Explicit Knowledge is the knowledge that is formalised and codified and is sometimes referred to as know-what. Explicit knowledge is relatively easy to identify, store, and retrieve. It is similar to information and involves management ensuring that employees have access to what they

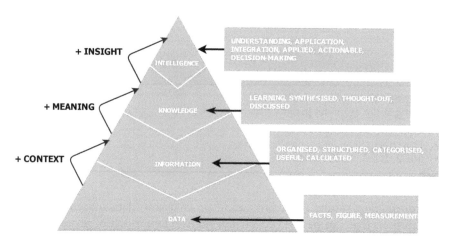

Figure 1.1 Relationship Between Data, Information, Knowledge, and Wisdom.

need. Explicit knowledge in the organisation should be stored, reviewed, updated, or destroyed.

Tacit Knowledge is difficult to pass from one person to another. It is knowing how to do something. Tacit knowledge is intuitive, which is hard to define and is mainly experience-based. It is also considered the most valuable source of knowledge and the most likely to lead to innovation and creativity. Tacit knowledge is used to provide companies with a competitive advantage when applied to business goals. It is also used to create or increase value for the company.

Implicit Knowledge is unconscious knowledge that is it lies outside of the individual's awareness. Implicit knowledge is difficult to verbalise and can only be inferred from behaviour. It is difficult to transfer. It emerges from task performance. Once the employee knows and understands the explicit knowledge as indicated by a manual or supervisor, it leads to more profound knowledge. An individual who implicitly understands the reason behind a specific set of instructions will better appreciate why a particular course of action occurs. This allows for collaboration and leads to new and improved ways for companies to operate.

Relationship Between Data, Information, and Knowledge

Based on the definitions of data, information, and knowledge, the relationships between data and information, information, and knowledge, are intertwined and consequently, they are often regarded as interchangeable. However, they are distinct entities (Table 1.2).

If we put Knowledge into an equation, it would look like this: Information + application or use = Knowledge

Transforming Data to Information

Data + Meaning = Information

Table 1.2 Provides an Outline of the Intricate Relationship between Data, Information and Knowledge

---

Example 1 of data:
Looking at the examples given for data:

- 4,8,12,16, and 20
- lion, tiger, elephant, snakes, monkey
- 161.2, 175.3, 166.4, 164.7, 169.3

Only when assigned a context or meaning, does the data become information. It all becomes meaningful when we are told:

- 4,8,12,16, and 20 are the first five answers in the 4x table
- lion, tiger, elephant, snakes, and monkey is a list of zoo animals
- 161.2, 175.3, 166.4, 164.7, 169.3 are the heights of a 15-year-old student

---

Intelligence

Intelligence is the ability to sense the environment, make decisions, and control action. An individual or system can transform information into behaviours. Higher levels of intelligence can include the ability to recognise objects and events, present knowledge in a world model, and reason about future strategic directions. Advanced forms of intelligence provide the capacity to perceive and understand, choose wisely, and act successfully under a wide range of circumstances.

Paradigms of intelligence include natural intelligence, artificial intelligence, machine intelligence, and computational intelligence. In addition, the development of cognitive robots, cognitive computers, intelligent systems, and software agents indicates that intelligence may also be created or implemented by machines and manufactured systems.

Categories of Data

Data can be divided into two main categories: structured or unstructured data.

Structured Data

Structured data refers to data that exists in a fixed field within a file or record. It is data that adheres to a predefined data model and is, therefore, easier to analyse. Structured data follows a tabular format with relationships between the different rows and columns. Each of these has structured rows and columns that can be sorted. It depends on creating a data model, defining what types of data to include, storing, processing, and accessing it. In a data model, each field is discrete and can be accessed separately or jointly with other areas. This makes structured data exceptionally powerful. It is possible to aggregate data from various locations in the database quickly. It is considered the most traditional form of data storage. The programming language employed for structured data is SQL (Structured Query Language). Classic examples of structured data include names, addresses, credit card numbers, and geolocation.

Unstructured Data

Unstructured data is data that is not structured in a predefined way. It is typically text-based but may contain dates, numbers, and facts as well. There is no data model as the data is stored in its native format. Typical examples of unstructured data include rich media, text, social media activity, surveillance imagery, audio, video files, or No-SQL databases. The capability to store and produce unstructured data has increased significantly in recent years, with many new technologies and tools available to store specialised unstructured data types. The ability to analyse unstructured data is especially relevant in Big Data since it makes up 80% or more of all enterprise data. The ability to extract information or value from unstructured data is one of the main drivers behind the rapid growth of Big Data. Therefore, companies that are not using unstructured data miss the opportunity to gain valuable business intelligence.

Data Science

Data science is a multi-disciplinary approach that involves algorithm development, data inference, and predictive modelling to solve analytically complex business problems. It is used for discovering valuable insights from the massive volumes of datasets by performing various operations. Data science involves organising, analysing, and processing data. There are different components of data science. This includes (Figure 1.2):

1 Data: the raw dataset forms the foundation or the core of Data Science. Raw data can be found in different types of structured and unstructured data.
2 Programming: the data is managed and analysed using computer programming. A variety of programming languages can be used for this purpose.
3 Statistics and Probability: data is manipulated in different ways to extract valuable information. Statistics and probability provide an intrinsic way to analyse large numerical data volumes and find meaningful insights from them.
4 Machine Learning: machine learning seeks to make machines more intelligent by learning from the data by training them using various algorithms.

Components of Data Science

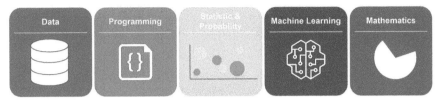

Figure 1.2 Components of Data Science.

5 Mathematics: mathematics is one of the main components of Data Science. It helps the data scientist to identify patterns in the data and then design algorithms accordingly.

Phases in Data Science

1 Discovery

The life cycle of Data Science starts with discovering data and involves collecting data from multiple sources like social media platforms, online sources, and logs.

As part of the discovery phase, it is crucial to determine whether there is enough information. The data scientist must know the available resources (people, time, technology, data). Several factors may affect this phase, such as the various requirements of the project, and the overall expenses, time, and technologies.

2 Data Preparation

Data preparation is also called data cleaning and involves cleaning and transforming raw data before processing and analysis. It often includes reformatting data, making corrections to data, and combining data sets to enrich data. Data preparation is often a lengthy process but is an essential prerequisite as it allows the data scientists to:

- Locate and remove the outliers and anomalies, biases, and errors from the data before processing.
- Discover various trends and relationships.
- Produce high-quality data by reformatting datasets.
- Make better business decisions. High-quality data that are easily and quickly analysed will result in more timely, efficient, and high-quality business decisions.

3 Modelling

Data modelling is where the data is analysed to extract meaningful information. Data modelling is the foundation of data science and forms the foundation for adaptive, predictive analytics critical to the current data ecosystem. Before data scientists can refine cognitive computing

Figure 1.3 Fields of Data Science.

models or build applications required to solve specific business problems, they must rectify differences in data models to leverage different data types for a single-use case. Data modelling is used to create the most efficient storage method while still providing complete access and reporting. It requires knowledge from several areas of mathematics like statistics, probability, linear regression, and logistic regression.

The most commonly used tool for data modelling purposes is R. However, there are several other tools like SQL and Tableau. The primary purpose of this phase is to identify suitable machine learning algorithms and build models that match the business needs.

4 Evaluation

Evaluating the performance of a data mining technique is an essential aspect of machine learning. Evaluation methods can differ from model to model. However, the most popular data processing techniques are classification, clustering, and regression.

5 Communication

Communication is a critical phase in the Data Science life-cycle. It is used to present all the key findings of the project to stakeholders and decision-makers. Communication is used to evaluate the results' accuracy and ensure that the project satisfies all the user requirements. The data scientist is responsible for designing and constructing new data modelling and production processes using prototypes, algorithms, predictive models, and custom analysis.

Data Science vs Data Analytics

Data science is the broad term that incorporates data analytics, data mining, machine learning, and several other related disciplines. While a data scientist is expected to predict the future based on past patterns, data analytics extract meaningful insights from different data sources. Thus, a data scientist produces questions while a data analyst finds answers to the existing questions. (Figure 1.3).

APPLICATION CASE 1.1

Big Data in the 1800s (The Hollerith Tabulator Machine)

The United States conducts a population census every ten years. There was a big problem in the 1800s census data tabulation. For example, it took almost eight years to complete the tabulation of the 1880 census results. When the government finally knew the actual population and its demographic makeup, it was time to start counting again. And since most government policies were based on population and demographics data provided by the census, the government was governing without good information.

As the 1880 census tabulation was awaiting completion almost eight years after the count was made, another problem was looming. A flood of new arrivals was ongoing and census bureau officials knew that the US population was exploding, and that the 1890 census might take years to be tabulated completely. They realised that the manual tabulation process in use then would not only take years to complete but will be an administrative and logistical nightmare. They decided to find a solution to the problem. In 1888, they decided to hold a competition to find a more efficient and faster method to tabulate and process the census data. They used the 1880 census data from St Louis, Missouri, and asked contestants to tabulate and process the data. Whosoever tabulated and processed the data fastest would be given the contract to process the 1890 census.

Herman Hollerith, who had worked for the census bureau, was one of the contestants. He invented the machine that not only won the contest but also changed information and data processing forever. Some believe he is the father of data analytics and the device he invented was the Hollerith Tabulator. The company that came into existence later became known as IBM (International Business Machine). The Hollerith Tabulator took 72.5 hours for data capture and 5.5 hours for data tabulation, while the others took 144.5 hours for data capture and 44.5 hours for data tabulation. He was awarded the contract, and the census bureau used a modified version of his machine up to the 1950s.

(Continued)

Hollerith's machine was based on punch cards. The device has a punch card reading station equipped with electrically operated components to read holes in the punch card. The punch card was 3 inches by 7 inches, the size of a dollar bill, and held one person's data. The punch card was placed on the tabulating machine, and the pins in the device went through the holes that made contact with the bottom plate of the machine filled with mercury. When the two touched, it completed an electric circuit, transmitted an electric impulse that read the card, and displayed the result on the machine's board. His machine only took two years to tabulate the 1890 census. Thus, the US government saved millions of dollars, time, and avoided administrative nightmares. The result was so impressive that soon other countries started using the machine.

The impact of the Hollerith machine, which became the Tabulating Machine Company, did not end with census data processing. Soon the question arose that if it could count and analyse demographic data, what about business data? Insurance companies, electric companies, department stores, oil companies, railroads, and drug manufacturing companies started using the machine to collect and analyse data. This electromechanical card reading machine was used for over 60 years until the advent of computers in the 1950s. This machine made IBM one of the world's most valuable companies at the time and survive the Great Depression.

Source: British Broadcasting Corporation: *The man who got rich on data - years before Google* : https://www.bbc.com/news/business-50578234: *Source*: United States Census Bureau History: https://www.census.gov/history/www/innovations/technology/the_hollerith_tabulator.html: *Source*: IBM; The Punched Card Tabulator: https://www.ibm.com/ibm/history/ibm100/us/en/icons/tabulator/

Key Term

Data; Qualitative Data; Quantitative Data; Unstructured Data; Structured Data; Data Science; Data Analytics; Knowledge

Chapter Key Takeaways

*   Data is raw or unprocessed facts. Therefore, it lacks meaning and is generally unorganised.
*   Data is everywhere and has no meaning in itself.
*   Information is data that has been cleaned of errors, analysed, and processed to give meaning. Therefore, information helps organisations make better and more informed decisions leading to successful outcomes and competitive advantage.

- Knowledge is closely connected to doing and implies the capacity to act (know-how), cognition or recognition (know-what), and understanding (know why).
- There are different types of knowledge: tacit, implicit, and explicit.
- Intelligence is the ability to sense the environment, make decisions, and control action.
- Paradigms of intelligence include natural intelligence, artificial intelligence, machine intelligence, and computational intelligence.
- Data can be divided into the main categories: structured or unstructured data.
- Data science is a multi-disciplinary approach that involves algorithm development, data inference, and predictive modelling to solve analytically complex business problems.
- The components of data science are Data, Programming, Statistics, and Probability, Machine Learning, and Mathematics.

Discussion Questions

1 Discuss the different phases of data science.
2 What is data?
3 Explain when data becomes information.
4 In the context of data analytics, what is information?
5 List and explain the three types of knowledge and give an example for each.
6 Explain the relationship between data, information, and knowledge.
7 What are the categories of data?
8 What is the difference between structured and unstructured data?
9 List and explain the components of data science.

2 Data Mining and Analytics

Data mining, also known as data discovery, is an automated analytical method that allows businesses to extract usable information from large datasets. It focuses on identifying and predicting patterns, behaviours, and future trends that emerge from a specific dataset, thus allowing companies to make better decisions. Several types of pattern detection are commonly used. These include cluster analysis, anomaly detection, association learning, classification, regression, and sequential pattern mining, emphasising connections and dependencies in data. In addition to pattern detection, this chapter also examines how data and text mining leads to a better decision-making process for businesses.

LEARNING OBJECTIVES:

At the end of this chapter, students should be able to:

- Assess the role of data mining in businesses
- Know the steps in the data mining process
- Identify and evaluate the different data mining techniques
- Understand text mining and its techniques

Data Mining

Data mining is also referred to as knowledge discovery, knowledge extraction, pattern analysis, and data dredging. It is the process of discovering anomalies, patterns, and correlations within large datasets to predict outcomes. Companies use several software tools to identify patterns in large batches of data. Data mining combines statistics and artificial intelligence (such as neural networks and machine learning) with database management to analyse extensive digital datasets. Data mining depends on significant data collection and warehousing as well as computer processing. It is used in industries such as in business (insurance, banking, retail), science (astronomy, medicine), and government (security detection of criminals and terrorists).

DOI: 10.4324/9781003129356-2

The evolution of data mining started with the storage of business data in computers and technologies, allowing users to navigate data in real time. The change is due to the vast volume of data collection, high-performance computing, and data mining algorithms.

Key features of data mining are:

- Pattern predictions based on trend and behaviour analysis.
- Prediction of likely outcomes.
- Creation of decision-oriented or actionable intelligence
- Focus on big datasets and databases for research.
- Clustering is based on finding and visually documenting facts not previously known.

Data mining can help businesses learn more about customers to develop more effective marketing strategies, improve customer relationships, better decisions, reduce risks, increase revenue, and decrease costs. Data mining can provide solutions for the banking and credit industry in the business field, such as credit scoring, fraud detection, customer segmentation, and maintaining a competitive environment. It can also develop proprietary bureau scores for general risk, bankruptcy, revenue, response, and optimising business needs. Therefore, data mining techniques allow credit managers and underwriters to rapidly build and analyse credit application scorecards, allowing increased acceptances and reduced bad debt.

The Internet is currently one of the most important markets and channels in the business environment. The Internet provides the potential for web mining to measure return on investment (ROI), improve online business decisions, increase cross-selling and up-selling, and deepen customers' loyalty and uncover relationships among products. In addition, data mining can assist coaches and other stakeholders to organise and interpret vast volumes of data amassed at every game in sports and entertainment. Using data mining, a coach can quickly review and detect patterns in the statistics. Data mining techniques can also predict individuals who are at high risks of specific significant illnesses. Therefore, presenting timely medical intervention and preventative treatment opportunities promotes the patients' health and reduces costs.

Data Mining Process

Three steps are involved in the data mining process:

- Exploration
- Pattern Recognition
- Deployment

Data Exploration is the first step in data analysis. Data analysts employ data visualisation and statistical techniques to define dataset characterisations, such as size, quantity, and accuracy, to understand the nature of the data. Data exploration techniques include both manual and automated analysis. Data exploration solutions visually investigate and identify relationships between different data variables, the dataset structure, the presence of outliers, and the distribution of data values to expose patterns and points of interest, enabling data analysts to understand the raw data. Data is collected in large, unstructured volumes from different sources, and data analysts must develop a comprehensive outlook of the data before extracting pertinent data for further analysis. The analyst employs techniques such as univariate, bivariate, multivariate, and principal components analysis. Manual data exploration entails manually filtering data into spreadsheets. Automated data exploration tools, like visualisation software, allow users to monitor the different data sources and conduct data exploration on otherwise overwhelmingly large datasets. Graphical data displays, such as bar charts and scatter plots, are valuable for visual data exploration. Data exploration uses visualisation to create a detailed view of datasets rather than thoroughly examining thousands of individual numbers or names.

Data cleaning and preparation is an essential aspect of the data mining process and accounts for nearly 80% of the data mining process. This task requires enormous effort as raw data is cleaned and formatted to be helpful in different analytic methods. It includes various elements of data modelling, transformation, data migration, Extract, Transform, and Load (ETL), data integration, and aggregation. In addition, data cleaning and preparation are crucial to understanding data's basic features and attributes to identify how to obtain the best use.

The business value of data cleaning and preparation is apparent. Without it, data is meaningless to an organisation, incomplete or unreliable due to its low quality. Companies must trust their data, the results of their analytics, and the decisions from those results.

Pattern Recognition examines the available data and seeks to identify any regularities or patterns within the data using machine-learning algorithms. It classifies data based on knowledge already gained or on statistical information extracted from patterns and/or their representation. One of the essential features of pattern recognition is its application capabilities. Pattern recognition methods apply to different systems and provide real-time characteristics. Machine recognition, description, classification, and grouping patterns are significant challenges in various disciplines, including biology, psychology, medicine, marketing, computer vision, artificial intelligence, and remote sensing.

Given a specific pattern, the recognition or classification may consist of:

- Supervised classification techniques which employ the class association of the samples to a particular group (class or category) to classify new unknown samples in one of the known classes based on its pattern of measurements.
- Unsupervised classification (e.g., clustering) in which the pattern is assigned to a formerly unknown class.

The classification is either established by the system designer (in supervised classification) or determined based on the similarity of patterns (in unsupervised classification).

Data used for pattern recognition can include:

- Texts or words
- Images
- Mood, sentiments, or emotions
- Sounds
- Other elements and information

The information collected from pattern recognition can be used for Big Data analytics. The most crucial goal of pattern recognition is to extract meaningful patterns from data and bring knowledge into an understandable format to the decision-maker. Thus, the pattern recognition process aims to obtain high-level data from low-level data.

The four best-known approaches to pattern recognition are:

- Template Matching: matches the attributes of an object using predefined variables and analyses the object by proxy. An example of template matching is "Plagiarism Checking."
- Syntactic or Structural: interprets a complex association between components, such as "parts of speech."
- Statistical classification: determines where the particular items belong – for example, identifying whether an object is a motorcycle or not (Figure 2.1).

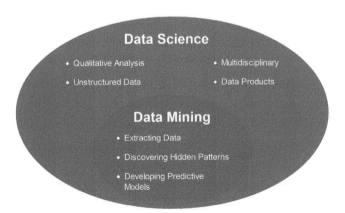

Figure 2.1 Summary of Data Mining Process.

Deployment comprises all the activities used to organise knowledge gained through data mining models and present valuable decision-making insights.

Data Mining Techniques

There are ten data mining techniques (Figure 2.2), namely:

- Tracking patterns
- Classification
- Association
- Outlier Detection
- Clustering
- Regression
- Prediction
- Sequential Patterns
- Statistical Techniques
- Visualisation

1 Tracking Patterns

Tracking patterns is a basic data mining technique. Pattern tracking involves identifying and monitoring trends or patterns in data to make intelligent decisions about business outcomes. It is also used to identify regular occurrences of similar events from historical data. Therefore, organisations use tracking patterns to identify trends in sales data. For example, suppose that a specific product sells more than others for a particular demographic. In that case, businesses can use this knowledge to develop similar products or services or keep a better inventory of the original product for a specific demographic. Another example is where historical sales data can be used to discover items that buyers purchase together at different times of the year.

2 Classification

Classification is a popular data mining technique for real-world problems. It involves analysing the various attributes associated with different types of data. Once businesses identify the characteristics of the data

Figure 2.2 Data Mining Techniques.

types, they can categorise or classify related data. Classification is beneficial for Big Data Analysis and is widely applied in various fields. For example, classification is used to identify the default risks and risk groups in the banking and insurance industries, specify the most appropriate insurance options for individual customers, increase customer satisfaction, and identify credit card fraud. The classification algorithms are widely used, and successful results are obtained from them to determine credit risks. Which classification algorithm to choose is a significant decision. The models can differentiate new data in the classification technique by observing how previous observations were classified. Several factors are considered when assessing classification models. These are:

- Predictive accuracy: assesses the ability of the model to predict the class label of newly or previously unseen data. It is the most commonly used assessment factor for classification models.
- Speed: examines how fast the data is processed.
- Robustness: the ability of the model to make reasonably accurate predictions when dealing with incomplete data or insufficient quality data.
- Scalability: the ability to construct prediction models efficiently when given a large volume of data.
- Interpretability: the level or depth of knowledge provided from analysing the data.

Classification considers the following business activities:

- Is this credit card transaction fraudulent?
- Which type of subscription should be offered to a particular customer?
- Will a specific customer buy a bicycle?
- Why is a business process failing?

To aid businesses in answering these questions, several primary classification methods are used, including:

- Bayesian networks
- Decision tree induction
- k-nearest neighbour classifier

3 Association

Association is a data mining technique that discovers the probability of the co-occurrence of items in a collection. It indicates that specific data (or events found in data) are associated with other data or data-driven results. It is similar to the concept of co-occurrence in machine learning, where the presence of another indicates the likelihood of one data-driven event. Association shows the relationship between two data events. For example, French fries frequently accompany the purchase of hamburgers.

The relationships between co-occurring items are expressed as association rules. This use of association modelling is called market-basket analysis. It is used for direct marketing, sales promotions, and the identification of business trends. It can also be used to design store layout, catalogue design, and cross-sell. Association modelling has essential applications in areas such as e-commerce applications, including website personalisation. For example, the association model can discover that users who visit pages A and B are 70% likely to see page C in the same session. Based on this rule, a dynamic link could be created for users interested in page C. Association helps businesses to identify:

1   What products should be recommended to customers?
2   Which services can be used together?
3   Which products are most likely to be purchased together in a supermarket?
4   Which set of books are most likely to be borrowed together in a library?
5   Which courses or recipes from a cookbook go well together?

4 Outlier Detection

Outlier detection determines any anomalies in datasets. For example, they can indicate variability in measurement, experimental errors, or novelty. An outlier may result from chance, but it may also show measurement error or a particular dataset with a heavy-tailed distribution. That is, an outlier is an observation that diverges from an overall pattern on a sample. Once organisations find outliers in their data, it becomes easier to understand why these anomalies happen and prepare for future occurrences to achieve business objectives. For example, suppose there is an increase in the usage of transactional systems for credit cards at a particular time of day. In that case, businesses can capitalise on this information by identifying why it is happening to optimise sales during the rest of the day.

There are four Outlier Detection techniques in general.

• Numeric Outlier
• Z-Score
• DBSCAN
• Isolation Forest

5 Clustering

Clustering analysis locates groups of data objects that are similar in some sense to one another. The objects of a particular cluster are more like each other than they are members of other clusters. The clustering analysis aims to find high-quality clusters such that the inter-cluster similarity is low and the intra-cluster similarity is high. It is used for data exploration. If there are several cases and no obvious groupings, clustering algorithms can find natural groupings. Clustering can also serve as a practical data-preprocessing step to identify homogeneous groups to build supervised models. It can also be used for anomaly detection. Once the data has been segmented into clusters, it is easy to identify anomalies or outliers.

Clustering relies on visual approaches to understand data. Graphs are ideal for using cluster analytics as each element in the cluster shows different types of metrics.

6 Regression

Regression techniques help identify the nature of the relationship between variables in a dataset. Regression is a data mining function. It can be used to predict profit, sales, mortgage rates, house values, square footage, temperature, or distance. Regression is used across disciplines and industries for business and marketing planning, financial forecasting, environmental modelling, and trends analysis.

A regression analysis begins with a specific set of data where the target values are known. In addition to value, the data can track the average age, square footage, the number of rooms, taxes, school district, and proximity to shopping centres.

The simplest form of regression is linear regression, which is used to estimate a relationship between two variables. Linear regression uses the mathematical formula of a straight line ($y = mx + b$). That is given a graph with a Y-axis and an X-axis. The relationship between X and Y is a straight line with some outliers. For example, it is fair to assume that an increase in population would increase food production at the same rate – it requires a strong, linear relationship between the two figures. To visualise this, on a graph where the Y-axis records population increase and the X-axis tracks food production. As the Y value increases, the X value also increases simultaneously. Therefore, the relationship between both variables is a straight line.

7 Prediction

A prediction is a potent tool of data mining that represents one of four branches of analytics. Predictive analytics use patterns identified in current or historical data to make organisational decisions. It gives organisations insight into data trends. There are different approaches to predictive analytics. The more advanced involve aspects of machine learning (ML) and artificial intelligence or algorithms.

Predictive analytics indicates what might happen in the future, providing respective probabilities of likelihoods given the examined variables. Businesses utilise predictive analytics to explore hypothetical situations through a holistic lens. Companies can use predictions to predict:

• The number of customers that the company will lose over time
• Which cable customers will order an upgrade on their package?

8 Sequential patterns

This data mining technique focuses on uncovering a series of events that takes place in a sequence. Sequence data is everywhere, and it is beneficial for data mining transactional data. Each sequence is a list of transactions, where each transaction is a set of literals, called items. Examples include customer shopping sequences, stocks, market data, telephone calling patterns, weblog click streams, and medical data. Typically, there is a transaction time associated with each transaction. A sequential pattern consists of sets of items. For instance, this technique can reveal what clothing customers are more likely to buy following an initial handbag purchase. Understanding sequential patterns can help organisations recommend additional items to customers to increase the volume of sales.

Traditionally, sequential pattern mining is employed to find subsequences that often appear in a sequence database, i.e., common to several sequences. Those subsequences are called frequent sequential patterns. Therefore, this can be useful to understand the behaviour of customers to make marketing decisions.

9 Statistical Techniques

Statistical techniques are central to most analytics techniques involving the data mining process. The different analytics models are based on statistical concepts, which output numerical values to specific business objectives. For example, neural networks use complex statistics based on different weights and measures to determine if a picture is a dog or a cat in image recognition systems. Statistical models represent one of the two main areas of artificial intelligence. Some statistical techniques are static, while others involving machine learning.

10 Visualisation

Data visualisation is another crucial element of data mining. Without visualisation, mining and analysis have no importance as data mining is finding inferences by analysing the data through patterns. Different visualisation techniques can only represent those patterns. A picture is worth thousands of numbers. Visualisation grants users insight into data based on visual sensory perceptions. Modern data visualisations are dynamic, useful for streaming data in real-time, and characterised by colours that reveal other trends and patterns in data.

Uses of data visualisation:

- A practical method of exploring data with presentable results
- For preprocessing portion of the data mining process
- Supports the data cleaning process by finding incorrect and missing values
- For variable derivation and selection, i.e., to determine which variable to include or discard in the analysis.
- Assist in combining categories as part of the data reduction process

Dashboards are an effective way to use data visualisations to uncover data mining intelligence. Dashboards can base on different metrics and visualisations to visually highlight patterns in data. There are several well-known techniques for visualising multi-dimensional datasets: scatterplot matrices, copilots, parallel coordinates, projection matrices, and other geometric projection techniques such as icon-based.

Data Sources

Data sources are related to several forms of data. They can reside on several platforms and contain structured information, such as tables or spreadsheets, or unstructured information, such as plaintext files or pictures and other multimedia information. These can be internal, operational databases, external data, market research companies, the Internet, or the existing data warehouse environment. The different data sources contain the raw data that can be processed using software that creates actionable information usable at all the organisational levels and in various divisions.

Text Mining

Text mining is also text analytics or text data mining that uses natural language processing (NLP) to transform the unstructured text in documents and databases into structured data. The data then becomes suitable for analysis or to drive ML algorithms. Text mining uses interdisciplinary techniques to discover patterns and trends in unstructured data or textual information. The goal of text mining is to process extensive textual data to extract high-quality information. Such information is helpful to provide insights into the specific scenario to which the text mining is being applied. Text mining has several applications, including text clustering, concept extraction, sentiment analysis, and summarisation. By mining text data, companies are saving on operational costs and gaining insights into future trends (Figure 2.3).

IBM's Watson text mining application is one of the most popular and performed very well when competing against humans on the Jeopardy game show. Watson uses a search and comparison technique similar to search engines such as n-grams and stemming. Watson has access to hundreds of millions of structured and unstructured documents (text documents), including the full content of Wikipedia entries. When a Jeopardy question is transcribed to Watson, it searches for and identifies documents that score a close match to the words of the question. Once it identifies relevant documents, it uses other text mining methods such as NLP to rank them. If the search result matches the terms in the sentence, a high score is assigned to the inserted term.[1]

Text mining also finds uses in various business activities such as email spam filtering, consumer sentiment analysis, and patent mining, to name a few. In

Figure 2.3 Data Mining: a Subset of Data Science.

addition, text data includes call centre transcripts, online reviews and chats, customer surveys, and other text documents. Text mining and analytics are allowing businesses to transform words into business actions.

Text Mining Techniques

According to IBM (2021),[2] the process of text mining involves several activities, such as:

- Text preprocessing, which consists of cleaning and transforming text data into a usable format. Text prepossessing practice is a core aspect of NLP. It usually involves techniques such as language identification, tokenisation, part-of-speech tagging, chunking, and syntax parsing to format data appropriately for analysis.
- Text mining algorithms are used to derive useful information from the data.

Examples of text mining techniques include:

1 Information Retrieval
2 Natural language processing (NLP)
3 Information Extraction

Information Retrieval

Information retrieval (IR) returns relevant information or documents based on a predefined set of queries or phrases. IR systems utilise algorithms to track user behaviours and identify relevant data. Information retrieval is used in library catalogue systems and popular search engines such as Google. Some common IR sub-tasks include:

Tokenisation: This is the process of separating a long-form text into sentences and units called "tokens." Tokens can either be words, characters or sub-words (n-gram characters). These tokens are used in the models for text clustering and document matching tasks.

Stemming: This is the process of separating the prefixes and suffixes from words to derive the root word form and meaning known as a lemma. Stemming improves information retrieval by reducing indexing files and consequently is critical to search queries and IR.

Natural Language Processing (NLP)

NLP uses various disciplines, such as computer science, artificial intelligence, linguistics, and data science, to enable computers to understand human language in written and verbal forms. For example, by analysing sentence structure and grammar, NLP sub-tasks allow computers to "read." Examples of sub-tasks include:

Summarisation: provides a synopsis or shortened version of longer text to generate a concise, coherent summary of the intended message.

Part-of-Speech (PoS) tagging: assigns a tag to every token in a document based on its part of speech. There are eight main PoS: nouns, verbs, adjectives, pronouns, adverbs, conjunctions, prepositions, and interjections. Tagging is essential for semantic analysis of unstructured text and creating lemmatisers.

Text categorisation refers to analysing text documents and sorting them into groups based on predefined topics or categories. This sub-task is particularly helpful when categorising synonyms and abbreviations. In addition, it is beneficial to understand customer perception and spam detection.

Sentiment analysis identifies positive, negative, or neutral emotions from internal or external data sources. It allows companies to track and measure changes in customer attitudes over time. It also provides companies with the audience perceptions of brands, products, and services. These insights can drive businesses to connect with customers and improve processes and user experiences.

Information Extraction

Information extraction (IE) is extracting information from the relevant pieces of data when searching various unstructured textual sources. It also focuses on extracting structured data from free text and storing these entities, attributes, and related information in a database. Common information extraction sub-tasks include:

Feature selection, or attribute selection, selects the critical features (dimensions) that contribute the most to the output of a predictive analytics model.

Feature extraction selects a subset of features to increase the accuracy of a classification task. It is essential for dimensionality reduction.

Named-entity recognition (NER), or entity identification or entity extraction, seeks to discover and categorise specific entities in text, such as names or locations.

APPLICATION CASE 2.1

Nestlé Corporation Use Big Data to Answer Business Questions

Nestlé was founded in 1866 and is headquartered at Vevey, Switzerland. It is a food and beverage multinational company. Nestlé corporation company has subsidiaries in North America, Europe, Middle East, and North Africa with over 2000 brands and has a presence in over 185 countries worldwide. Its brands include Zone, Cerelac, Gerber, NaturNes, Poland Spring, Nesquick, and Cheerios. As of September 6, 2021, the company's market value is $345 billion. Revenue for the year 2020 was $84.7 billion, down from $92.9b in 2019 due primarily to COVID-19.

The company has many subsidiaries and affiliates around the US and worldwide. One of its most challenging issues is moving its food and beverages to supermarkets, grocery stores, and other retail outlets worldwide. The most pressing issue is that most of its food products are perishable items, and making sure that they reach their destination on time and intact is a logistical challenge. In addition, they have to consider many variables such as traffic, drivers, scheduling, weather, and other unseen events.

Nestlé uses data analytics to determine the best and most cost-effective way to deliver its products to its affiliate stores and customers. They collect real-time data about products' whereabouts, traffic, drivers' locations, weather and predict when a shipment should be made. Additionally, the analytics will tell them if a load is running late and when to intervene to alleviate the situation. Because of the Big Data and predictive analytics, the company has increased on-time deliveries in all their shipments. On-time delivery increases customer satisfaction and increases company sales and profitability because there is less spoilage, especially in perishable products.

Big Data also allows them to analyse retail data and help them understand customer preferences in food items. The analytics also help them identify patterns in purchase behaviour and possible new trends in food choice. Identifying early food trends is very important to the company because it gives them time for product development. The company believes that Big Data and data analytics is making them faster and stronger as a company. Because of the good results they have seen, they are pushing to become a data-driven organisation in all of their operations, from the board room to human resources, finance, sales, supply chain to shelving products in the grocery stores.

Source: Nestlé corporation 2020 annual report. https://
www.nestle.com/investors/annual-report and https://
www.nestle.com/, and https://finance.yahoo.com/quote/
NSRGY?p=NSRGY&.tsrc=fin-srch and Nestle. Business
Analytics with a Purpose. *At Nestlé, we're using Big Data to
answer burning business questions and bring our consumers amazing
foods at the perfect time and place.* https://medium.com/nestle-usa/
business-analytics-with-a-purpose-fa2fe8b56f8e

Key Term

Data Mining; Text Mining; Outlier Detection; Tracking Patterns; Statistical Techniques; Isolation Forest; Decision Trees; Infographics

Chapter Key Takeaways

- Data mining is used to discover anomalies, patterns, and correlations within large datasets to predict outcomes.
- Data mining help businesses learn more about their customers to develop more effective marketing strategies, improve customer relationships, better decisions, reduce risks, increase revenue, and decrease costs.
- Data mining combines statistics and artificial intelligence with database management to analyse extensive digital datasets.
- Three steps are involved in the data mining process:
  - Exploration
  - Pattern identification
  - Deployment
- Data mining techniques include
  - Tracking patterns
  - Classification
  - Association
  - Outlier Detection
  - Clustering

- Regression
- Prediction
- Sequential patterns

Discussion Questions

1 The first step in the data mining process is data exploration, discuss how is it used to shift through Big Data.
2 How do companies use pattern recognition in data mining?
3 Describe the different approaches to pattern recognition.
4 How are classification methods used to assist companies with data mining?
5 List the factors influencing data visualisation. Then, discuss in detail any three of these factors outlining their contributions to businesses.
6 What is the value of data mining in business? Give at least one example.
7 What is data exploration, and what is the business value of the data exploration process?
8 List five types of data mining techniques and explain each of them
9 List and explain three primary classification methods in data mining.
10 What is the sequential patterns data mining technique? Give two examples of its business application.
11 What is data visualisation? Give three uses of data visualisation.

References

1 Kotu, V. & Deshpande, B. (2019). *Data science* (Second Edition), https://www.ibm.com/cloud/learn/text-mining
2 IBM (2020). *Text mining*, https://www.ibm.com/cloud/learn/text-mining

3 Data Analytics Tools

Currently, there is a considerable amount of interest in the topic of Big Data. Big Data is an operational reality for some companies, providing unprecedented ability to store and analyse large volumes of data critical to the organisation's competitive advantage. Business users are continually challenged to efficiently access, filter, and analyse data and gain insight. Collecting and analysing Big Data requires complex and technical solutions. Nevertheless, businesses realise their ability to improve business development agility and support timely and accurate business decisions. Companies seek faster, more efficient ways to navigate massive amounts of data to determine critical organisational issues and get answers to specific business questions to improve decision-making. This chapter provides a brief overview of some of the fundamental technologies for businesses to operate efficiently. Data analytics tools can add value and meaning to the data and give users more significant insights into their customers, business, and industry.

LEARNING OBJECTIVES:

At the end of the chapter, students should be able to:

- Identify Data Analytics tools and their characteristics
- Understand Embedded Analytics
- Determine how Business Intelligence is used in companies to drive core competencies and provide a competitive advantage
- Understand self-service analytics and its benefits

What Is Big Data?

Companies now understand that they can apply analytics and gain significant value by capturing all the data streams into their businesses. The concept of Big Data is not new, and since the 1950s, decades before the term "Big Data" was coined, companies have been using basic analytics in the form of spreadsheets to uncover insights and trends. Big Data consists of large and complex

DOI: 10.4324/9781003129356-3

datasets that can be structured, semi-structured, or unstructured and will typically not fit into memory to be processed. Big Data relates to datasets that could not be perceived, acquired, managed, and processed by relational databases, IT, and software/hardware tools within a tolerable time. The techniques for Big Data analytics comprise a wide range of mathematical, statistical, and modelling techniques that involves historical or current data and visualisation. It requires Big Data analytics to use data mining to discover knowledge from an extensive dataset. Accuracy in Big Data may result in more confident decision-making. Better decisions mean greater operational efficiency, cost reduction, increased value to the customer and organisation, and reduced risk. As an essential part of Big Data analytics, data visualisation techniques make knowledge patterns and information for decision-making in figures, tables, or multimedia.

Therefore, Big Data analytics is used to facilitate business decision-making and realisation of business objectives through:

• Analysing current problems and future trends
• Creating predictive models to forecast future threats and opportunities
• Analysing or optimising business processes based on detailed historical or current data to enhance organisational performance using the techniques mentioned

Characteristics of Big Data

Big Data is data whose scale, distribution, diversity, and/or timeliness require the use of new technical architectures, analytics, and tools to enable insights that unlock new sources of business value. Moreover, these datasets are so voluminous that traditional data processing software cannot interrogate them. Consequently, there is typically a 5Vs model of Big Data. These are velocity, volume, variety, value, and veracity (Figure 3.1).

Velocity: refers to the rapid generation and is the real-time speed at which data is generated, collected, and analysed. Typically, the highest velocity of data streams directly into memory versus being written to disk. Big Data technology allows the analysis of data without storing it in databases.

Volume: The amount of data available to the organisation matters, and vast quantities of data can be generated every second from different sources such as images, video, audio, emails, and sensor data shared.

Big Data analytics tools process high volumes of low-density, unstructured data. For example, this can be data of unknown value, such as Twitter data feed or mobile applications. For some organisations, the amount of data generated ranges from tens of terabytes to hundreds of petabytes. Big Data is measured in petabytes. An excellent example is Google Inc., which process over 20 petabytes of data every day. Companies must implement modern business intelligence tools to capture, store effectively, and process this vast quantity of data in real time.

Figure 3.1 Characteristics of Big Data.

A large volume of datasets is not only a problem to analyse but also presents a storage issue. These are examples of by-the-minute volumes of data:

- eBay: it has 40 PB of data and captures 50 TB/day
- Netflix hours of video streamed: 694,444 (2019); 97,222 (2018)
- Amazon sales generated per minute: $533,713.85 (2019); $270,015.22 (2018)
- YouTube videos watched: 4.5M (2019); 4.333M (2018)

The unparalleled growth in the volume of data suggests a continued increase in business intelligence.

Variety: This refers to the different modalities of data that are available. Traditional data types are structured. However, with the increased use of the internet, data comes in new unstructured data types. Unstructured and semi-structured data types include text, audio, and video, which require additional pre-processing to derive meaning and support metadata. One of the main reasons for the rise in Big Data is the wide variety of sources, including logs, clickstreams, and social media, from which they are generated. Using multiple sources for analytics means that standard structured data is mixed with unstructured data, such as text and human language, and semi-structured data, such as eXtensible Markup Language (XML) or Rich Site Summary (RSS) feeds. There is also data which is hard to categorise since it comes from audio and video. Furthermore, multi-dimensional data can be obtained from a data warehouse to add historical context to Big Data. Thus, with Big Data, the variety is just as huge as volume.

Veracity/Validity: Unstructured data has inconsistencies and uncertainty, sometimes affecting its quality and accuracy, making it difficult to control.

Veracity guarantees the assurance of the quality or credibility of the collected data. Validity is used to characterise the data quality as either good, bad, or undefined. Validity classification is due to data inconsistency, incompleteness, ambiguity, latency, deception, and approximations. Common questions that should be answered when the veracity of the data is unknown include:

- Can the data be trusted?
- Is this data credible enough to gather intelligence?
- Can business decisions be based on this data?

Value: The majority of data have a low-value density in its raw and unstructured manner.

Therefore data manipulation and analytics are required for it to become functional. While many organisations have invested heavily in developing data aggregation and storage infrastructure, they fail to realise that data aggregation is not equivalent to the added value and decision-making process. Data is of no use or importance, but it needs to be converted into something valuable to extract information. Hence, value has been considered the most critical V of all the 5Vs. It presents new opportunities for discovering new values and gaining an in-depth understanding of the hidden benefits.

Business Benefits of Big Data

Big Data offers strategic advantages for businesses, including the following (Table 3.1):

Customer relationships and sales can also benefit from utilising Big Data. Some of the benefits in these areas include the following (Table 3.2):

The business functions of Big Data, as seen in Figure 3.2, are:

- Understand customer needs
- Improve process efficiency
- Reduce costs
- Identify and mitigate risks

Table 3.1 Strategic Benefits of Big Data

Better Strategic Decisions	*Increased Creativity and Faster Development Lifecycle for New Products and Services to Market*
Increased innovation	Better insight into the business
Increase competitive advantage	Provide real-time change for existing products, services, or offers

Table 3.2 Customer Relationships and Sales Benefits of Big Data

Improved Customer Satisfaction	*Enhanced Customer Service*
Improved sales results via cross-selling and up-selling Increased targeted marketing via social media	Increased attraction and retention of customers

Figure 3.2 Business Benefits of Big Data.

Drivers of Big Data

The technological developments in storage, processing, and analysis of Big Data include:

1 The decreasing cost of storage and CPU power
2 The increasing flexibility and cost-effectiveness of datacentres and cloud computing
3 The development of new frameworks allows users to store large quantities of data through flexible parallel processing (Figure 3.3)

Big Data Analytics

Big Data analytics is the process of assessing large and varied datasets (Big Data). These datasets are often unexploited by traditional business intelligence and analytics programs. They include unstructured and semi-structured data from social media contents, mobile phone records, web server logs, and clickstream data. Also analysed are text from survey responses, customer

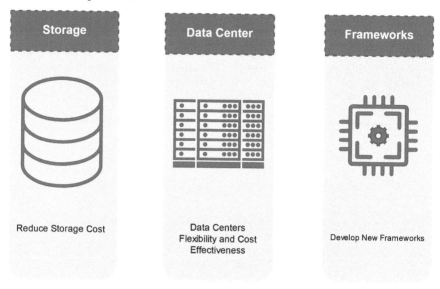

Figure 3.3 Drivers of Big Data.

emails, and machine data captured by sensors connected to the Internet of Things (IoT). It uses analytic techniques such as data mining, machine learning, artificial learning, statistics, and natural language processing. Analysts, researchers, and IT teams often employ data analytics tools to access business data efficiently.

Big Data analytics is used to discover relevant information, patterns, trends, or correlations to help a company make informed decisions. As a result, Big Data analytics enables a company to improve its operational efficiency, enhance customer service, develop and adopt more effective marketing strategies, discover new revenue opportunities, and gain a competitive advantage.

Big Data Analytics Techniques

Several types of analytics techniques are available to analyse Big Data for different purposes. These are:

- Descriptive Analytics
- Prescriptive Analytics
- Predictive Analytics

Descriptive Analytics

Descriptive analytics is a conventional form of business intelligence and data analysis. It seeks to depict or summarise the facts and figures in an understandable format to inform or prepare data for further analysis. Descriptive analytics uses two primary techniques, namely, data aggregation or clustering and data mining. It presents data in an easily digestible format, therefore, benefitting a broad business audience. It uses techniques such as online analytical processing (OLAP) or drill down and aims at identifying problems and opportunities within existing processes and functions. It does not go beyond surface analysis. It seeks to discover, "What has happened?" Descriptive analytics is helpful to understand how past events might influence future outcomes. Examples of descriptive analytics include web analytics for pay-per-click or email marketing data. Another example of data analytics is fraud detection, which uses clustering to identify individuals with similar purchasing patterns.

Prescriptive Analytics

Prescriptive analytics represents a more advanced use of predictive analytics. It addresses questions such as:

- What should we do?
- Why should we do it?
- What should happen under uncertain situations?

Prescriptive analytics can suggest all favourable outcomes according to a specified course of action and recommend several courses of action to achieve a particular result. Hence, it uses a reliable feedback system that continually learns and updates the relationship between the action and the outcome. For example, Big Data prescriptive analytics can provide an optimal marketing strategy for an e-commerce company. It can be achieved through simulations.

Predictive Analytics

Predictive analytics seeks to determine what will happen by analysing historical data and trends. It uses statistical models and programming to discover explanatory and predictive patterns within data to understand the future. An example of predictive analytics is classification. A set of data is divided into predefined groups, and the analyst then searches for patterns in the data that differentiate those groups. Another method employed in predictive modelling is regression analysis used when the target attribute is numeric. The aim is to predict the value of new data. It is enabled by the use of techniques such as data mining and forecasting. It seeks to answer, "What could happen, and why will it happen?" For example, predictive analytics can determine where the next attack target of terrorists might be.

APPLICATION CASE 3.1

How Hadoop, Apache Spark, and Hive made Uber operates efficiently

Uber, founded in March 2009, is the world's largest ride-sharing company. It has operations in Africa, Asia, Canada, Europe, Latin America, Middle East, and the United States. The company connects drivers and riders for ride-sharing services. The company also connects consumers and riders with grocery stores and restaurants to provide delivery services. As a result, its operations grow very fast in a brief period. Uber became a publicly traded company on May 9, 2019. As of September 2021, the company is valued at over $75 billion.

When Uber started operation in 2009, the amount of online data needed and collected was small and stored in their PostgreSQL and MySQL databases. However, one of their problems was that their database was scattered across the globe and on different Online Transaction Processing (OLTP) databases. As a result, they did not have a global view of all their data in one place. Nevertheless, their data scientists developed a bespoke system that was very inefficient even though it was functional. However, it was around a few terabytes, and the speed was reasonably fast.

However, when Uber started to grow at a fast pace, the need for a better integrated database was necessary. The company expanded its operations in more than 200 cities around the globe. As a result, the number of drivers and riders also increase tremendously. As a result, their data users also triple in number. Their three primary data users were:

1   On-the-ground city operators who responded to riders' and drivers' specific questions around the clock
2   Data users were data scientists scattered on different geographical locations around the globe to help make sure that the data was updated and accessible to drivers, riders, and other users
3   Primary data users were engineers whose main job was to build applications that make drivers' onboarding quick and efficient and prevent fraud

Because of the vast amount of data collected every second, data ingestion into the warehouse was slow and fragile. Data ingestion is the process of receiving and adjusting incoming data from various sources and formats into a format and structure needed for analysis. As a result, the same data is ingested multiple times, causing a system overload and questions the quality of data in the warehouse. In addition, as the number of users increases, it generates more data adding extra pressure to the system. Because of these ingestion problems, data latency, which is the time it takes to store and retrieve data, was far from where it needed to be for the company to operate efficiently.

All of these primary users helping to make Uber operate smoothly were growing in the thousands, and the company needed to make sure that their data warehouse was in one place and access to these data was fast and easy. They developed various ETL (extract, transform, and load) jobs that copied data from different sources and loaded them to their data warehouse to solve these problems. They standardised their SQL to streamline data access. They reconfigured their Big Data warehouse around Hadoop, which made a big difference. The Hadoop architecture allows data to be ingested from all the various online data sources only once. This significantly reduces the pressure on their Big Data platform. They also introduce Apache Spark to facilitate access to raw data in both non-SQL and SQL format. The company uses Hive data analytic tools to process extensive queries, and for ad hoc user queries, the company's Big Data platform also uses Presto. The introduction of these data analytical tools enables their data platform to be accessible and flexible for all users.

With this aggregation of data into one data warehouse, Uber data users could have a global view of the data and could easily access it in one place. In addition, on-the-ground city operators could use the data without having to understand the technologies behind it. By 2017, Uber's Big Data platform was available to all users across the company, including engineers, on-the-ground operating teams, data scientists, riders, and drivers. In addition, users can easily access the data through Presto, Hive, Vertica, or Spark data analytic tools. Most importantly, the latency period was reduced from 24 hours to just 10–15 minutes.

Source: Uber engineering: "Uber's Data Platform in 2019: Transforming Information to Intelligence". https://eng.uber.com/uber-data-platform-2019. Source: https://www.uber.com/newsroom/history/: Source: "Uber's Big Data Platform: 100+ Petabytes with Minute Latency". https://eng.uber.com/uber-big-data-platform/. Source: UBER TECHNOLOGIES, INC. December 31, 2020, annual report – SEC Form 10-K: https://investor.uber.com/financials/default.aspx

Overview of Data Analytics Tools

Below are some popular Data Analytics Tools:

- R
- Python
- RapidMiner
- HADOOP
- Tableau

R

R is an Open Source software program and service developed by a group of volunteers. The R language is a dialect of S that was designed in the 1980s. R is used widely by statisticians and researchers. The software environment of R is created using C, Fortran, and R itself. The fact that R is based on open source projects means that it is updated frequently for new features and repairs for bugs are done promptly. R remains one of the most popular for data analytics as the program has an excellent command-line interface, and all the commands are easy to apply and understand. Several graphical front-ends such as R studio, IntelliJ, Visual Studio are available. The analytical capacity of R is virtually unmatched. It is a flexible program with many additional features that can be downloaded in coding packages. R specialises in a small subset of statistical data and is much easier for a data analyst.

R allows data analytics by various statistical and machine learning operations such as:

- Regression
- Classification
- Clustering
- Recommendation
- Text mining

Data Analytics in R

R Markdown provides a unified authoring framework for Big Data analytics that combines the code, results, and prose commentary. In addition, R Markdown documents are reproducible and support several output formats, such as PDFs, Word files, PowerPoint presentations, amongst others.

R Markdown files are used in three ways:

- For decision-makers, the primary focus is on the conclusions and recommendations drawn from the analysis and not the processes behind the investigation
- For collaboration with stakeholders and data scientists interested in the findings and the process behind the study
- To provide an environment in which thought processes and work can be captured

In addition, the R environment contains many classical and modern statistical techniques. Several of these techniques are built into the base R environment, but many are supplied as packages. There are about 25 packages provided with R (called "standard" and "recommended" packages), and many more are available through the CRAN family of Internet sites.

R Functionality

R functionality is divided into several packages. Some of these packages include:

- The "**Base**" R system contains, among other things, the base package which is required to run R and includes the most fundamental functions. The base packages include utils, stats, datasets, graphics, grDevices, grid, methods, tools, parallel, compiler, splines, tcltk, stats4
- The "**Recommended**" packages include boot, class, cluster, codetools, foreign, KernSmooth, lattice, mgcv, nlme, rpart, survival, MASS, spatial, nnet, Matrix
- The **dplyr** packages provide essential functionalities for subsetting, summarising, rearranging, and joining together datasets. The primary functions to operate with dplyr are filter, selection, arrange, mutate, and summarise
- The **data.table** is an enhanced version of data. It sorts data in R. It allows data manipulation operations such as *subset, group, update, join* that are all inherently related. Keeping these related operations together allows for R's faster manipulation.
- The **Read Rectangular Text Data readr** provides a fast and easy way to read rectangular data like csv (comma separated values), tsv (tab-separated values), delim (delimited values), and fwf (fixed-width files).
- The **tidyr** makes the R data tidy. Tidying data is essential to ensure that more time is spent analysing the data. It provides tools for changing the layout of the datasets using the gather and spread functions to convert your data into a tidy format.
- The **stringr** package provides a comprehensive set of functions designed to work with regular expressions and character strings.

Python

Python is an easy tool to learn, powerful, and fast programming language. It consists of an extensive standard library that is structured and focuses on general programming. It is open source, which means it is freely usable and distributable, even for commercial purposes. In addition, Python is explicitly designed so that code written in Python would be easy for humans to read and minimise time spent writing codes.

Data Analytics in Python

Python applies to all the stages of data analysis. The Data Scientist can use Python for Data mining, data processing, and modelling along with data visualisation. Using Python for data analytics is appropriate because of its statistical analysis capacity and its easy readability. Python libraries for data analytics are as follows:

- The **Panda** library is used for data manipulation and data analysis. Pandas provide sophisticated indexing functionality that makes it easy to restructure, perform aggregations, and select subsets of data. Panda in Python provides rich data structures and functions designed to make working with structured data fast, easy, and expressive. For financial users, Pandas offer easy to manipulate high-performance numerical and time-series data. Statsmodels module helps users to explore data, estimate the statistical models, and to perform statistical tests.

- **NumPy,** short for Numerical Python, is the foundational package for mathematical computing with arrays such as trigonometric, statistical, and algebraic routines and mathematical expressions such as defining, optimising, evaluating data. In addition, it is used to analyse large datasets. Because NumPy arrays are stored at one continuous place in memory, processes can access and manipulate them very efficiently.

- **statsmodels** provide classes and functions to estimate many different statistical models and conduct statistical computations, including descriptive statistics and estimation and inference for statistical models and data exploration.

- **Scikit-learn** is used for data modelling of medium-scale supervised and unsupervised problems. Emphasis is placed on ease of use, performance, documentation, and API consistency.

- **Mlpy** provides a variety of machine learning methods for supervised and unsupervised problems. Mlpy seeks a reasonable compromise among modularity, maintainability, reproducibility, usability, and efficiency. Mlpy is multi-platform.

- **Matplotlib** is a visualisation library in Python for 2D plots of arrays. It supports interactive and non-interactive plotting and can save images in several formats. The dual nature of Matplotlib supports both interactive and non-interactive scripts. On web pages, Matplotlib allows visual access to vast amounts of data in easily digestible visuals. It consists of several plots like line, bar, scatter diagrams, pie charts, 3D graphs, geographic map graphs, and histograms. Matplotlib is highly customisable, flexible, and easy to use.

Python has gained popularity in recent years because its syntax allows programmers to code using fewer steps than Java or C++.

RapidMiner

It is coded using Java programming language, and it supports most of the machine learning process steps. It was developed in 2001 and is one of the world's most-used solutions for data analyses. RapidMiner allows data mining, text mining, and predictive analytics. It is a software program that empowers users to enter raw data, such as databases and text, which is automatically analysed on a large scale. RapidMiner has business and industrial applications. It is used for research, education, training, prototyping, and data mining, including results visualisation, validation, and optimisation.

Data Analytics and Rapid Miner

RapidMiner is a data analytic tool that offers machine learning and data mining measures, including statistical modelling, processing, visualisation, product deployment, evaluation, and predictive analytics.

RapidMiner offers a GUI-based data science platform, which best suits beginner and expert data analysts. RapidMiner is an integrated environment used for data preparation, machine learning, deep learning, text mining, and predictive analytics. It uses both descriptive and predictive techniques useful for decision-making and business intelligence. Companies employ Rapid Miner for business and commercial applications and research, education, training, rapid prototyping, and application development and support machine learning, including data preparation, visualisation, model validation, and optimisation. Therefore, RapidMiner is ideal for data analytics for several reasons, namely:

- It is easy to use a visual environment for building analytics processes: a graphical design environment makes it fast and straightforward to create better models.
- Data Access and Management: RapidMiner provides access, load, and analyses any type of data, traditional structured and unstructured data like text, images, and media. It can also obtain information from these data types and transform unstructured data into structured.
- Data Exploration: users can understand and create a plan to prepare the data automatically extract statistics and critical information. It can produce descriptive statistics such as univariate and bivariate statistics and plots.
- Data Preparation: RapidMiner formats, creates the optimal dataset, and blends structured with unstructured data for predictive analysis.

Hadoop

Hadoop (High-Availability Distributed Object-Oriented Platform) is an open-source platform for scalable, reliable, and distributed computing. It is a software library that allows for the distributed processing of large datasets that efficiently and cost-effectively work on any platform. As a result, Hadoop is the most widely used Big Data technology for analysing large datasets.

Data Analytics in Hadoop

Hadoop provides the technology to process large volumes of data while keeping the data in the original data clusters. Hadoop is ideal for capturing and refining many multi-structured data types with an unknown initial value. It also serves as a cost-effective platform for retaining large volumes of data and files for long periods. Hadoop assists companies in overcoming the challenges of Big Data because of its resilience, low cost, and diversity of data formats such as unstructured (videos), semi-structured (XML files), and structured.

Features of Hadoop

The main features of Hadoop are:

- **MapReduce**, which consists of a Mapper and Reducer. MapReduce is used to support distributed processing of the standard map and reduction operations. Because both the map and reduce functions can be distributed to clusters of commodity hardware and performed in parallel, MapReduce techniques are appropriate for larger datasets.
- **NameNode** is a master server that maintains and manages the file system Namespace and regulates client's access to files. It supports the directory tree of all files and tracks where the file data is held across the cluster. NameNode does not store data. Instead, the NameNode responds to the successful requests by returning a relevant DataNode server where the data lives.
- **DataNode** stores the actual data in HDFS. The NameNode and DataNode are in constant communication. When a DataNode starts up, it announces itself to the NameNode along with the list of blocks. DataNode is usually configured using hard disk space since the actual data is stored in the DataNode.
- **Secondary NameNode** works concurrently with the primary NameNode as a helper daemon. Its principal function is to take checkpoints of the file system metadata present on NameNode.
- **Job Tracker** is the master daemon for both Job resource management and scheduling/monitoring of jobs. It assigns client requests to Task-Trackers on DataNodes, where the data required is locally present.
- **Yet Another Resource Negotiator Yarn** is a resource management and job scheduling platform responsible for managing the compute resources in clusters and using them for scheduling users' applications. Through its various components, it can dynamically allocate various resources and schedule the application processing. For significant volume data processing, it is necessary to manage the available resources appropriately so that every application can leverage them. Therefore, the Resource Manager has two main components: Scheduler and Applications Manager.

Tableau

Tableau Desktop is a business intelligence and data visualisation tool. It provides organisations with the tools to transform tabulated data into elegant graphs and representations capable of communicating business insights. Tableau requires no coding skills. It allows for easy upgrade and integration with third-party Big Data platforms and offers Google Big Query API support. Tableau provides the tools to transform vast volumes of business-generated data into manageable, understandable, and actionable information. Companies can use the data generated from Tableau to drive business decision-making, form strategies, and plan operations.

Data Analytics in Tableau

Tableau provides companies with the tools to transform massive volumes of business-generated data into manageable, logical, and actionable information. It allows users to prep, analyse, collaborate, and share Big Data insights. Therefore, business decision-makers use the information generated to form strategies and plan operations. Tableau, as a business intelligence platform, is designed for the individual. However, its scalability allows businesses to convert information into valuable insights.

Tableau is a data analysis and visualisation tool that connects with several data sources. It utilises application integration innovations such as JavaScript APIs and single sign-on applications to include Tableau analytics into basic business applications consistently. Tableau is used to create a variety of visualisation to present data and highlight new insights. In addition, it provides real-time data analytics capacity and cloud support.

Features of Tableau

Tableau has different components, including desktop design and analysis tools used to create and consume data.

- **Tableau** Server allows larger enterprises to access reports in a secure environment without the need to load software. Tableau Server also enables reports to be created on iOS or Android tablet computers.
- **Tableau** Desktop is a data visualisation application that allows users to quickly analyse structured data and produce highly interactive graphs, dashboards, and reports. It can connect to virtually any data source and display information from multiple graphic perspectives.
- **Tableau** Public is a free service where anyone can publish interactive data on the web. Once on the web, anyone can interact, download it, or create their data visualisations.
- **Tableau** Online is an analytics platform that is fully hosted in the cloud. It is easily accessible from a browser or mobile apps. Here users can

publish, discover, and explore hidden opportunities with interactive visualisations and accurate data.

- **Tableau** Mobile provides on-demand access to the organisation's Tableau Server or Tableau Online site. Having Tableau Mobile allows users
to make better decisions and develop a deeper understanding of the internal business environment.
- **Tableau** Data Prep is designed to quickly and confidently combine shape
and clean data for analysis. In addition, the direct, visual experience provides a deeper understanding of the data.

Self-Service Analytics

The concept of self-service is related to different tasks such as direct access to
data and functions, preparation of reports or data resources, or creation of new
resources. The system support varies with each task. Self-Service Analytics
(SSA) allows end-users to analyse data by building and modifying existing
reports quickly. It refers to business intelligence (BI) platforms that directly
enable business users to access and interact with their data. This differs from
traditional reporting systems by the fact that not only a few standard reports are
provided. The advantage of this approach is that it is well suited for casual users
with minimal analytical or tool skills. Basic insights can be derived easily if the
needed information is found and interpreted correctly. Users can dynamically
analyse data by modifying, drilling through, or adding calculation functions
to a report. Therefore, ad hoc reporting can be done as users can now develop
reports quickly. As business processes increase, the frequency of changes to
reporting and analytics also increases. Such flexibility decreases the demand
for resources. SSA tools have numerous benefits, but they also create new challenges as users may not understand the application of the tool to validate business rules. However, SSA relies on the validity and consistency of the data.

For an SSA tool to function efficiently, users should have easy access to the
data they need across the organisation, including siloed data existing in various systems. Then, the data can be applied for greater business insight and results. Integrating data from different systems and devices requires a complete
understanding of the organisation's data map and journey and its association
with other similar – or sometimes conflicting – data. Such insights can be
achieved using data governance.

Advantages of SSA

Big Data and analytics is a central component of every organisation. However, owing to the widespread acceptance, organisations are finding it difficult to manage. Consequently, companies rely on SSA as it offers advantages.

- **Democratise Big Data**: SSA increases the number of people accessing
and using Big Data. In addition, it spreads awareness among business
users involved in SSA tasks.

- **Empower business users:** with the rapid increase in volume and growth of data, data analytics tasks cannot be confined to a small group of users since this limits the ability of the organisation to leverage the power of analytics. SSA empowers business users to perform their tasks independently.
- **Allowed focus on core analytics tasks**: SSA enable end-users to perform minor tasks like data exploration, verification, visualisation, and reporting. Data scientists can then focus on critical and complex analytics tasks, thus providing additional business value.
- **Improve collaboration and increase productivity**: SSA business users and the core data science team can work together for the best result. With SSA, end users can perform basic tasks within their understanding of the data. The data scientists can collect input from the SSA team for other advanced analytics or complex tasks.

Embedded Analytics

Embedded analytics uses analytics and reporting capabilities in transactional business applications. Therefore, companies are increasingly empowering employees with analytics tools to access data and improve decision-making. Thus, businesses are embedding analytics into their core business applications. As a result, embedded analytics seeks to broaden the business reach and improve business insights. In addition, the technology for the integration of reports, charts, dashboards, and SSA tools has rapidly evolved. Although the current users of embedded analytics are primarily large corporations, there are numerous industries and organisations where embedded analytics tools could advantageously assist decision-makers.

Embedded analytics allows for tightly integrated capabilities into existing CRM, ERP, marketing automation, and financial systems. These systems bring awareness, context, or analytic ability that support decision-making for specific tasks in the company. For example, task assignment and completion may require data from several systems or aggregated views, but the output is not a centralised overview of information. Embedded analytics allows decision-makers to support a decision or action within the context in which that decision or action occurs. Using embedding tools helps with the reporting of BI added to existing business applications allows for the efficient presentation of data. By using embedding tools, businesses can confidently extract essential insight from data within the applications. With this analysis, users can identify and mitigate issues and identify opportunities.

The Evolution of Embedded Analytics

Traditional BI is specifically developed to be operated by an analyst who will aggregate data and information from across the organisation to optimise decision-making process. These platforms focus on data preparation and integration and provide analysis via scripting, reports, interactive visualisations, and static dashboards. However, an essential shortcoming of traditional BI is its underdevelopment in receiving reports. Quite often, decision-makers receive business reports when it is too late to undertake any action. Embedded analytics addresses this latency by shifting from reactive analytics to proactive analytics. Embedded analytics also inserts intelligence or a set of tightly integrated capabilities inside everyday systems or applications. Consequently, there is no need for users to switch between multiple applications to derive insights and take action. Embedded analytics is built on three principles:

1 Synthesis: facilitates the rapid integration of multiple sources and large volumes of data
2 Enabling in-the-Moment Analysis: allows users to function within the typical business applications and for a wide range of scenarios. Embedding makes analytics available when and where required, providing users with a powerful experience
3 Democratising Analytics: permit a broad population of users to understand and use analytics results in an easy-to-use, easy-to-share interface

The Rise of Embedded Analytics

Technology and software companies, financial services, manufacturing, and retail are among the highest users of the embedded analytics. The use of embedded analytics continues to grow and exceed that of standard data recovery. Companies have gone beyond simply adding open-source charts or static visualisations. Businesses are willing to dedicate time and resources to embed sophisticated analytics to impress end-users. Investment in embedded analytics continues to grow as companies believe that embedded analytics plays a critical role in improving customer satisfaction and user experience. It has gained traction among decision-makers as they use embedded analytics to win and retain customers.

The most common analytics capabilities include:

• Dashboards and data visualisations
• Static and interactive reports
• SSA and ad hoc querying
• Benchmarking
• Mobile reporting
• Visual workflows
• Predictive analytics

Forces Driving Embedded Analytics

Managers and executives are seeking analytics solutions that are flexible, scalable, embeddable, and easy-to-implement. Three forces are driving embedded analytics: technology, people, and business, as shown in Figure 3.4.

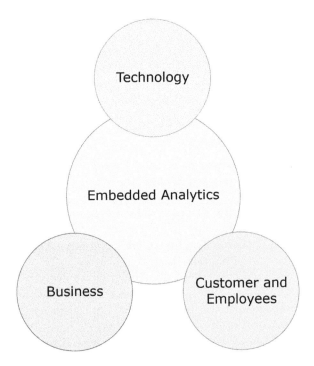

Figure 3.4 Forces Driving Embedded Analytics.

1 Technology: the increasing volume and availability of data, advances in data collections, computational power and storage capacity, advances in analytical techniques and technologies are all resulting in the formation of new business models;
2 Business: businesses are looking for real-time analytics that can help them to stay agile and competitive. Business leaders demand platforms to store and analyse massive amounts of data from various disparate data sources to make data-driven decisions. Companies also require the ability to:

    a Facilitate fast access to data
    b Blend and make seamless connections with a wide range of data from various data sources
    c Analyse vast volumes of data using data science algorithms
    d Provide the outputs of analytics in a visualised, easy-to-use, customisable interface
    e Integrate market data with real-time network feeds (Twitter, Instagram) to correlate business activity with social reaction

3 Customers and Employees: customers are looking for visual analytics that requires no training nor technical expertise. These visual analytics must also be available from a variety of data sources. Internal employees desire

a solution that allows them to push data in and return easy-to-read analytics, allowing them to produce results and solve problems quickly.

Key Term

Big Data; Big Data Analytics; Data Mining; Self Service Analytics; Embedded Analytics; Tableau; Python; RapidMiner; Hadoop

Chapter Key Takeaways

- Big Data is large and complex datasets that can be structured, semi-structured, or unstructured and will typically not fit into memory to be processed
- The 5Vs model of Big Data are velocity, volume, variety, value, and veracity
- The Big Data Analytics Techniques are Descriptive Analytics, Prescriptive Analytics, and Predictive analytics
- The business benefits of Big Data Analytics are decision-making, customer intelligence, Supply Chain and Performance Management, Quality Management and Improvement, Risk management, and Fraud Detection
- Examples of data analytics tools are R, Python, RapidMiner, Hadoop, and Tableau
- Self-Service Analytics allows end-users to analyse data by building and modifying existing reports quickly
- Embedded analytics seeks to broaden the business reach and to improve the timeliness of insights. Embedded analytics allows for tightly integrated capabilities into existing CRM, ERP, marketing automation, and financial systems

Discussion Questions

1 Discuss the characteristics of Big Data. Explain how these characteristics have changed and the mechanisms that companies are implementing to adapt to these changes.
2 Explain how the characteristics of Big Data assist companies in gathering Business Intelligence. Also, discuss how it can be overwhelming for SMEs.
3 Identify and discuss the different techniques that businesses use to analyse Big Data.
4 What are the steps involved in the discovery phase of the data analytics life cycle? How does this step help identify and prepare data for analysis?
5 Outline the different techniques used in transforming data.

6 Explain how companies can use Big Data to manage risks and detect fraud. Which industry is the most likely to be impacted by these risks and why?

7 List five data analytics tools. Explain in detail how any one of these tools is used by companies to analyse Big Data.

8 Data analytics is critical to the success of self-service analytics. So how can companies overcome the challenges of siloed data to create seamless data communication and empower employees using self-service analytics?

9 Discuss how embedded analytics is used to broaden business reach and support managerial decision-making.

10 Discuss the driving forces of embedded analytics.

4 Business Analytics and Intelligence

Big Data analytics and Business Intelligence (BI) are common buzzwords used in the technology sector. Both concepts offer businesses the opportunity to delve deeper and perform a detailed analysis of the data collected. Even though they overlap, they are different and offer organisations two unique ways to handle their data streams. BI focuses on leveraging business information, business analyses, and decision support to improve profitability. BI and analytical tools are predictive and analytical platforms that assist in analysing and interpreting vast amounts of data to gain insightful information about business and the industry in which the company operates. The demand for these tools has increased tremendously by small and mid-size companies. This chapter provides insight into customer behaviour, supply chain efficiency, marketing effectiveness, social media analytics, and pricing analytics. It explores the strategic planning for BI and analytics in the world of Big Data. The chapter also identifies how BI can be leveraged to improve specific business processes and enhance performance management techniques.

LEARNING OBJECTIVES:

At the end of this chapter, students should be able to:

- Understand the need for business analytics
- Understand the foundations of BI
- Learn the significant frameworks of computerised decision support: analytics and BI
- Understand the various types of analytics
- Recognise the role of Mobile Business Analytics and Intelligence in business decision-making

Business Analytics (BA)

Business analytics combines skills, technologies, and practices to examine business data and performance to gain insights and make data-driven

DOI: 10.4324/9781003129356-4

decisions using statistical analysis. It seeks to narrow down which datasets are valuable and increase revenue, productivity, and efficiency. BA, in most cases, can accurately predict future events relating to the actions of consumers and market trends. It can also assist in creating more efficient processes that can potentially lead to an increase in revenue.

Business analytics can be applied to customer relationship management, finance and marketing, supply-chain management, human resource management, pricing, and team game strategies in sports. Its application facilitates and equips enterprises with a better understanding of data for decision-making. As a result, the practical application of BA can help companies improve performance and profitability, align resources and strategies, increase market share and revenue, provide a better return to a shareholder, enhance competitive advantage, and reduce risks.

The growing significance of BA is evident based on recent development in BI, such as prescriptive analytics, which predicts future business trends and suggests the actions managers should take to capitalise on them. As a result, BA techniques enable analysts to make quick and intelligent decisions and provide stable leadership to compete in the market effectively.

Business Analytics Applications

Marketing

BA integrates market and customer-related data, technology, quantitative analysis, and computer-based models to provide decision-makers with various significant prospects for more reliable and optimal decision-making. For example, it is used to understand how different demographics respond to many advertising forms or chart how product desirability depends on context and environment. Relationship management with customers is an important area that requires continuous monitoring by service firms to provide a competitive advantage. Business analytics is also used for:

- **Segmentation**: enables the preparation of segment-wise reports. Therefore decision-makers can determine where to concentrate the company's resources.
- **Marketing Mix Optimisation:** The '6P's of marketing help determine the right marketing mix resulting in optimum sales. BA tools can help determine the correct marketing mix through the combinations.
- **Competitor Analysis:** The manager can compare the information with competitors, determining the areas of improvement or tactics to achieve a competitive edge.
- **Sales Performance Analysis:** The sales team can increase the company's revenue by gauging the sales performance, determining the area that needs modifications, and help raise the performance bar.

- **Sales Pipeline Analysis:** BA helps detect and eliminate any gaps in the sales process, which will help develop faster and more efficient operations.
- **Campaign Analysis:** Historical data can assist the marketing manager in directing future campaigns to those consumers who are more likely to respond to different adverts.

Finance

The finance industry harnesses the power of business analytics to transform freshly collected, raw, complex sets of data into understandable and usable insights. Financial institutions can be considered as one of the critical users of the most substantial and complex data. Recent advances in technology and techniques allow companies to leverage BA to improve decision-making across the enterprise. Business analytics is used in the financial industry for fraud detection, risk analysis, customer management, algorithmic trade, loan, and investment management for personal and commercial purposes. The finance sector is increasingly reliant on predictive analytics to boost efficiency, enhance customer service, identify potential issues, and much more. BA technologies are also prevalent in the banking industry including optimisation and segmentation.

BA is also vital in increasing business revenue, removing trade wastes, and making reliable business decisions. Client profitability analytics, predictive sales analytics, cash flow analytics, product profitability analytics, value-driven analytics, and shareholder value analytics are examples of BA technologies employed in the finance industry. As a result, business analytics technology has changed the way the finance industry functions.

Human Resources

Understanding organisation and people management has gained immense attention due to the value attached to human aspects to provide a sustainable competitive advantage. Human resources possess the creative capabilities to upgrade the innovative and creative domain of an organisation. Businesses use BA in the HR department for the following:

MEASURING PERFORMANCE

Organisations can use BA tools to establish performance benchmarks and provide existing and incoming employees guidelines to understand those qualities and their impact. For example, along with other companies, Deloitte analyses employee performance data and billing hours to help boost professional performance. Companies can even use data gathered from high-performing teams or individual employees to understand effective processes and establish benchmarks for other groups to emulate.

It can be demotivating for many high-performing employees to see under-performing peers receive promotions. By using business analytics, managers can determine the key factors that drive these decisions for promotions and raises. In addition, using different data sources, companies can employ AI algorithms to support decision-makers in making less-biased decisions and ensure performance-generated data.

UNDERSTANDING *ATTRITION AND INCREASING RETENTION*

BA is also used to predict employee turnover while also indicating those factors that contribute to attrition. Companies may also apply BA to identify at-risk workers. Organisations can also collect data on staff turnover rates to uncovered trends and address sudden surges.

EXAMINING *EMPLOYEE ENGAGEMENT*

A crucial metric for any personnel department is employee engagement. Such data is usually gathered via employee engagement surveys conducted by the HR department to monitor engagement regularly and with the help of AI tools, gain immediate insights into the data.

MEASURING *EMPLOYEE DEVELOPMENT AND LEARNING OUTCOMES*

A vibrant training program can benefit organisations with a more productive workforce and improved retention. Companies can employ predictive ana-lytics to customise training content that meets employee learning styles at an individual level. At an organisational level, it can assess weaknesses in the train-ing program. Businesses can then focus on the comprehension of the training program and track the employee's actual progress throughout the program.

Telecommunications

The telecommunications industry has a considerable customer base whose needs and desires are constantly evolving and changing. In a highly dynamic and competitive environment, each decision is crucial to maintain a compet-itive edge. Therefore, companies must make decisions based on extensive BA to ensure efficient and effective use of available resources. Although analytics is instrumental in the telecom industry in many ways, some of the significant applications include the following:

CUSTOMER RETENTION/IMPROVING CUSTOMER LOYALTY

Competition between the numerous players in the telecommunications in-dustry is robust. Therefore, customer retention is essential. Increasingly, telecom companies employ analytical tools to identify cross-selling opportunities and make meaningful decisions to retain their customers. Analytics help determine trends in customer behaviour, which is used to predict customer behaviour, buying patterns, and telecommunication preferences. When dealing with a large customer base, broad-spectrum marketing can be expensive and ineffective. Hence, BA can help direct marketing efforts by identifying target groups, thus increasing its opportunity to return its marketing investment.

NETWORK OPTIMISATION

Telecom companies must ensure that all customers have access to and full operational capabilities of their products at all times. At the same time, companies need to be frugal in allocating resources to the network since any unused capacity is a waste of resources. BA improves better monitoring traffic and aids in facilitating capacity planning decisions. Analytical tools leverage data collected through daily transactions and support short-term optimisation and long-term strategic decision-making.

SOCIAL MEDIA BRANDING

As in most industries, the branding of telecom companies on social media plays a crucial role in customer accrual and retention. Data generated through social media can be analysed and used to provide meaningful insights using social analytical tools. For example, customer sentiment analysis, customer experience, and company positioning can enrich customer experience. Also, data generated from social media platforms are more diverse geographically and demographically, providing a more in-depth understanding of customer information.

USES OF BUSINESS ANALYTICS

Regardless of the industry, BA is used for the following purposes:

1 To make a sound commercial decision. It affects the organisation's functioning as it helps to improve the profitability of the business, increases market share and revenue, and provides a better return on investment for shareholders. Likewise, BA can evaluate supplier performance based on customer ratings, order fulfilment speed, and quality, which helps companies decide which supplier works best.
2 Facilitates comprehensive understanding of available primary and secondary data, which again affects departments' operational efficiency. In addition, since business efficiency is not limited to employees' performance, businesses can also analyse other resources to learn more about their performance.

3   Provides a competitive advantage to companies. BA is used to make sound commercial decisions as it influences the functioning of the entire organisation. In this digital age, flow of information is utilised to make a company competitive. BA combines available data with various thought models to improve business decisions. Therefore, it enhances its profitability, boosts its market share and revenue, and provides a better ROI.

4   BA converts data into valuable information that businesses can use to plan for the unexpected. This information can be presented in the required format for the decision-maker. It can also model business trends, such as sales and profits, making it easy for larger organisations to predict order volume and minimise waste.

Business Intelligence

Traditionally, business intelligence (BI) is an umbrella term describing the concepts and methods to improve business decision-making using fact-based support systems. BI uses techniques and tools to acquire and transform raw data into meaningful and valuable information. The purpose of BI is to allow for the straightforward interpretation of Big Data. Identifying new opportunities and develop an effective strategy based on insights can provide businesses with a competitive market advantage and long-term stability. It is also used to provide historical, current, and predictive views of business operations and support different business decisions ranging from operational to strategic management. Examples of operating decisions include product positioning or pricing, while strategic business decisions have the company's priorities, goals, and directions at the highest level. For BI to be effective, it must combine data from the external with internal company sources such as financial and operations data. Combining external and internal data can provide a more holistic view for the company to make accurate decisions, gain insight into new markets, assess demand and appropriateness of products and services for various market segments, and measure the effect of marketing strategies.

The importance of BI has grown from the need to make real-time decisions and maintain a competitive advantage. BI is often used to produce reports, forecasts, improve companies' marketing strategies, and make better management decisions. Thus, BI can be the source of competitive advantages. It can provide the necessary information to users to make decisions that benefit the firm. This is especially true when firms can extrapolate information based on indicators in the external environment and make accurate forecasts about future occurrences or economic trends. Organisations also require actionable information to be accessed faster. BI reduces operational costs and time in analysing data and increases income by helping with better predictions and forecasts. Apart from these things, the business environment has become increasingly complex, and companies want to keep their IT costs to a minimum.

In addition, BI allows companies to:

- improve the timeliness and quality of information which improves the accuracy of the decision-making
- benchmark against competitors
- monitor changes in customer behaviour and spending habits
- monitor market social, regulatory, and political environment

BI technologies can handle large volumes of structured and unstructured data to help identify, develop, and create new strategic business opportunities. As a data-centric approach, BI relies on various advanced data collection, extraction, and analysis technologies. These technologies are collectively called business analytics (BA) and include the underlying architectures, tools, databases, applications, and methodologies. Data warehousing forms the foundation of BI. At the same time, data marts and tools for extraction, transformation, and load (ETL) are essential for converting and integrating business-specific data. Database queries, online analytical processing (OLAP), and advanced reporting tools are used to explore essential data characteristics. The primary objectives are to enable interactive and easy access to diverse data, enable manipulation and transformation of these data, and provide business managers and analysts the ability to conduct appropriate analyses and perform actions. In addition, BI initiatives provide various accounting, finance, and marketing applications, such as enterprise risk assessment and management, credit rating and analysis, stock and portfolio performance prediction.

Components of Business Intelligence

BI consists of an increasing number of components, including (Figure 4.1):

- Business Process Reengineering (BPR)
- Data Warehouse
- Reporting
- OLAP
- Advanced Analytics
- Data Mining

BUSINESS PROCESS REENGINEERING (BPR)

BPR seeks to radically redesign business processes to gain significant improvements in cost, quality, and service. Thus, BPR helps companies achieve excellent performance in various parameters like time, customer service, and quality. It is also used to improve business processes, thus creating value for the users through products or services and strengthen competitiveness through the fundamental redesign of business processes. Therefore, BPR is often employed to overcome challenges involving inefficiencies and inflated operating costs.

Figure 4.1 Component of Business Intelligence.

BPR is not necessarily dependent on technology. However, IT has been widely recognised as an essential enabler, and BPR is crucial in achieving IT business value. Furthermore, from a broader perspective, IT is a basis for process innovation, while process innovation is the catalyst for realising IT business value. Finally, some organisational changes as a result of BPR are:

- Modifications to the jobs and skill requirements as there is a shift from simple tasks to multi-dimensional work
- The roles of employees change from controlled to empowered
- The organisational structures change from hierarchical to flat

Performing such process improvement can be overwhelming to a company. BI allows companies to measure changes and provide answers to move the process improvement initiative to a new level. This is often achieved using Key Performance Indicators (KPIs) such as lead conversion rate (in sales) and inventory turnover (in inventory management).

DATA WAREHOUSE

A data warehouse is a repository of data that, when analysed, companies use to make informed decisions. Data flows into a data warehouse from heterogeneous sources such as transactional systems and relational databases. The data is processed, transformed, and ingested to access the processed data using BI tools, SQL clients, and spreadsheets. A data warehouse consolidates information from different sources into one comprehensive location. It can contain several databases. Within the database, data is organised into tables and columns. Each column includes a description of the data, such as integer, data field, or string. Tables can be arranged inside schemas, which operate as folders. Data warehouses generally consist of structured, semi-structured, and unstructured data. When data is ingested, it is stored in different tables described by the schema. Query tools use the schema to decide which data tables to access and analyse.

Business analysts, data engineers, data scientists, and decision-makers access the data through BI tools, SQL clients, and other analytics applications. As seen in Figure 4.2, the primary components of the database architecture are:

*   Data Sources including CRM (customer relationship management) and ERP systems
*   Applications and Database Management systems
*   Data warehouse: these feed data in the data mart. End-users access these for different organisational functions.

By merging the information in one place, an organisation can analyse its customers more holistically. Data warehousing makes data mining possible.

Data Warehouse Architecture

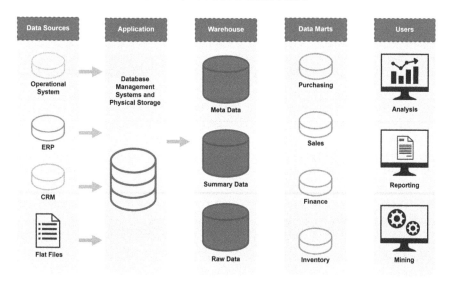

Figure 4.2 Data Warehouse Architecture.

From a business perspective, data warehousing is a storehouse of knowledge about company performance. It is essential for any organisation that hosts an extensive collection of available data to users. Typically, information is dispersed around the organisation, with no summaries or methods to retrieve and analyse this data. In addition, there needs to be consistency for more effective decision-making, especially when there is no commonality to the information. Each department views and uses the data differently. Data warehousing allows businesses to sift through data layers and examine inter-related components that can help drive decision-making, product development, and improve business performance. Data warehousing is considered the core component of a business intelligence system and is subject-oriented and integrated. It supports the physical propagation of data by handling the different enterprise records for integration, cleansing, aggregation, and query tasks. It can also contain the operational data used for organisational-wide tactical decision-making of a particular subject area. The data warehouse has live enterprise data and retains minimal historical data. The key to a successful BI system lies in consolidating data from numerous company operational systems into a data warehouse. Companies can distinguish themselves by leveraging information about their marketplace, customers, and operations to capitalise on business opportunities.

Decision-makers and analysts need direct access to the data in the warehouse. The connection must be instant and on-demand to improve performance, especially when rapidly making decisions to stay ahead of the competition due to market changes. A data warehouse is crucial to assist an organisation in achieving its strategic management goal, which guides the decision support system. Data warehouse allows for strategic analysis by examining external and internal aspects of the organisation.

Data and analytics have become vital to businesses to maintain a competitive advantage. Managers and other decision-makers rely on reports, dashboards, and analytics tools to extract intelligence from their data, monitor business performance, and support decision-making. Data warehouses are used to power these reports, dashboards, and analytics tools by storing data efficiently to reduce the input and output (I/O) of data and deliver query results quickly to users concurrently. In addition, a data warehouse supports analytical reporting, structured and ad hoc queries, and decision-making. The information collected in a data warehouse can be used for the following:

- **Production Strategies** – Product strategies can be adjusted by repositioning the products and managing the product portfolios by comparing quarterly or yearly sales.
- **Customer Analysis** – This is used to analyse customers' buying preferences, buying time, budget cycles, and other variables.
- **Operations Analysis** – it allows for the analysis of business operations, as it is beneficial for customer relationship management and making environmental corrections.

Benefits of a Data Warehouse

Once a data warehouse is implemented into the company's BI framework, it can benefit them in numerous ways. These benefits include:

1 Enhanced business intelligence
   By having access to information from different sources from a single platform, decision-makers will no longer need to rely on instinct or limited data. Additionally, data warehouses can be applied to business processes, such as market segmentation, sales, risk, inventory, and financial management.
2 Saves times
   It standardises, preserves, and stores data from various sources, thus consolidating and integrating data. Critical data is available to all users and allows them to make informed decisions. Likewise, management can query the data with little to no IT support, saving more time and money. A data warehouse enables high-quality, standardised data to be available on time and for rapid data mining. This power and speed allow for the development of competitive advantage.
3 Enhances data quality and consistency
   A data warehouse converts data from different sources into a consistent format. Since the data is standardised, the results from each department are consistent. Consistency of data also leads to increase data accuracy, thus forming the basis for solid decisions. Furthermore, a data warehouse is specifically geared to handle massive levels of data and complex queries.
4 Generates a high Return on Investment (ROI)
   Companies investing in data warehouses experience higher revenue generation. Creating more regulated and better quality data is the main strength of a data warehouse. In addition, BI improves the decision-making in the organisation. Improved decision-making strengthens the business, thus creating a higher ROI.
5 Provides a competitive advantage
   Data warehouses give companies a holistic view of their current standing and evaluate opportunities and risks, thus providing them with a competitive advantage. By using a data warehouse, businesses can strategise and effectively compete against competitors. In addition, a data warehouse improves business decision-making, which is crucial in providing any business with a competitive advantage.
6 Improves the decision-making process
   It provides better insights to users by maintaining a cohesive database of current and historical data. By transforming data into meaningful information, decision-makers can perform more practical, precise, and reliable analysis and generate more valuable reports.
7 Enables Forecasting
   A data warehouse stores large quantities of historical data to analyse different periods and trends to forecast. Data analysts and scientists can analyse the data to predict market trends, identify KPIs, and gauge indicated

results, allowing key personnel to plan accordingly. Such data typically cannot be stored in a transactional database.

Reporting

Companies are always seeking to improve business performance, create better products, and discover how customers respond. As a result, BI reporting is fundamental to every business. It is the process of preparing and analysing data, extracting valuable insights, and creating shareable reports to inform business decisions. The data is collected from different tools and platforms, including CRM, finance, and HR management systems. Centralising these data sources in a data warehouse allows businesses to perform queries, manipulate the data, and present it in report form. These reports can take different formats such as tables, spreadsheets, and PDFs. Visualisations can include charts and graphs. Reports can also be customised dashboards that are accessible through a web browser. With current technology, BI reports can be automated and run on a pre-determined schedule.

It primarily consists of two categories:

- **Managed reporting** occurs when a technical employee such as a data analyst prepares the data for managerial or non-technical users.
- **Ad hoc reporting** occurs when a non-technical user creates reports from scratch or edits pre-existing reports without making requests from IT.

Reporting allows business users to examine data trends over time and determine relationships between variables. In addition, smart BI tools have features such as Natural Language Processing (NLP), so users can query the data using questions without coding.

Common BI Reporting Challenges

Traditionally, there are several common challenges to BI reporting:

- **Data wrangling** – Tracking and analysing data across platforms and services can be time-consuming without the correct automation tools.
- **Data silos** – in enterprises, data can become siloed. As a result, users often have access to limited data within a specific domain but cannot obtain a holistic picture of events across the organisation.
- **Reporting inconsistencies** – Usually, these platforms and tools have built-in analytics and reporting features. Inconsistencies across platforms and tools make it challenging to create accurate reports and dashboards.
- **Manual data preparation** – Because of inconsistencies and data silos, BI users must extract data and compile relevant data sources themselves. The culmination of these activities requires additional time to produce reports and tell a coherent data story.

OLAP (Online Analytical Processing)

This component stands behind most BI applications that executives use to sort and select data clusters for monitoring purposes. OLAP deals with data discovery and capabilities for report viewing, complex calculations, to "what if" scenario planning. Businesses are constantly bringing information together to perform further analysis, and OLAP is used to optimise the searching of enormous data files by using the automatic generation of SQL queries. They need to get all the data in one location to achieve an accurate and reliable understanding of different aspects of the data.

OLAP allows the end-user to explore multi-dimensional summarised views of business data to obtain the necessary insight for making a decision. The multi-dimensional perspective will enable managers to analyse data from different perspectives and discover hidden information. It produces readable, interactive report generation, analysis, modelling, planning for optimising the business, and strategic decision-making. These systems process queries required to discover trends and analyse critical factors. OLAP techniques and tools are used in data warehouses or data marts design for sophisticated enterprise intelligence systems. Most companies have data with multiple dimensions or categories of data for presentation, tracking, or analysis. For example, sales prices may have different sizes related to location (region, country, state/province, city/town, store), time (year, quarter, month, week, day), product (clothing, men/women/children, brand, type), and more.

Therefore, companies use OLAP to enable fast and intuitive access to centralised data that also provides related calculations for analysis and reporting purposes. An OLAP solution improves a data warehouse or other relational database with aggregate data and business predictions for the IT team. In addition, by enabling users to perform their analyses and reporting, OLAP systems reduce demands on IT resources.

OLAP offers five key benefits to businesses:

- Business-focused multi-dimensional data
- Trustworthy data and calculations
- Speed-of-thought analysis
- Flexible, self-service reporting
- Ad hoc Analysis

Business-focused Calculations

OLAP systems allow for the computation of pre-aggregate values. The calculation engine aggregates data and business calculations. In an OLAP system, the analytic capabilities are independent of how the results are presented. The analytical calculations are centrally stored in the metadata for the system, not in each report.

Trustworthy Data and Calculations

Many companies have multiple reporting systems, each with its database. As a result, when data proliferates, it can be challenging to ensure that it is trustworthy. OLAP systems centralise data and calculations, providing a single data source for all end-users, ensuring that they can access consistently defined data and calculations to support BI.

Ad Hoc Analysis

The analysts can pose queries and get immediate responses from the OLAP system. In addition, users can immediately pose another query based on the findings, thus leading the analyst down the road of discovery. As a result, companies have fast response times and in-depth insights into relationships that otherwise might be missed with the intuitive multi-dimensional data.

OLAP systems respond rapidly to end-user queries because of the pre-aggregate data. Pre-aggregation indicates that there is no need for time-consuming calculations when an end-user query is processed. In addition, OLAP systems optimise business calculations, so they take less time to execute.

Flexible, Self-Service Reporting

Enabling decision-makers and other business users to create their reports is a hallmark of an OLAP system. OLAP systems allow users to query data and create reports using familiar tools. The familiarity of end-users with these tools increases the chance of using the system. Also, with the commercial and customised spreadsheet applications, OLAP systems support additional front-end reporting tools designed with business users in mind. For example, it includes user-friendly tools that enable report designers to create and publish web-based dashboards and interactive reports using live OLAP data. When business users can build their reports, it reduces the reliance on IT resources for generating reports.

Advanced Analytics

Advanced Analytics refers to data mining, forecasting or predictive analytics, semantic analysis, sentiment analysis, network, cluster analysis, multivariate statistics, graph analysis, simulation, complex event processing, neural networks, and more sophisticated statistical analysis techniques. Advanced analytics allows managers to examine the data of different products or services. When used for problem-solving, it is more proactive and pre-emptive and is used to uncover patterns and opportunities.

Advanced analytics provides businesses with the opportunity to operationalise and get more value from data assets. It represents a potential opportunity for companies to extract value from data stored in a data warehouse or real-time data created by business operations. Businesses that utilise advanced analytics tools can build upon knowledge discovery and problem-solving. In addition, it offers the functionality to anticipate future issues, providing greater confidence for more repeatable business results. For example, a restaurant chain may analyse the sale of certain items and make local, regional, and national modifications on menu board offerings. The data could also predict in which markets a new product may have the best success.

Benefits of Advanced Analytics

In addition to contributing to business value, the following are some of the benefits organisations derive from a successful advanced analytics program:

- Businesses using advanced analytics can act quickly and with a greater degree of confidence about future outcomes. It allows companies to make data-driven decisions and gain deeper insights on market trends, customer preferences, and critical business activities. Implementing advanced analytics will enable businesses to assess market conditions faster and react to changes before competitors, thus gaining a significant advantage.
- With more accurate predictions from advanced analytics, businesses can avoid making costly, risky decisions based on inaccurate predictions. Advanced analytics provides companies with a comprehensive understanding of the business operations, past, present, and future, to better identify and manage risk.
- It helps businesses solve challenges beyond the capabilities of traditional BI. For example, based on likelihood, it can prescribe actions to result in better business outcomes. As enterprises mature in advanced analytics, it can lead to lower costs and higher revenues.
- It directly improves demand capacity management by allowing real-time insights into the demand/capacity curve. Predictive insights provided by advanced analytics enable more accurate and consistent forecasting across the organisation, generally leading to more effective planning processes. For example, it leads to improving customer service.
- It eliminates problems from the supply chain. As a result, customers enjoy more reliable and consistent delivery times and product quality. Likewise, advanced analytics enables additive manufacturing that leads to higher margins and faster speed to market. Ultimately, advanced analytics offer greater production control across the supply chain and beyond.

Data Mining

Acquiring information through mining is referred to as business intelligence. Datasets are multiplying because of the use of information systems and data warehousing. Large telecommunications and mobile operators generate some of the most extensive datasets as they have millions of user accounts, resulting in millions of data per year. As these numbers increase, analytical processing such as OLAP and manual comprehension appears ineffective. It is worth mentioning that BI software is directed at knowledge workers, mainly executives, analysts, middle management, and to a lesser extent, operational management.

The central theme of BI is to utilise massive data to help organisations gain competitive advantages. Therefore, one of the primary uses of DM is for BI and risk management purposes. Furthermore, since companies must make business-critical decisions based on large datasets stored in their databases, DM directly affects decision-making. Therefore, DM is widely used in retail, telecommunication, investment, insurance, education, and healthcare. Thus, its applications in any sector depend on two main factors:

1   The available data and the business problems to be solved with BI;
2   DM technologies.

Real-Time Business Intelligence

Real-time BI is applying analytics and data processing tools to gain insight into relevant data and visualisations instantaneously. Real-time, in this case, means information is delivered in a range from milliseconds to a few seconds after the event occurred. Real-time BI is richly visual and allows for human-oriented data exploration. The information is used to make informed decisions quite rapidly. By using real-time BI, businesses remain responsive and adaptable in an ever-changing digital environment.

Consequently, real-time BI has emerged as a necessity. Advances in technology have made real-time BI achievable. The Internet and information communication technologies (ICT) have transformed how is information is shared. It is straightforward to capture all sorts of data and store them cheaply. BI has become an essential component of an increasingly mobile society that allows business owners to respond to real-time trends in email, messaging systems, or even digital displays. It can also help marketing professionals create better deals and limited-time offers. It also works on Big Data or past data repositories to combine them, derive inferences, or compare/correlate previous statistics. For example, it can help analyse customers' number, time, and location to provide better deals on a specific day or weekend. CEOs may also use real-time BI to track the exact location and time a user interacts with a website. The marketing team can offer special promotions while users are still engaging with the website.

Business Intelligence and Analytics

The concept of BI and BA are sometimes used interchangeably. BI involves acquiring data and information from a wide variety of sources and utilising them in decision-making. BA adds another dimension to BI using models and solutions. Companies conduct BA as part of their larger BI strategy. However, BA should not be considered a linear process but rather a series of data access, discovery, exploration, and information sharing.

BI collects business data to find information by asking questions, reporting, and online analytical processes. It is designed to answer specific queries and provide quick analysis for decisions or planning. BA, on the other hand, uses statistical and quantitative tools for explanatory and predictive modelling. Thus, BA can be considered a subset of BI focusing on statistics, prediction, and optimisation rather than the reporting functionality.

Used together, BI&A technologies facilitate data collection, analysis, and information delivery and are designed to support decision-making. BI&A allow decision-makers to gain data analysis and decision support, creating value for the company. These insights can improve products and services, achieve enhanced operational efficiency, and foster better customer relationships. In addition, BI&A is considered crucial for organisational learning and adjustments, refining operational efficiency, and consolidating companywide intelligence. BI&A has also increased companies' absorptive capacity by expanding their ability to receive, store, analyse, and transfer information with minimal errors.

BI and BA are data-driven. It is highly applied and is used to leverage opportunities presented by the vast volume of data. BI and BA allow for domain-specific analytics needed in many critical and high-impact application areas such as e-commerce and market intelligence, e-government, science and technology, health, and security. In addition to technical system implementation, significant business knowledge and effective communication skills are required to complete such business intelligence and analytics projects.

Business Intelligence and Analytics Components

BI and BA systems usually include:

Data Warehousing as a Service (DaaS)

Data Warehousing as a Service (DaaS) amplifies the use of BI and BA by providing actionable analytics and insights promoting digitally transformed business processes. DaaS allows companies to secure the input for data warehouse on cloud infrastructure, making data easily accessible to decision-makers while protecting it from unauthorised users and hackers. DaaS addresses that a company needs to aggregate, store, organise, and analyse data by providing the full-featured capabilities companies need without much administrative overhead. Companies considering DaaS should understand its benefits, how it can be integrated into their existing systems, and available options.

Key Performance Indicators

Performance Management – KPIs are another component of BI and BA. Performance- management focuses on aligning decisions and actions with the companies' strategic goals. Performance management assists companies depart from dealing with tedious voluminous reports and data dumps. With performance management, users can streamline their focus on what is relevant information. Performance metrics are crucial for monitoring and measuring progress toward goals. KPIs enable organisations to analyse data to interpret whether they successfully reduce customer dissatisfaction, improve on-time delivery, and other business performance goals.

Mobile Business Intelligence and Analytics

The increasing use of mobile devices and the development of ubiquitous computing with embedded processors have led to mobile BI and BA development. A mobile BI and BA system can offer similar functionality as traditional BI and BA. BI and BA applications are arriving on mobile devices primarily for communication and collaboration purposes. Increasingly, companies are using the mobility, geolocation, and interface features these devices offer to their advantage. By employing these mobile devices, organisations can deliver information in the context of an ongoing collaboration, enabling users to identify and highlight key points for shared decisions. Having access to content digitally, users will want to implement BI reports and data access functions to develop integrated information views. These views can bring together information that is important for reducing delays and streamlining business processes.

Mobile BI and BA systems are sources of essential data management concerns. Companies need to assess their readiness to meet data security, availability, performance scalability, real-time data, and other challenges likely to increase intensity as mobile utilisations grow. Companies also face new data management challenges in ensuring that mobile users access the same data as on-premises to desktop users. Data security is a complex problem for mobile BI and BA deployments. Data security and authentication concerns are among the top barriers to making the business or IT case for providing BI and BA on mobile devices. Concerns regarding potential violations of regulatory provisions are one of the main barriers to mobile usage. In addition, companies are concerned about the risks associated with sending data outside of systems boundaries. Typically, Secure Sockets Layer (SSL) protocols, encryption, and virtual private networks (VPNs) protect data transmission over mobile devices.

Employing mobile BI and BA increases the demand for data management capabilities to deliver right-time data insights. However, mobile BI and BA applications benefit from data management techniques such as operational data integration, in-memory analytics, reporting, multicore systems, grid computing, enabling faster query performance, and more frequent data updates toward real-time goals. These advances also increase data availability, which is essential to delivering data and analytics at the right time to users who are on the move – possibly around the globe – and may need data on demand.

APPLICATION CASE 4.1

Data Analytics Improves Efficiency and Accuracy of Operations – Rowan University

This case study teaches how Rowan University automated a manual process to assign appropriate courses for incoming first-year students. The project reduced required staff time, improved the accuracy of the registration process, and freed up advisors from tedious tasks, enabling them to return to the critical work of advising students.

The Challenge: A Beneficial but Time-Consuming Process

Rowan University is a public university in Glassboro, New Jersey. Founded in 1923, Rowan offers more than 70 bachelor's programs, over 50 master's degree programs, four doctoral programs, and two professional programs. Rowan University prides itself on its core inclusivity, agility, and a diverse, scholarly, and creative educational experience. Its student population is growing, and enrolment recently exceeded 19,000 total students across all campuses.

To ensure that students will be on track to graduate on time with all required courses and credits, Rowan uses a system to place incoming first-year students into the appropriate section of their required courses for their major, including evaluation of placement testing scores. The process utilises Freshman Instructional Guides (FIGS) to create freshman Fall schedules based on major-specific curriculum requirements. It greatly benefits incoming students by setting them down the right path and preventing them from running into graduation bottlenecks. However, manually evaluating and registering students became more and more time-consuming as Rowan's student population grew.

The traditional FIGS process involved the following steps:

1   Testing Services produced several student record spreadsheets, then manually reviewed and evaluated SAT or ACT results and AP or transfer credits to determine if a student was exempt from a placement test or required to take it.
2   University advisors then manually assigned students to appropriate classes and sections based on placement test results, exemptions, and degree requirements.

3   Curriculum Planners used the results of the steps above to determine how many of each section would be required to accommodate the incoming class.

4   The Office of the Registrar manually registered 2,700 students, one-by-one, in the Banner Student Information System.

The process was lengthy and bore the risk of human error. For example, a slight distraction could lead to a student being improperly assigned (or exempted from) a placement exam or mistakenly sorted into a course too basic or too advanced.

Since 2015, the student population at Rowan has approximately doubled, increasing from around 10,000 students to over 19,000. This meant that either additional staff time needed to be allocated to manually sorting and registering students, or Rowan needed a more efficient system.

The Solution: Automate the FIGS Process

Rowan's Information Resources & Technology Data Analytics team worked in collaboration with the University Advising, Testing Services, and Development & Innovation teams to take on the challenge of creating an automated system to rapidly and accurately perform the entire FIGS process.

To complete this work, the Data Analytics team at Rowan required data tools that would enable them to do the following efficiently:

- Connect to a variety of databases, information sources, and disparate file types
- Incorporate scoring rules to perform sorting calculations
- Output the information in an actionable format

Rowan University chose Rapid Insight's Construct to accomplish this task, citing its flexibility and vital customer service as deciding factors.

The FIGS Dashboard

The solution developed by Rowan's Data Analytics team is known as the FIGS Dashboard. The entire process of assigning students to placement exams and course sections now happens automatically, and the Registrar Office receives a clean, organised dashboard to work.

With the process saved in Construct and data automatically refreshed from Banner, no additional work is needed to implement the dashboard

(Continued)

using a new year's data. For example, suppose Testing Services has new scoring rules to implement, or the specific essential requirements change from year to year. In that case, the system can quickly and easily be updated to reflect the changes. The dashboard does the rest, automatically providing advisors with the exact list of courses to register each freshman for in Banner.

Lara Roberts LeBeau, the Assistant Director of Testing Services at Rowan University, described the improvements the FIGS Dashboard made for her department by saying,

> the Dashboard revolutionised the process of administering placement testing for incoming students. It reduced the number of hours required to determine which students require testing and the number of hours required to prepare for placement testing appointments. The Dashboard is accurate and simple and is truly a pleasure to use.

– Lara Roberts LeBeau, Assistant Director of Testing Services

Implementing the FIGS dashboard reduced the required staff time for Testing Services by 125 hours and saved student advisors an additional 90 hours. In total, the dashboard keeps 215 hours each year – over five weeks of FTE staff time. This freed Testing Services and student advisors to focus on critical work previously overshadowed by the lengthy manual task of sorting and ranking incoming students.

"The automation of the course mapping of degree requirements to freshman schedules reduces the number of time advisors needs to enter course information manually," said Amy Ruymann, Rowan's Director of University Advising Services. "The increased efficiency and accuracy of the overall system has been significant in that advisors can now spend more time on the important work of supporting students."

– Amy Ruymann, Director, University Advising Services

Additionally, the FIGS Dashboard removed the potential for human error; when records were checked manually, the chance existed that a student could be incorrectly flagged as needing to take a test when they already met the requirements for bypassing it. The FIGS Dashboard saves advisors and students additional time, as these errors no longer need to be corrected.

The FIGS dashboard also benefits curriculum planners. It delivers a more timely and accurate list of the sections required for the coming term. This allows planners to ensure there are enough sections of each course available earlier in the planning process, preventing over or understaffing for those sections.

> *Source*: Rapid insight case studies, a data analytics company: *Rowan University uses Rapid Insight to Transform Freshman Registration and Section Planning*, https://www.rapidinsight. com/why-rapid-insight/case-studies/rowan-university-uses-rapid-insight-to-transform-freshman-registration-and-section-planning/. Used by permission from Rapid Insight.

Key Term

Business Intelligence; Business Analytics; Online Analytical Processing; Key Performance Indicators(KPI); Real-Time

Business Intelligence; Advanced Analytics; Mobile Business Intelligence; Reporting; Business Process Reengineering (BPR)

Chapter Key Takeaways

- Business analytics combines skills, technologies, and practices used to examine business data and performance to gain insights and make data-driven decisions in the future using statistical analysis.
- Components of Business Intelligence include OLAP, Business Process Reengineering (BPR), Benchmarking, Data Warehouse, Reporting, Data Mining, and Advanced Analytics.
- Business Intelligence is used to produce real-time:
  - customer engagement, thus improving relationships, customer experience, encouraging loyalty, and turning leads into paying clients, even long-term customers;
  - collaboration that fosters better decision-making, which leads to increased sales and improved market share gains;
  - transactions that allow companies to make better, real-time transactions;
  - support, thus providing the correct information to the right people at the right time is essential;
  - reporting and business decisions that provide snapshots and more detailed insights into business activities. It allows companies to perform real-time decision-making processes critical to their operations.
- Business intelligence and business analytics are used interchangeably. Companies conduct business analytics as part of their larger business intelligence strategy.
- Mobile business intelligence and analytics systems offer similar functionality as traditional BI&A. These applications are arriving on mobile devices primarily for communication and collaboration purposes.

Discussion Questions

1   Identify the areas/industries where Business Analytics is used. Then, explain in detail how marketers employ it.
2   Describe how companies use real-time business intelligence to provide insights into business transactions.
3   What is the difference between descriptive, predictive, and prescriptive analytics?
4   List and explain why business analytics is used in most businesses.
5   What are the advantages of business analytics?
6   What is business intelligence? Give two examples of its uses in business.
7   What are the components of business intelligence?
8   What is a data warehouse?
9   List and explain the components of a data warehouse.
10   What is the value of a data warehouse to a business?

5 Customer Relationship Analytics, Cloud Computing, Blockchain, and Cognitive Computing

Every business needs customers. Retaining and gaining new customers is necessary for most companies to survive. Additionally, businesses, especially small enterprises, need a low-cost application platform and inexpensive third-party transaction costs to survive in this technologically driven business environment. This chapter looks at how cloud computing reduces the cost of doing business, decreases hardware requirements, and allows companies to use sophisticated enterprise application tools such as Customer Relationship Management (CRM) analytics. The chapter also examines how Blockchain help reduces transaction costs. Finally, it discusses how companies can eliminate third-party transaction costs and prevent the duplication of CRM data, the corruption of customer profile data, and maintain customer data privacy.

LEARNING OBJECTIVES:

At the end of this chapter, students should be able:

- Understand the role of CRM solutions in retaining and managing customers
- Identify the different types of cloud computing platforms available to business
- Know the benefits of cloud computing
- Understand Blockchain technologies and their benefits
- Recognise the business use of CRM analytics
- Know the relationship between CRM and Big Data
- Understand how customer relationship analytics function

Customer Relationship Management (CRM)

CRM amalgamates practices, strategies, and technologies to interact with customers. This entire relationship comprises direct interactions with customers through sales and service-related processes, forecasting, and customer

DOI: 10.4324/9781003129356-5

trends and behaviours from the company's perspective. Therefore, CRM serves to enhance the customer's overall experience.

CRM software is a tool that helps businesses obtain, retain, and maintain a good relationship with all customers. It does this by tracking customers' phone calls, website visits, complaints, buying habits, order history, and social media data across multiple sources. The data in the CRM is organised to provide critical business insights. In addition, the system customises and displays the data in one place on a dashboard that is available to all employees. With this information, organisations can stay connected with customers, improve business services and product offerings. However, it can be costly to get new customers. Therefore, finding ways to retain existing customers and attract new ones is the prime goal of CRM solutions. Data is one of the essential assets in a business, and CRM software collect this invaluable asset and put it in a central location for analysis.

CRM solutions allow the business to run successfully and efficiently as:

- It gives a complete overview of customers' status and behaviour and helps prioritise important customers and complaints.
- It categorises customers based on their expectations, shopping patterns, order history, feedback, likes and dislikes of a product, and other categories.
- It generates a good database that can be used to target promotional and loyalty programs.
- The data it collects will improve communication between businesses and customers and strengthen their relationship as companies know customers' needs and complaints.

Benefits of CRM

Improves Customer Service

CRM manages all the customer contacts and aggregates valuable new data. It allows companies to build customer profiles based on behavioural patterns, purchase records, and previous communications across different media channels. This information determines how best to reach the company's target audience. As a result, social media advertising offers companies one of the most effective tools to attract and keep new customers.

Increase in Sales

CRM tools help streamline and improve the sales process, automate tasks, and analyse sales data. The combination of these activities will inevitably lead to increased sales and sales productivity. CRM identifies which customer segments are more willing to consume more of the company's products or services. Organisational sales can be significantly increased by targeting prospects, customers, and other contacts from these segments. CRM increase sales by:

- Increasing efficiency into the sales process thus saving time and money
- Monitoring and organising customers' information in segmented lists to conduct targeted promotions
- Maintaining personalised interactions with prospects and clients

Increase Customer Retention

Customer retention is vital for a company's success. CRM service offers businesses a way to build and maintain relationships with a broad audience, creating loyalty and customer retention. Sentiment analysis, automated ticketing, customer support, and customer service automation can improve customer retention. In addition, most customers expect personalised, targeted service. CRM software manages relationships with customers and helps businesses keep abreast of client interactions by:

- Targeting customers with special offers. CRM software allows businesses to track customer's purchase history and determine which promotional offers are most appealing. Such practices increase relevancy and brand awareness. As a result, companies can offer special discounts or some additional value for products or services.
- Rewarding customer loyalty. Using customer data gathered from the CRM software, businesses can determine which customer accounts are most profitable. Knowing which accounts generate the most revenue allows enterprises to allocate time and resources efficiently and increase cross-selling or up-selling.
- Personalising customer follow-ups. CRM system makes it easier for businesses to establish and maintain relationships with customers by personalising future communications. The greater the details provided, the easier it is to tailor follow-up strategies.

Improved Analytics

CRM analytics is helpful for businesses of all sizes, substantial enterprises dealing with a large clientele daily. Using analytical CRM tools provides available, intelligible, and relevant data to match its business needs. Data from the different functions like sales, finance, and marketing flow into CRM system supported by data warehouse and data mining to assist with analytics. CRM analytics help companies gain insights into business services and optimise various business processes. It provides a single platform through which all authorised team members can access specific customer information and provide personalised service. The overall benefits to companies are more significant customer acquisition, customer retention, and better data management. Having all the essential day-to-day business functions in one location allows for better workflow, an easier collaboration between employees, and improved project management. In addition, CRM analytics can determine which groups of customers are most likely to bring in the highest ROI based on customer segmentation. As a result, businesses can focus on advertising, marketing, and sales, thus increasing profit margins over time.

Improved Knowledge Management and Sharing

Managing knowledge and connecting with customers to receive their loyalty are prerogatives for organisations seeking a competitive advantage. With knowledge management tools and company support, CRM can develop and enhance customer relationship strategies. Knowledge management helps companies understand the customer's needs and manage the relationship between the two entities. Building and managing lasting relationships between customer and supplier, based on trust, collaboration, and commitment, is beneficial to both customer and company.

Miscommunication and sharing of incomplete information cause inefficiencies in the organisation. CRM tools prevent redundancies and help streamline team activities by creating a knowledge base, establishing best practice workflows, and allowing frictionless communication between team members.

CRM Cloud Solutions

Cloud-based solutions provide real-time data to the sales team and increase accessibility to customer information. These solutions cover the entire customer lifecycle, including initial contact, inquiries, conversion, and long-term engagement. These solutions are:

* Cloud Computing Technologies
* Blockchain Technologies

Cloud Computing Technology

Cloud computing is an IT model where both the hardware and software services are provided on demand through networks independent of the terminal device and location. It is the process of delivering computing services, including data storage, over the Internet rather than on the personal computer. It offers a mobile platform on which to operate a business. Cloud computing technology makes business operations very flexible. It reduces the upfront cost of setting up systems, lowers transaction costs, and eliminates the need to implement a disaster recovery plan. In addition, it facilitates enhanced and faster responses, agility, and seamless communication.

Cloud computing is great for small businesses and start-up companies with little capital. It reduces or eliminates the initial setup cost of a technology system, such as buying software, hardware, paying an IT expert, and having an in-house IT management employee or team. Furthermore, cloud computing is significant for sharing and storing different types of data, and it also saves the time and energy of the users. In addition, cloud computing is efficiently secure because the service provider frequently upgrades the software, and data backup is constant.

Types of Cloud Computing

There are three primary cloud computing platforms, as seen in Figure 5.1:

1 IaaS
2 PaaS
3 SaaS

INFRASTRUCTURE AS A SERVICE (IAAS)

An Infrastructure as a Service (IaaS) offers computing, storage, and network resources to consumers on-demand, over the Internet, and on a pay-as-you-go basis. Businesses can load software, including operating systems and applications, onto the cloud, thus reducing the need for high, upfront capital expenditures or irrelevant infrastructure.

IaaS collects physical and virtualised resources that provide customers with the primary resources required to operate applications and workloads in the cloud. The IaaS platform and architecture consist of the following:

- **Physical data centres:** IaaS providers manage large data centres containing the physical machines available to end-users over the web. In some IaaS models, users do not interact directly with the physical infrastructure, but it is provided as a service.
- **Compute:** IaaS is typically perceived as virtualised computing resources or as a virtual machine. IaaS providers manage the thin layer of software that supports the entire cloud ecosystem called hypervisors.
- **Network:** Networking in the cloud is a type of software-defined networking. It involves using traditional networking hardware, such as routers and switches made available programmatically through APIs.
- **Storage:** There are three primary types of cloud storage, i.e., (1) block storage, (2) file storage, and (3) object storage. Block and file storage are standard in traditional data centres. However, these types of storage can face scalability and performance issues over the cloud. Object storage is the most basic storage mode in the cloud since it is highly distributed and resilient.

IaaS Characteristics
Characteristics that define IaaS include:

- Resources are available as a service
- Cost varies with consumption
- Services are very scalable
- Multiple users on a particular piece of hardware
- Companies retain complete control of the infrastructure
- Dynamic and flexible

PLATFORM AS A SERVICE (PAAS)

Platform as a Service (PaaS) provides developers with a software platform on which to build an application. It allows for the development, operation, and management of the applications without the cost, complexity, and inflexibility of creating and managing that platform on-premises.

Developers rely on cloud providers to supply the development tools, infrastructure, and operating systems, simplifying web application development as back-end activities occur behind the scenes. PaaS hosts the hardware and software on its infrastructure and delivers this platform to users as an integrated solution, solution stack, or service through an internet connection. Using PaaS allows for the scalability of the underlying hardware and software platform. A customer pays a monthly fee based on usage and can purchase more resources on-demand as needed. In this way, PaaS allows the development team to build, test, deploy, maintain, update, and scale applications faster and cheaper than managing an own on-premises platform.

PaaS Characteristics
The following are the essential characteristics when PaaS is being utilised:

- Utilise virtualisation technology which allows for scalability of resources based on business fluctuations
- Provide services that assist with the development, testing, and deployment of applications
- Allow various users to access the same development application
- Integrates web services and databases

SOFTWARE AS A SERVICE (SAAS)

Software as a Service (SaaS), also known as Web-based software, on-demand software, or hosted software, runs on providers' servers. Web-based email application services such as Outlook, Hotmail, or Yahoo! Mail are typical SaaS examples. SaaS providers manage access to the different applications, including security, availability, and performance. Therefore, SaaS reduces the complexity of software installation, maintenance, upgrades, and patches for

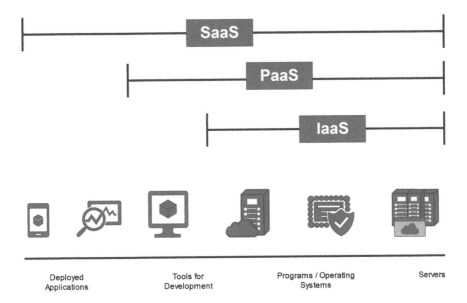

Figure 5.1 Types of Computing.

the in-house IT team since the software is centrally managed and monitored by SaaS providers.

SaaS Characteristics

The following are the essential characteristics when SaaS is being utilised:

- Managed from a central location
- Hosted on a remote server
- Accessible over the Internet
- Service providers are responsible for hardware or software updates

Benefits of Cloud Computing

Cloud computing offers a change from the traditional approach to how businesses use IT resources. There are several benefits to organisations using cloud computing services. These include:

Cost

Cloud computing helps companies to achieve economies of scale. Cloud computing reduces the capital expense of buying hardware and software by using racks of servers. In a cloud-based model, financing for capital investment is not the responsibility of the company. As a result, there is far less variability in cost, thus removing a significant barrier to growth.

In addition, companies will share server infrastructure with other organisations' computing needs rather than having dedicated servers to maintain and pay for regardless of demand. Therefore, businesses will not pay for idle infrastructure but rather what is used. The practicalities of cloud computing include high utilisation, smoothing peaks and troughs in workloads, and the demand for round-the-clock electricity for power and cooling.

Staffing can account for more than half of the operational cost for a business since the cost of IT experts for managing the infrastructure is often expensive. Cloud computing allows companies to improve the IT department's operations by deploying staff to other business areas, improving their bottomline capabilities.

Speed

Most cloud computing services are provided by self-service and on-demand. Cloud computing allows companies to deploy services quickly in fewer clicks. The faster deployment enables a business to receive the resources required within fewer minutes. Therefore, even vast amounts of computing resources can be provisioned in minutes, typically with just a few mouse clicks, giving businesses much flexibility and taking the pressure off capacity planning.

Productivity

Cloud computing contributes to several financial benefits by reducing the hardware requirement, which also helps to decrease IT maintenance costs. It has redefined the way businesses operate by increasing productivity and efficiency. In-house data centres require hardware setup, software patching and updating, and other time-consuming IT management activities. Cloud computing eliminates the need for several onsite tasks. Therefore, IT teams can achieve more important business goals. Employees can also access any required data or information and work remotely using mobile devices anywhere and anytime. Cloud-based tools also allow for remote collaboration, which assists teams in working more effectively and efficiently. It offers various tools that enable better connectivity and cooperation among the workforce regardless of geographical location. The fact that employees can access the same information improves collaboration among the team members and enhances performance. By choosing the appropriate service provider, companies can become more reliable and current, increasing overall productivity.

Another way cloud computing promotes increased productivity is via the efficient use of resources. The cloud is scalable, making provisions for fluctuations in business activities, development cycles, and growth. When a company grows, it is better to scale up its services with cloud platform help. The operational agility offered by cloud computing is one of the primary benefits.

Companies can either increase or decrease cloud services according to business activities and demand without interrupting or affecting performance.

Reliability

One of the factors that add to the success of a business is control. Unfortunately, even a tiny amount of unproductive downtime can have a resoundingly negative effect in today's market. Downtime in business services can lead to loss of productivity, revenue, and brand reputation. But while there may be challenges to prevent or anticipate the disasters that could potentially harm the company, there are mechanisms that can help speed up the recovery of business operations. For example, cloud-based services provide rapid data recovery for different emergency scenarios, from natural disasters to power outages. In addition, cloud computing makes data backup, disaster recovery, and business continuity more manageable and cheaper as data can be mirrored at many redundant sites on the provider's network.

Flexibility

Cloud computing provides businesses with a greater degree of flexibility than when hosted on a local server. A cloud-based service also offers extra bandwidth to instantly match increased demand rather than undergoing a complex, often expensive update to IT infrastructure. As a result, using cloud computing will improve the flexibility and ability of the company to quickly meet business demands, which makes a significant difference to the organisation's overall efficiency.

Security

Many companies have security concerns about adopting a cloud-computing solution. However, many cloud hosts offer a broad set of policies, technologies, and controls that strengthen many companies' overall security posture by protecting their data, applications, and infrastructure from potential threats. Systems are carefully monitored and are significantly more efficient than conventional in-house systems. A company must consider many IT concerns in a traditional approach, with security being only one of them. Most security vulnerabilities occur as a result of internal data theft, naïf acts, or carelessness. When this is the case, it can be much safer to keep sensitive information offsite. The critical cloud computing security is to encrypt the data being transmitted over networks and stored in databases. By using encryption, information is less accessible by hackers or anyone not authorised to view the data.

Blockchain Technology and CRM

A blockchain is an ever-growing list of interlinked records or chains of blocks. Each block contains transactional data and remains connected to the blocks both preceding and following it. These blocks are secure and resistant to any outside attack. It operates as an open, decentralised ledger that efficiently records transactions between parties. Some businesses have found blockchain technology valuable and adopt it because it reduces transaction costs and human error. Blockchain technology provides CRM systems with a complete customer profile and interoperable data infrastructure. It offers a unique solution to the data corruption problem by enabling customers to own a single block. The inherent structure of blockchain technology prevents duplication of CRM data or the corruption of information from causing problems. Blockchain technology can improve CRM based on the following:

1 Enhanced security
   In a Blockchain, blocks are joined to adjacent blocks cryptographically. These blocks are secured in such a manner that users employ network keys to restrict unauthorised access. In addition, blockchains tend to be decentralised and distributed across regularly synchronised peer-to-peer networks. Therefore, tampering with them is nearly impossible, as it would require massive computing power to access the entire chain.
   It enables companies to interact with customers securely and transparently without relying on intermediary financial institutions like banks or third-party brokers. Furthermore, it allows the encryption, authentication, and storage of personal data without divulging details to third parties. Security of private data is crucial as cases of cyber incidents such as viruses and malware increase. Therefore, it is not surprising that CRM systems are expected to address IT security issues by modifying their private data. Hence, chances of fraud and repudiation are also eliminated.

2 Improve Transparency
   Blockchain is a digital ledger that holds transactional records that have been verified by all parties involved, and payment can be executed without the involvement of a third-party intermediary such as a financial institution. This increases transactional efficiency and speed. The records of the transactions are held in a network of computers. One individual cannot alter the records without changing the records maintained in the other computers. Thus, a blockchain is a decentralised entity.
   Trust is one of the reasons a customer will choose and remain with a company. However, creating a trusted brand image requires extensive campaigns with high overheads, resources, and creativity. Blockchain technology creates transparency in the business process that allows customers to access information that builds trust. For example, a retail enterprise can gain customer trust by using blockchain-enabled product tracking to let the customer know exactly where the product was sourced, clarifying authenticity. This is especially useful when the product in question is a luxury item.

3 Ensuring User Privacy Control

Customers are growing increasingly concerned about personal data security. Therefore, companies must adjust how they handle customer data in the CRM systems hosted on cloud servers. Cloud-security issues remain a prevalent concern for companies and customers alike. Because of its decentralised and secure nature, Blockchain allows users to have control over their identity. Using blockchains to create token IDs for customer profiles ensures the privacy of customer data, which is collected for the personalisation of services.

Furthermore, it can store or encrypt personal data and verify it without sharing any specifics among the concerned parties. This grants users greater control over their information and identity. In addition, the system makes it difficult for organisation employees to link customer profiles, therefore keeping customers' identities safe, preventing identity theft and other forms of data abuse.

4 Data Cleansing

CRM systems are prone to inaccurate or duplicate data resulting from either negligence or inept data import. With blockchain technology, customers can have a personal key that presents companies with clean and valuable data. Furthermore, it offers a unified and accurate picture of customer personal information, past transactions, subscriptions, and other vital data by eliminating duplication or corruption of customer information. Therefore, Blockchain assists companies to circumvent concerns with inaccurate, obsolete, and duplicate data records by enabling customers to own a single block. Consequently, this yields better insights into customer's behaviour and helps businesses engage with them more effectively.

5 Loyalty Programs

In today's hypercompetitive environment, companies are increasingly adopting customer-centric business models to gain market advantage. However, even though the loyalty management market in 2021 is valued at USD $24.6 billion, several companies cannot engage customers meaningfully. Customer engagement and retention are the critical elements of loyalty programs, and are effective strategic investments in achieving these goals. Loyalty programs broaden the brand relationship through cross-selling services, peripherals, or companion devices for companies selling products. For service-based companies, reward programs seek to increase the usage of the services offered.

A blockchain-powered loyalty network can disrupt the traditional loyalty program practices by eliminating the limitations and inefficiencies and heightening customer experience with secure and immediate redemption options across several vendors. Blockchain technology provides consumers with a single decentralised wallet that is compatible with all brands. It reduces the rules and limitations associated with individual brands, point redemption, and dramatically simplifies the reward system. As a result, consumers will have greater control over their shopping experience. Brands will also compete for customers by offering better deals. Brands use block-chain technology to reimagine and reinvigorate their loyalty programs.

In sum, Blockchain will not replace existing loyalty and reward systems but will instead facilitate the interaction with legacy systems and drive improvements in traditional processes.

APPLICATION CASE 5.1

Cloud Computing Enhances Operational Efficiency at UBank

UBank, a financial technology bank, was founded in 2008. Its headquarters is in Sydney, Australia. The company offers banking services online and on the phone. They are an online bank. Since the company bank's operations are entirely online, they wanted to find a way to operate efficiently. In addition, they wanted to have virtual interaction with their customers since they have no physical bank branches. Their success depends on innovation and bringing new financial products quickly to the market without spending much money. Cost savings is significant for UBank because of their business model. Since they have no physical bank branches, the savings from lean operations are passed on to their customers through low fees and lower interest rates on their home loans and other financial products.

Their challenge was to construct a platform that was cheap yet effective and flexible. The bank decided to explore a PaaS cloud-based data analytic platform. They rationalised that a cloud-based PaaS will enable them to work effectively and will cost less. Therefore, they selected an IBM Cloud solution. First, to attract customers to their mortgage home loan programs, they built an app on their platform that plugs in directly into Facebook. This allows their customers to refer their Facebook friends and connections to their home loan financial products. This innovative app was built quickly, and it was effective and inexpensive. With such impressive results, they went further by creating their cloud-based platform integrating IBM cloud, a virtual agent enabled by conversation technology by IBM Watson. The virtual agent they called RoboChat could interact with their customers virtually, answering questions regarding the bank's product and services. That is, they had virtual staff 24 hours, seven days a week.

The PaaS cloud-based platform they developed allows them to be effective in their day-to-day operations. The cloud-based platform they developed help reduce the cost of doing business and hardware requirements. The bank could use sophisticated data analytic application tools such as IBM Watson and virtual agents without spending a tremendous amount of money on start-up costs and platform maintenance.

The most significant value of the PaaS deployed by UBank is that it provides the bank's data analytic tools developers with a platform to build whatever application they want. The platform allows for the development, operation, and management of their applications without the cost, complexity, and inflexibility of creating and managing their platform on-premises. Cloud-based computing has allowed big and small companies like UBank to scale up their operations and use sophisticated enterprise software at minimal costs. In addition, because the cloud providers supply the infrastructure, development tools, operating system, and take care of the back-end activities, it helped UBank streamline its workflows when multiple developers work on the same project. This allowed UBank to launch its new financial products and services to the market at a faster pace.

Source: IBM: UBank. Bringing digital banking capabilities to market faster with an IBM Cloud solution: https://www.ibm.com/case-studies/ubank: *Source*: UBank: https://www.ubank.com.au/: *Source*: IBM Cloud: https://www.ibm.com/cloud

Cognitive Computing and CRM

There is no consensus definition of cognitive computing technology. Still, the general idea is to use machine learning, robotic process, natural language, speech recognition, and AI to simulate human thinking and judgement to solve problems and provide solutions. Cognitive computing allows companies to extract meaning from vast volumes of customer data – both static and dynamic. For example, banks use cognitive computing to connect external and internal information in the financial sector to increase revenue across corporate accounts managed by a decreasing number of bankers. Wealth management companies enhance their internal data with customer records obtained from external public social and professional data sources used by advisors to proactively up-sell existing clients. It helps companies substantially reduce the time and resources spent resolving issues raised by customers for customer care operations. Cognitive computing allows companies to extract actionable intelligence from structured and unstructured customer data by providing suggested activities or best practice recommendations. Sales agents and customer relationship professionals can employ best practice recommendations to identify up-sell and cross-sell opportunities.

Cognitive computing technology assists humans and is beneficial for a smooth transition to an intelligent CRM model. It can create a customer knowledge layer that enriches data collected over an extended period about customer interaction and domain experience. Once the information has been enhanced, the technology continuously applies data enrichments, predictive recommendation algorithms, and unsupervised semantic learning to the different layers. The process is both continuous and dynamic, and the technology is self-learning, real-time, and contextual. Every interaction and result educates the platform, thus increasing its effectiveness over time.

Consequently, these are the benefits of using cognitive computing:

- Increase customer engagement activities: cognitive CRM tools allow businesses to follow up with customers based on their responses to communication techniques. Companies use this information to determine when and how to respond to messages left by customers. In addition, companies can learn from the data and enrich their learnings with data from external sources.
- Increase competitive advantage: cognitive computing offers companies a competitive advantage and aids in unlocking the value of data. This allows companies to counter emerging threats from non-traditional market entrants and competitors. As a result, it is a key technology used by businesses to reduce competition, increase revenue from existing customers and thrive in fast-changing market conditions.
- Reduce customer complaints: cognitive CRM tools deliver relevant and easily understandable solutions to common issues related to the industry autonomously. Therefore, customer service managers focus on the critical and unique, as cognitive CRMs reduce the number of complaints they need to address.

Barriers to Cognitive CRM Implementation

- The need for massive volumes of high-quality data: cognitive CRM requires large quantities of structured, high-quality data. Otherwise, the cognitive solution will be meaningless. However, currently, large amounts of human cognitive data are already available, which increases with use.
- The cost of implementation: cognitive CRM solutions are costlier than traditional CRM and may not be suitable or feasible for small and medium-sized enterprises. However, larger organisations can expect a better ROI over time with CRMs than traditional ones.

CRM and Big Data

Big Data presents companies the opportunity to obtain detailed insights from vast volumes of data. Consequently, companies are investing in CRM software to derive additional customer benefits from Big Data. This software traces customers' behaviours and patterns on different online platforms and presents the data rationally and coherently. Companies rely on CRM to develop lifelong relationships with customers. However, understanding customers has become problematic because the amount of daily information generated on the Internet needs to be analysed and utilised. In addition, companies must adapt quickly to the changing customer needs or be driven out of the market. Hence, having a CRM system integrated with analytical tools provides companies with a competitive edge to solve customer problems more efficiently.

Customer Relationship Analytics

Customer relationship analysis or analytics (CRA) involves processing data about customers and their relationship with the company to improve business performance and service at a lower cost. It is considered a form of on-line analytical processing (OLAP) and may employ data mining. Companies are increasingly interacting with customers, which presents the opportunity to collect valuable data. Consequently, software companies have developed products that conduct customer data analysis. Likewise, integrating analytics with CRM systems allows for the development of more intelligent systems. As a result, CRA empowers companies to make data-driven decisions.

Customer relationship analysis provides companies with meaningful insights into:

- Customer segmentation groupings (cluster individuals into group least likely to repurchase a product);
- Profitability analysis (the ability to identify customers who will provide the company with the most profit over time);
- Personalisation (tailoring or targeting an experience or communication based on data collected and learned about individual customers);
- Event monitoring (provides insight into website activity, content downloads, sales interaction, customer purchase volumes); what-if scenarios (the probability of a customer buying a particular or similar product);
- Predictive modelling (comparing different product development plans).

Data collection and analysis are a continuous and iterative process that allows for business decisions to be refined based on feedback from earlier analysis and subsequent choices.

Benefits of CRA

There are several benefits of customer relationship analysis. Some are:

- Increase productivity and improve customer relations in sales and service
- Improve supply chain management (lower inventory and faster delivery), lower costs, and more competitive pricing

CRM Analytics involves analysing customer and market-level information to provide the intelligence and insights that guide the company's strategic marketing, CRM, service, and go-to-market choices. CRM analytics allows companies to identify – Who are the most valuable customers? Which customers will most likely respond to promotional events? Which sales channels should be used to access and interact with customers? CRM analytics allows customers to receive personalised, timely, and relevant products and services through desirable channels.

Business Use of CRM Analytics

Marketing

Companies use CRA to identify customers interested in purchasing goods and services. From the data, companies design their marketing campaigns based on customer's tastes and preferences. Using CRA increases the effectiveness of enterprise marketing campaigns, thereby producing the desired ROI. Companies target their marketing campaigns to customers who demonstrate an interest in their products and services.

Sales

CRM analytics provide companies with detailed insights into customers' demographics, tastes, preferences, and buying behaviour, amongst others. The CRM analytics tool allows the sales and marketing team to track key metrics and manage the customer's journey. The data points are then analysed to reveal how businesses can improve selling and nurture customer relationships. Using CRM analytics to access advanced analytics enhances the sales team's decision-making abilities, enabling them to rethink, improve their decisions, and take advantage of opportunities.

CRM analytics can improve sales outcomes by enabling companies to:

- Obtain an end-to-end view of the sales processes and more easily drive the desired outcomes
- Provide indicators to drive sales in the right direction
- Leverage historical data to receive analytics-based information to finalise transactions
- Develop a perspective and anticipate potential challenges to customers before it becomes a problem
- Identify sales opportunities and receive recommendations for data-driven actions
- Provide feedback and help improve offers

Sales solutions built on advanced analytics models increase the ability of the sales team to make informed decisions, provide data about each customer opportunity, and offer suggestions for specific actions.

Customer Service

The CRA provides easy access to analytics dashboards and reporting features that display these indicators and impact business and forecasting. CRM analytics improve customer retention and enrich customer experiences by tracking online behaviour. It determines how consumers perceive a product, service, or brand. Companies can also contact and connect with customers to assess satisfaction or dissatisfaction by identifying positive and negative signals based on their actions.

Predictive Modelling

Predictive analytics allows data mining technology to uses customer data to automatically build a predictive model specifically in response to business needs. CRM analytics enable companies to use predictive modelling to determine outcomes using available data. By analysing custom data, businesses can accurately assess the likelihood of success or failure of a particular program or campaign. In addition, predictive modelling offers a glimpse into the future should a specific action be taken, allowing businesses to mitigate the associated risks. One of the significant challenges implicit in CRA is integrating the analytical software with existing legacy systems and other new systems.

What to Measure with CRM Analytics

CRM analytics measure two significant categories of customer relationship engagement activities: presales engagement and post-sales engagement. Presales engagement measures interactions before the sales, while post-sales measures activities that occur after the sale.

Presales Engagement

Measuring presales engagement activities helps the company to become more efficient at closing deals. In addition, it provides companies with the mechanisms for identifying the activities that most resonated with predictions. There are several presales activities to consider measuring the effectiveness of CRM analytics tools.

- **Prospecting:** this is the initial step in the sales process and consists of identifying potential customers. Prospecting seeks to develop a database of potential customers and converting them to current customers.
- **New opportunities:** once the company's goal and areas of expertise are established, the sales and marketing team needs to analyse the market and assess consumer needs. To identify market opportunities, the business model must be evaluated by identifying consumers, competitors, brand

value propositions, supply chains, prevailing regulations, and the micro and macro environment of the enterprise.

- **Product demonstrations:** allows prospective customers or investors to become interested and excited about the company's product or services. It is one of the most persuasive marketing tools available since the product is always the best tool for a demonstration. Product demonstration allows customers to see the product, its durability, and its functionality.

Post-sales Engagement

Retaining customers involves engaging and interacting with them at appropriate times and intervals. Post-sales engagement is as essential for customer retention as presales engagement. Monitoring post-sales data is critical to improving customer retention. It is used to measure interactions and activities that occur after the sale. Various post-sales engagement activities include tracking billing patterns, monitoring customer service, and determining project status.

- **Post-Sale Marketing:** after-sale customer engagement allows companies to recommend related products, accessories, and maintenance services. Post-sales marketing is hyper-targeted and personalised, and it only provides relevant product suggestions. As a result, it increases the chance of further sales while decreasing the advertising budget.
- **Increase Customer Retention:** to increase customer retention rates, businesses should consider the factors that impact customer satisfaction, customer service, and customer relationship. The following are some activities of after-sale customer engagement that help to improve customer retention:
  - Send out targeted recommendations
  - Provide comprehensive care and maintenance instructions
  - Follow up with questions and after-sale care
- **Help Save Time:** providing after-sales care, and maintenance support can help customers save time during troubleshooting and find any relevant information needed after purchase. Unfortunately, this also prevents customers from seeking general advice online, which may ruin the product image.

Key Term

Customer Relationship Management (CRM); Customer Relationship Analytics (CRA); Cloud Computing; Software as a Service (SaaS); Internet as a Service (IaaS); Platform as a Service (PaaS); Blockchain Technology; Cognitive Computing Technology

Chapter Key Takeaways

- Customer Relationship Management (CRM) software helps businesses obtain and retain customers and maintain good relationships.
- Cloud computing technology makes business operations very flexible. It reduces the upfront cost of setting up systems, lowers transaction costs, and eliminates the need to implement a disaster recovery plan. In addition, it facilitates faster responses, agility, and seamless communication.
- Infrastructure as a Service (IaaS) allows businesses to load software, including operating systems and applications, onto the cloud, thus reducing the need for high, upfront capital expenditures or irrelevant infrastructure.
- Platform-as-a-Service (PaaS) allows for the development, operation, and management of the applications without the cost, complexity, and inflexibility of creating and managing that platform on-premises.
- SaaS reduces the complexity of software installation, maintenance, upgrades, and patches for the in-house IT team since the software is centrally managed and monitored by SaaS providers.
- Blockchain technology provides CRM systems with a complete customer profile and interoperable data infrastructure. Also, the inherent structure of blockchain technology prevents duplication of CRM data or the corruption of information from causing problems.
- Cognitive computing allows companies to extract meaning from vast volumes of customer data – both static and dynamic.
- Cognitive CRM tools allow businesses to follow up with customers based on their responses to communication techniques. Companies use this information to determine when and how to respond to messages left by customers. In addition, companies can learn from the data and enrich their learnings with data from external sources.
- Customer relationship analytics (CRA) involves processing customer relationships to improve business performance and service and lower costs.

Discussion Questions

1 What is a CRM? Explain to a manager the benefits and potential pitfalls of using CRM analytics.
2 Explain why businesses need CRM systems. Which types of companies would most benefit from their implementations?
3 Describe how IaaS helps an organisation achieve a competitive advantage. Also, discuss how it can be used to achieve strategic objectives.
4 Describe how cloud computing is used to improve IT operations.
5 Describe the growth in the popularity of Blockchain technology. What are some of the reasons for its popularity amongst businesses?
6 How can cognitive computing help companies predict customer behaviour and enhance their experience?

7 Discuss how CRM analytics is used by businesses to measure operations.
8 Explain how businesses can use Customer Relation Analytics to their advantage?
9 How does CRM software help in customer retention?
10 What are the three primary cloud computing platforms? Please give a brief description of each of them.

6 Cybersecurity and Data Analytics

The concept of a corporate security perimeter has almost disappeared in recent years owing to the growing adoption of cloud and mobile services. As a result, organisational security has experienced a profound paradigm shift from traditional perimeter protection tools toward monitoring and detecting potential vulnerabilities and malicious activities within corporate networks. Increasingly, sophisticated attack methods used by cybercriminals and the growing role of malicious insiders in several recent large-scale security breaches indicate that traditional approaches to information security can no longer keep up. Data Analytics is the crucial element in leveraging cyber resilience, as companies need to move beyond prevention towards the Prevent – Detect – Respond paradigm. With Big Data solutions, behavioural analytics, and high-performance analytics, organisations now have the technology to manage cybersecurity issues. This chapter examines the role of data analytics in identifying and mitigating any risks, improving data–management techniques and cyber threat detection mechanisms.

LEARNING OBJECTIVES:

At the end of the chapter, students should be able to:

- Know the importance of cybersecurity to protect companies against intruders
- Understand how cloud computing and mobile services have changed how companies protect networks
- Identify the relationship between machine learning and cyber analytics
- Recognise how companies are using Big Data analytics to prevent cyber-attacks
- Understand the prevent, detect, and respond paradigm
- Understand the relationship between artificial intelligence and cybersecurity

DOI: 10.4324/9781003129356-6

Cyber Security

Cybercrime continues to rise at an alarming rate. As a result, companies need to protect sensitive data. Malware attacks have become more sophisticated, and protecting business data against malware and hacking is one of the biggest challenges. The increase of the Internet of Things (IoT) and bring your own device (BYOD) policies create additional access into the company's network. The volume and variety of portable devices connected to the network, plus the extension of the network to third parties via the supply chain, provide attackers with more entry points into the organisation than before. In addition to the increased access points, companies are also prone to human error and carelessness. As a result, businesses are as secure as their weakest link.

Historically firewalls, encryption, and other traditional techniques have been used to protect against cyber-attacks. These systems are a vital component of any security strategy. However, they are geared towards solving a narrow and specific problem, as they offer no data integration solution to better mitigate against cyber risk. With cyber-attacks constantly evolving, these technologies cannot regularly always successfully protect the network or sensitive data. Cyber analytics can be performed in real-time to provide the organisation with immediate situational awareness of the potential risks.

Big Data can store large quantities of data and further support analysts in examining, observing, and detecting irregularities within a network. Therefore, Big Data analytics is an appealing approach to prevent cybercrimes. Using Big Data analytics reduces the amount of time required to detect and resolve an incident. Big Data analytics tools can be used to identify cybersecurity threats, including malware or ransomware attacks, compromised and weak devices, and malicious insider programs.

Cybersecurity Analytics

In general, cybersecurity is the practice of defending computers, servers, mobile devices, electronic systems, networks, and data from malicious attacks. With the increase in cyber-attacks in volume and complexity, traditional tools and infrastructure are now redundant. To address the escalating number of cyber-attacks, Big Data analytics has been utilised to counter such attacks. Ultimately, Big Data analytics can help companies learn more about attackers' activities on the network. Cybersecurity analytics employs data to detect anomalies, identify vulnerabilities, unusual user behaviour, and other threats. Cybersecurity analytics aggregates data from across the entire organisation ecosystem and transform it into actionable intelligence that the IT team can utilise to mitigate and minimise risks. Advanced features such as AI and ML further assist by automating the detection and remediation process. Cybersecurity analytics combines Big Data capabilities with risk intelligence to help identify, analyse, and prevent insider threats and attacks from external hackers and persistent cyber threats.

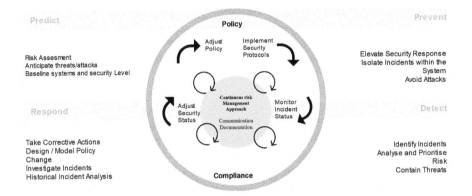

Figure 6.1 Security Analytics Process.

The cybersecurity environment is constantly evolving as cyber-attacks continue to increase in intensity and complexity. Managing the risks of cyber-attacks resembles dealing with any other sort of business risks that require trade-offs. As a result, companies must proactively align assets to reduce the probability of cyber incidents and limit the impact when a cyber-attack inevitably enters corporate networks. Part of this proactive approach, as seen in Figure 6.1, is to:

- Monitor incident status
- Adjust security status
- Adjust policy
- Implement security protocol

Contributing Factors of Cyber-Attacks

Factors influencing the rise of cyber-attacks include:

- Threats in the IoT
- Software defects
- Race condition
- Buffer overflow
- SQL injection
- Malware
- Spam and Phishing

Threats in the Internet of Things

With the advent of IoT, regular household items such as coffee makers, TV, and vehicles can be connected with individuals' electronic devices. The IoT sensors collect and communicate data that creates new opportunities for it to be compromised by hackers. The vulnerability arising from these systems serves as a means for an adversary to infiltrate a network. Often IoT devices are mass-produced and identical, providing opportunities for attackers to learn how to penetrate them. For example, an IoT device with default or weak passwords could be hacked using a list of common default passwords readily available on the internet. IoT devices that are not routinely patched or updated could be compromised by exploiting known software flaws. Compromised IoT devices can be used to disrupt a company's networks. For example, malware could be on the office network through a connected IoT device that has been compromised.

Software Defects

Software bugs are a common phenomenon that refers to an error, flaw, mistake, or fault in a computer program such as internal OS, external I/O interface drivers, and applications. Cybercriminals often exploit these software bugs to cause the systems to behave differently from their original intent. The majority of cyber-attacks today still occur due to exploiting software vulnerabilities caused by software bugs and design flaws. These vulnerabilities often happen due to using bugs in the memory, race condition, user input validation, and user access privileges.

Race Condition

Exploiting race condition errors: these vulnerabilities affect the security control mechanism. Hackers use flaws or induce a situation where a sensitive action is executed before complete security control. Therefore the system is trying to perform two or more operations at the same time. The time of check to time of use is an error caused by changes in a system between checking a condition and using the check results. For this reason, race condition vulnerabilities are also referred to as Time of Check/Time of Use vulnerabilities.

Buffer Overflow

A buffer overflow vulnerability exists when a program attempts to input more data in a buffer than it can hold or when it tries to input data in a memory area past a buffer. The excess data corrupts nearby space in memory and may alter other data, crash the program, or cause the execution of malicious code. This is particularly dangerous as an attacker can cause the web application to execute arbitrary codes.

SQL Injection

SQL injection is a web security vulnerability that permits an attacker to interfere with an application's queries to a database. It generally allows an attacker to view, modify, or delete unauthorised data. An SQL injection attack can result in unapproved access to sensitive data, such as credit card details or personal user information. In addition, an SQL injection attack can further escalate to compromise the underlying server or other back-end infrastructure or perform a denial-of-service attack. These attacks can go unnoticed for an extended period. However, several high-profile data breaches that have been in the media were due to SQL injection attacks leading to reputational damage and regulatory fines.

Malware

Malware or malicious software refers to a collective name for several malicious software variants, including viruses, ransomware, and spyware. Malware is typically developed by hackers and designed to cause extensive damage to data and systems or gain unauthorised access to a network. There are different types of malware:

- **Worms:** a form of malware that operates as a self-contained application and can transfer and copy itself from computer to computer. The ability to work autonomously without a host file or hijack code on the host computer leads to their notoriety. Worms are spread through pre-existing software vulnerabilities or phishing attacks. Many of the most popular and destructive types of malware attacks have been because of worms.
- **Computer Viruses.** Viruses cannot reproduce or spread on their own. Instead, viruses insert or attach malicious code into existing legitimate applications and use their functionality to execute their code. Computer viruses are written to harm the computer by damaging programs, deleting files, or reformatting the hard drive. Others replicate or overwhelm a network with traffic, rendering it impossible to perform any internet activity. Even less malicious computer viruses can significantly disrupt the system's performance, exhaust computer memory, and cause frequent computer crashes.
- **Bots and Botnets.** Bots are computer programs or software applications used to execute a series of operations automatically. Botnets are large networks of bots coordinated by a command and control centre instructing them on specific malicious actions. Once infected, malware or viruses can spread the bot infection to other computers to create massive botnets. They are one of the most common methods of malware deployment used to infect computers. As botnets infect new technologies, including devices in the homes, public spaces, and secure areas, these compromised systems place unsuspecting users at tremendous risk. They are commonly used to:
  - Steal financial and personal information. For example, attackers may use botnets to send spam, phishing, or other scams to convince consumers to provide them with money. These criminals may also collect data from the bot-infected machines and use them for identity theft.

- Attack legitimate web services. For example, hackers may use botnets to create Denial of Service (DoS) and Distributed Denial of Service (DDoS) attacks that overwhelm a legitimate service or network with a crushing quantity of traffic. The volume may severely slow down the service or network's ability to respond, causing it to shut them down.
- Extort money from victims. Revenue generated from DoS attacks often comes through extortion (pay or have your site taken down) or through hacktivism.
- Make money from zombie and botnet systems. Cyber attackers may lease their botnets to other criminals so they can spam, scam, phish, steal identities, and attack legitimate websites and networks.

- **Trojan Horse**. Malicious code or software that disguises itself as legitimate but can control a computer. A Trojan horse is designed to damage, disrupt, steal, or in general, inflict some other harmful action on data or network. A Trojan cannot replicate itself. Instead, it has to be executed by a user. There are different types of Trojans, and these include:
  - *Backdoor Trojans* – allow remote access and control of a computer, often uploading, downloading, or executing files on demand.
  - *Exploit Trojans* – inject a machine with codes deliberately designed to take advantage of inherent weakness in software.
  - *Rootkit Trojans* – prevent the discovery of malware already infecting a system to allow maximum damage to the system.
  - *Banker Trojans* – target personal information used for banking and other online transactions.
  - *Distributed Denial of Service (DDoS) Trojans* – execute DDoS attacks by flooding the network with requests from different sources.
  - *Downloader Trojans* – download additional malware or viruses, often including more Trojans, onto a device.

- **Ransomware.** Ransomware infects machines and displays messages demanding a fee to be paid. Ransomware is used to lock a computer screen or encrypt important, pre-determined files with a password. They are installed through deceptive links in an email message, instant message, or website. Criminals use these types of malicious codes to make money. Ransomware attacks can severely impact business processes and leave companies without the data they need to operate and deliver mission-critical services. In addition, hackers use tactics, such as deleting system backups that make restoration and recovery more difficult or infeasible for the impacted organisation. As a result, ransomware incidents have economic and reputational repercussions for companies. Typically, the amount of money that the attackers seek is based on whether the attacker knows the value of data being held hostage or can cause a significant direct financial loss to a company.

- **Adware and Scams**. Adware is intrusive software displays or advertisements. Adware can become a severe problem if it installs itself on the machine: it can add spyware, hijack the browser to display more ads, gather unauthorised data from a Web browser, change the browser's homepage and prevent from uninstalling it. The most common issues with adware are that it can:
  - Slow down the Internet connection
  - Render computer unstable
  - Cause constant crashing
  - Distract and waste your time

There are different types of adware: legitimate adware or potentially unwanted applications (PUAs). Legitimate adware requires consent to ads and software promotions. Some users may find the accompanying personalised ads or sponsored third-party software desirable. Legitimate adwares are a valid, legal, and ethical way to provide customers with a free product. However, not all application downloads are consensual such as PUAs. PUA adware may be legal malicious, or illegal. It depends on the goals of the software and those who distribute it.

- **Spyware.** Spyware is used to collect small pieces of information without users knowing secretly. In addition, spyware initiates a variety of illegal activities, including:
  - Identity theft or a data breach
  - Keylogging
  - Recording audio and video, and screenshot capture
  - Remote control of the device
  - Capturing content from email, messaging, and social apps
  - Recording and capturing browser history

In addition to monitoring computer activities, spyware interferes with computer operations by installing additional software, redirecting the browser, changing computer settings, and slowing or cutting off the Internet connection. Spyware is used for many purposes. Usually, its primary goal is to track and sell internet usage data, capture credit card or bank account information, or steal personal identity. The longer spyware goes undetected, the more damage it can cause. Spyware works by using the following actions on a computer or mobile device:

1. Infiltrate: via an app install package, malicious website, or file attachment.
2. Monitor and capture data: via keystrokes, screen captures, and other tracking codes.
3. Send stolen data: to the spyware author to be used directly or sold to other parties.

Spam and Phishing

Spam and phishing are based on social engineering to reveal personal information to an attacker. Spam is the electronic unsolicited, bulk, or junk mail, often unwanted and sent in massive volume by botnets. Spams are also prevalent on social networking sites. Other than annoying, spams can be dangerous, especially when they are part of a phishing scam. Spams are sent out in mass quantities by cybercriminals looking to do one or more of the following:

- Make money from recipients that respond to the message
- Run phishing scams – to obtain sensitive information such as passwords, credit card numbers, bank account details, and more
- Propagate malicious code onto recipients' computers

Phishing attacks use email, malicious websites (clicking on a link), or other communication to collect personal and financial information or infect the system with malware and viruses. Phishing messages are made to appear as though they come from a trusted sender. The victims are then deceived into providing confidential information or sending money, often on a scam website.

APPLICATION CASE 6.1

Cybersecurity and Fraud Prevention at PayPal

PayPal, valued at $324 billion at the close of the market on September 17, 2021, was founded in 1998 in San Jose, California. The company enables digital and mobile payments on behalf of consumers and merchants worldwide. PayPal's holdings include PayPal credit, PayPal, Venmo, Xoom Braintree, iZettle, and Hyperwallet products. The company's payments platform allows its customers to send and receive payments. The platform also allows customers to hold balances in their PayPal accounts in various currencies and enables businesses to accept payments online with credit, debit cards, and digital wallets.

The concept of corporate security has shifted from traditional perimeter protection tools toward monitoring and detecting potential vulnerabilities and malicious activities within corporate networks. For companies like PayPal, whose business transaction is entirely online, cybersecurity and fraud prevention are a basic necessity for its survival and to protect its vast customer data and information. The company has to protect both its corporate data and its customer information.

Today, most cases of cybersecurity threats are a result of employee-related incidences, also known as insider threats. Therefore, PayPal's cybersecurity

---

and fraud prevention measure focuses on threats from outside the organisation and within its employees. The threats range from spam and phishing emails, malware such as worms, computer viruses, Trojan Horse, ransomware, adware, and scams. In addition, as cybercriminals increasingly use sophisticated attack methods, PayPal needed a better way to detect and prevent fraud. Hui Wang, VP of Data Science at PayPal since 2018, knows that detecting and stopping fraudulent transactions before they happen is the only way to secure the company's good name.

Fraud and Cybercrime have continued to rise at an alarming rate from 2014 onwards – the need for a solution to protect corporate data and consumer information is increasing. Hui Wang's team at PayPal decided to invest in predictive analytics. PayPal's data analytics team uses historical data to predict impending attacks. Using Big Data analytics, companies can develop reference points based on statistical information that highlight normal or abnormal patterns in the data. For PayPal, the device used, the state or country where the transaction originated are all considered in their ML algorithms to determine fraudulent transactions. Because the company continues to grow in size and the volume of transactions continues to rise, they needed a more robust data analytics platform to run more complex analytics. They use open-source data analytics tools such as Spark and Hadoop to give their data scientists the flexibility to work with the tools they are accustomed to. In addition to open-source analytics tools, they use tools from Oracle, SAS, and Teradata to build a data analytics platform that can run complex algorithms to meet the increasing threats from cybercriminals and scammers who are threatening PayPal's business operations. The analytics made them more efficient and reduced the time required to detect and resolve suspected fraud and cyber incidents.

Source: Yahoo Finance: https://finance.yahoo.com/quote/ PYPL?p=PYPL&.tsrc=fin-srch: Source:PayPal: https://investor. pypl.com/financials/annual-reports/default.aspx. *Source*: PayPal annual SEC report: https://www.sec.gov/Archives/edgar/ data/1633917/000163391716000113/pypl201510-k.htm

Source: TechTarget: How PayPal fights fraud with predictive data analysis. https://searchbusinessanalytics.techtarget.com/feature/ How-PayPal-fights-fraud-with-predictive-data-analysis

Machine Learning and Cyber Analytics

ML consists of algorithms driven by mathematics and statistics. These algorithms are used to discover patterns, correlations, and anomalies. ML is critical to cybersecurity. It enables computers to use and adapt various algorithms based on their data, learn from it, and understand the required enhancements.

ML can help cybersecurity teams be more proactive in preventing threats and responding to active attacks in real time. Understanding and answering real issues has led to ML adoption in several areas, such as computer vision, medical analysis, gaming, social media marketing, and cybersecurity. ML can decrease the quantity of time spent on routine tasks and enable organisations to use resources strategically. It allows a computer to predict threats and detect anomalies more accurately than security analysts in a cybersecurity context.

Applications of Machine Learning Algorithms to Cyber Security

Intrusion Detection

The most common risk to the security of a network is an intrusion such as brute force, DoS, or infiltration from within a network. With the changing patterns in a network, switching to a dynamic approach to detect and prevent such intrusions is necessary. For example, intrusion detection aims to discover unauthorised activities within a computer or a network through Intrusion Detection Systems (IDS). An IDS allows the network to resist external attacks by providing a wall of defence against various attacks and detecting malicious network communications. IDS can be divided into two categories depending on the methods used to detect suspicious activities. These are:

- **Misuse or Signature-based intrusion detection** – These compare the incoming traffic with a pre-existing database of known attacks of weak spot patterns known as signatures to identify intrusions. Detecting new attacks is difficult.
- **Anomaly-based intrusion detection** – This employs statistics to form a baseline usage of the networks at different time intervals to determine whether deviation from the established standard usage patterns can be flagged as intrusions. Then, they are used to detect unknown attacks. ML creates a model simulating regular activity and then compares new behaviour with the existing model.

Artificial Intelligence and Cybersecurity

Cybersecurity is often reactive to breaches and threats. Responses to attacks generally take place long after the cyber incident has occurred. Threat signatures which are most widely used to address cyber-attacks employ patterns based on previous attacks. However, these approaches are often very limited in preventing new types of attacks. At the same time, technology is not the panacea for solving all cybersecurity vulnerabilities. By employing Artificial Intelligence and Machine Learning (AI-ML) based systems, companies can be proactive in cyber threats and attacks. Rather than waiting for a vulnerability to be exploited, these AI-based systems proactively seek potential vulnerabilities in organisational information systems. AI-based systems are effective cybersecurity prevention and detection tools. They effectively merge a multiplicity of factors, such as the reputation of the hacker or patterns used to determine how and when the threats may materialise and impact vulnerable targets.

ML plays a significant role in preventing and deterring phishing attacks. It proactively detects and tracks active phishing sources and reacts and remediates much more rapidly than humans. Moreover, AI-ML works at scanning phishing threats from all over the world. AI has made it possible to effectively differentiate between a fake website and a genuine one quickly.

The Need for Security Analytics

Companies increasingly integrate BYOD policies into daily business activities to increase productivity. Unfortunately, these mobile devices open the company to additional vulnerabilities and increase the complexity of attacks. Cybersecurity analytics is growing and offers a robust solution for companies seeking to prevent or detect vulnerabilities and threats. It combines data from various sources and aims to discover correlations and anomalies within the data. Security analytics tools can use a variety of methods to analyse data. These include traditional rules-based methods, statistical analysis, and ML. Typically, as seen in Figure 6.2, security analytics is employed for the following purposes:

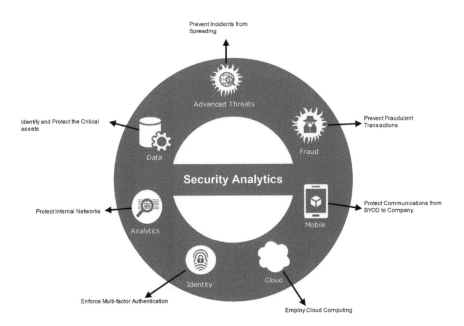

Figure 6.2 Security Analytics.

- Identify and protect critical assets
- Prevent cyber incidents from spreading
- Prevent fraudulent transactions
- Protect communication networks against BYOD type infiltrations
- Employ cloud computing to add another layer of protection
- Enforce multi-factor authentication
- Protect internal networks

There are several drivers key to the growth of security analytics. These include:

- **Change in focus from protection to detection** – Many attack mechanisms are available, and cybercriminals often exploit them, resulting in multiple vulnerabilities. Security analytics tools can explore common threat patterns and send alerts when an anomaly is discovered. Unlike traditional security tools, it allows for early detection by analysing user account activities for insider threat behaviours.
- **An integrated view of the organisation** – Security analytics offers both real-time and historical data. Such data sources include network traffic volume and types, server logs, third-party threat intelligence feeds, and real-time alerts from workstations, servers, sensors, mobile devices, and other endpoints. Structuring security data in this format provides a unified understanding of threats and security breaches, allowing for more innovative planning, faster resolution, and better decision-making. In addition, employing security analytics provides companies with insights into complex attack techniques such as compromised credentials, lateral movement, and data exfiltration.
- **Return on investment**: Organisations can easily connect various alerts and events by analysing real-time and historical data. Cybersecurity analytics can provide time-to-resolution metrics and fewer false positives that allow analysts to identify threats and respond to cyber-attacks rapidly. The result is proactive security incident detection and faster response times that help the business protect systems and data integrity.

Big Data Analytics and Cyber Security

Business data, information, and knowledge form a company's intellectual property and are among the most valuable assets any business has. With the influx of mobile devices and wearable technology, businesses collect vast volumes of data about their users. Consequently, security and privacy have become the primary concern. As a result, companies use Big Data analytics to compete with the continuously changing, sophisticated cyber-attacks resulting from increased daily data volumes. By employing Big Data analytics and ML, the business can thoroughly analyse the data generated and collected.

These results are used to identify vulnerabilities and potential threats to the integrity of the network and enterprise. These Big Data analysis tools operate in real-time and produce security alerts as per their severity level. Companies utilise Big Data analytics to address cybersecurity threats by examining historical data, looking at workflows, deploying intrusion detection systems. These are further discussed below:

Analysing Historical Data

Companies use historical data to predict impending attacks. Using Big Data analytics, companies can develop reference points based on statistical information that highlight normal or abnormal patterns in the data. Security data can be stored in a dedicated repository that combines and analyses real-time and historical data. These repositories are used to obtain beneficial information from large-scale and complicated data. The related technologies allow for the extension of traditional information security systems by facilitating the storage, maintenance, and analysis of security data to identify and recognise patterns to stay ahead of malicious activities or attacks.

The use of risk assessment techniques and a quantitative prediction of susceptibility to cyber-attacks can help businesses develop their counterattack measures. Historical data can also be used to create statistical models and AI-based algorithms. When ML is paired with Big Data analytics, businesses can address cyber threats and provide the necessary protection to networks. Big Data analytics collects, analyses, and prepares data based on previous cyber-attacks, while ML allows for cyber-attack defence responses. Big Data analytics and ML capabilities can detect vulnerabilities within a network, discover breaches in real time, and correlate information from multiple sources.

Monitoring and Automating Workflows

Most cases of cybersecurity threats are a result of employee-related incidences, also known as insider threats. Cybersecurity measures frequently focus on threats from outside an organisation rather than its employees. With Big Data analytics, companies can significantly reduce the risk of these insider threats by monitoring and automating workflows. One way of decreasing insider threats is to restrict access to sensitive information only to authorised employees. Authorised individuals should be given specific logins and other system applications to view files and change data. The IT team should work with the HR department to approve authorised members based on their role and responsibility.

Big Data analytics is used in mitigating cybersecurity breaches by facilitating the timely and efficient submission of any suspicious activities to a security service for additional analysis. In addition, the automation of reporting suspicious activities enables the system to respond to detected threats, such as malware attacks.

Deploying an Intrusion Detection System

IDS monitor the organisation's network, network node, or host traffic and flag any intrusions. They use either a statistical anomaly-based technique or a signature-based technique to detect any intrusion into the network. Signature-based techniques observe, monitor, and compare network packets and traffic patterns against signatures of known attacks. Attacks are considered to be those that are outside of everyday activities. The significant advantage of anomaly detection techniques over signature-based techniques is that they can detect new and known attacks.

When Big Data analytics is used to discover irregularities, it detects anomalies and suspicious activities from network flows, logs, and system events. Given the increasing sophistication of cyber breaches, IDS such as network-based intrusion detection systems (NIDS) are valued as practical tools for detecting cybersecurity threats. Using Big Data analytics for intrusion detection and mitigating network security problems has been increasingly attracting attention. It promotes the investigation of vast volumes of complex and disparate data with different formats from heterogeneous sources and combats cyber-attacks. A holistic view and situational awareness of intrusion or attacks can be determined by correlating the security incidents from heterogeneous sources. However, the more heterogeneous data sources available, the greater the challenges and the more complicated the Big Data. Utilising Big Data analysis that conducts stream processing (real-time analytics) and batch processing is the best defence to detect intrusion and protect critical information infrastructures. Network intrusion prediction and detection are time-sensitive and need a highly efficient approach. The prevention and mitigation of cyber threats largely depends on the risk management and actionable intelligence provided by Big Data analysis. Therefore, it is crucial to have automated tools that automatically relay essential data to the right people.

There are several cybersecurity frameworks available today to assist businesses in assessing risks. An example includes the National Institute of Standards and Technology (NIST) Framework, which presents a framework of computer security guidelines for evaluating and boosting a company's ability to detect, prevent, and deal with cyber-attacks.

Securing Businesses with Big Data Analytics

Cyber and data security are increasingly driven by Big Data, reducing the severity and even reducing instances of those breaches. Big Data analytics supported by AI and ML allows for real-time detection of attacks, thus preventing further damage or predicting and preventing cyber-attacks before they occur. These security data originate from several sources, including business application data, network metadata, DNS/DHCP, IaaS, PaaS, and SaaS. Additionally, Big Data analytics allows for identifying and comprehending the who, what, and why behind attacks, allowing the security team to secure the data processes from hacking or cybersecurity breach.

These systems also enable analysts to classify and categorise cybersecurity threats quite rapidly. By utilising the power of Big Data analytics, businesses can enhance their cyber threat-detection mechanisms and improve data management techniques. Big Data analytics can assist systems in collecting internal data by merging with relevant external data to detect known vulnerabilities and keep ahead of malicious activities or intruders. Several Big Data technologies, tools, services, and techniques were developed to cope with the increased volume, velocity, and variety of network-related data. Big Data systems form part of a cyber defence strategy for companies seeking to meet complex and large-scale Big Data analytics needs. This section describes examples of Big Data analytics used for security purposes.

Network Security

Network security protects the integrity and usability of the organisation's entire network and data connection. Network security consists of practices and policies that monitor and prevent data misuse, unauthorised access, and unauthorised modification of the existing data in the system. In addition, it is concerned with protecting computer networks from cyber-attacks. While Big Data analytics focuses on extracting useful information from large volumes of data, network security deals with creating strategies to protect the networks. Being in the era of connected devices has created the need for a system to track or detect any attack before it occurs. In addition, data storage facilities have introduced Big Data, which contains unprecedented amounts of helpful information.

Cyber-attacks are becoming increasingly sophisticated and advanced, and one successful attempt on the organisation's networks can have an adverse effect. Companies must move beyond prevention towards the "Prevent, Detect, and Respond" paradigm to protect their assets. Big Data analysis focuses primarily on the Detect function when considering network security. Big Data analysis helps with enhanced detection capabilities. The networks can identify pattern changes.

Quick complex analysis and correlations can be performed through various data sources in response to any detected network changes. The analyst can discover important intrusion detection and prevention information by utilising computers, networks, cloud systems, and sensors. Combining Big Data analytics with network security allows organisations to identify vulnerabilities, predict cyber-attacks, and develop calculated network security solutions to improve their ability to protect networks from cyber-attacks. Cyber analytics plays a vital role in detecting advanced threats and insider threats. Monitoring systems can be used to minimise false alarms by providing Big Data analytics and improving threat detection.

Enterprise Events Analytics

Enterprises consistently collect vast volumes of security-relevant data (e.g., network events, software application events, and people action events) for many different reasons, such as the need for regulatory compliance forensic analysis. Unfortunately, such vast volumes of data quickly become overwhelming and pose challenges in harnessing its usefulness to the organisation. Existing analytical techniques cannot cope with the increased volume of data and typically generate many false positives that undermine their efficacy. The problem is further exacerbated as companies move to cloud architectures and accumulate more data which becomes less actionable. Algorithms and systems must be designed and implemented to identify actionable security information and reduce false-positive rates to manageable levels to maximise the benefits of upsurging in data. Using enterprise events analytics, an increase in data collection increases its value to the company.

Advanced Persistent Threats Detection

Advanced persistent threats (APT) are targeted attacks. Individuals or organisations exploit a vulnerability to access a network, remain undetected, steal information, monitor activity, or deploy malware. APTs are among the most insidious information security threats as they steal intellectual property, customer personal data, or access strategic business information. These attacks can be costly due to data corruption, illegal insider trading, or business disruption. Attackers also seek financial gains through blackmail and cause reputational damage to an organisation. However, by employing advanced persistent threat detection technology, companies can prevent these types of attacks. Unfortunately, detection techniques rely on human analysts to create custom signatures and perform the manual investigation, which tends to be labour-intensive and unscalable. In addition, these anomaly detection techniques typically focus on obvious outliers but are inappropriate for low and slow APT attacks and suffer from high false-positive rates. Likewise, a challenge in detecting APTs is the large amount of data to analyse to identify anomalies.

Therefore, Big Data analytics is suitable for APT detection. It can save time, hardware performance, network resources and simplify large quantities of data. However, the success of APT is to adopt multiple security layers to protect against attempts to exploit network vulnerabilities. Viruses, malware, spear-phishing, and zero-day attack threats must be addressed for an effective APT detection strategy.

Intelligent Risk Management

Cybersecurity mainly relies on actionable intelligence and risk management. Big Data analytics tools enhance cybersecurity efforts with intelligent risk management insights. Security experts can leverage these insights to evaluate data more quickly and efficiently. Consequently, organisations can handle security incidents without any delay.

Protect, Detect, and Respond

To secure and protect business assets, three general areas of cybersecurity must be addressed:

- Prevention (protect)
- Detection
- Response

Every company should have a cybersecurity plan that protects the organisation from cyber-attacks and the consequences of a data breach.

Prevention of Cybersecurity Incidents

Data is an asset that must be protected like any other organisation asset. Security measures must be taken to protect this intellectual asset from unauthorised modification, destruction, or disclosure, whether accidental or intentional. Since the goal of the security framework is to prevent an incident or a breach, the prevention phase of the framework should design and implement the security policies, procedures, controls and processes, and training. As part of the prevention plan for action, a culture of cybersecurity awareness should be developed where employees follow best practices and understand specific cyber threats within the network. Risk assessment should be conducted and based on the results. The tasks and events should be prioritised to strategically secure the systems, networks, and applications.

Prevention is the most cost-effective tool a company can employ to guard against an attack. However, in addition to dealing with the internal issues, companies should also assess the external entities such as third-party companies and suppliers.

Prevention Techniques

Prevention techniques include:

- Security Policy
- Security awareness
- Access Control

SECURITY POLICY

The first objective in developing a cybersecurity prevention strategy is to determine "what" must be protected. Once this is established, it should be documented to create a formal policy that defines its role and responsibilities, the employees, and management. The policy should also determine circumstances for implementation, enforcement, audit, and review. Finally, it must be written in a manner that is transparent, concise, coherent, and consistent to ensure effective implementation and subsequent enforcement, audit, and assessment.

SECURITY AWARENESS

Prevention is more affordable than responding to a security issue. Companies can save millions of dollars annually using security awareness training to prevent attacks on company systems. Security awareness training is the ideal investment for the growing business intent on harnessing the newest technology. Security awareness educates employees on the significance of security framework, the use of security measures, reporting procedures for security violations, and identifying employees' roles and responsibilities as outlined in the security policy. Employees should not know the cyber threats that exist or what to do without their input. Security awareness and training programs should educate employees about the different security threats and their policies and procedures for addressing them. Training programs should be a continuous process and help employees maintain a heightened awareness level. It should also provide instructions on dealing with threats and best practices for keeping the organisation secure. The security awareness program should address organisation-wide issues and focused specialised training needs of the individual employees. By empowering employees to take the measures required to protect the company, companies can minimise the potential for attackers to target individuals and networks. Once the training program is completed, issues relating to social engineering and other individually-focused attacks can be reduced.

ACCESS CONTROLS

Access control is the method used to guarantee that users have the appropriate access to company data equal to their status. Based on the roles and functions in the company, users will be assigned specific privileges to certain areas of a system and its information. Access should be restricted and granted on a need-to-know basis.

Any access control system, whether physical or logical, has the following main components:

Authentication: is the method of validating the identity of a person or computer user. For example, it might involve validating personal identity, verifying the authenticity of a website with a digital certificate, or checking login credentials against stored information. Authentication is used to provide a level of trust.

Three main authentication techniques can be employed:

a   *Passwords and pins* – These are private bits of information that only the specific user would know. These are the cheapest and most common authentication means and are the least secure due to poor password selection and storage.

b   *Access cards and keys* – Cryptographic keys and smartcards or tokens provide a digital signature or two-factor or multi-level authentication, ensuring a high level of security. Each requires the user to possess "something" for authentication.

c   *Biometrics* – is the most expensive and secure authentication methodology. It confirms a person's identity by using a unique genetic attribute, DNA, behaviour, or physical characteristics. Typical biometric scans include:

- Retina scan
- Iris scan
- Fingerprint
- Palm scan
- Facial scan
- Hand topography
- Voiceprint
- Signature or keyboard dynamics

Authorisation: is the function of specifying user access rights or privileges to company resources. Authorisation determines the level of access and the user's ability to change, edit, or disseminate specific information. For example, HR staff are usually authorised to access employee records, and this policy is generally formalised as access control rules in a computer system. The processes of authorisation also consider Authorization Management which deals with creating authorisation rules. For instance, an administrator can create a rule that lets another user publish content on a web page. Authorisation technologies enable companies to control what employees can access, where, and on which device this data can be accessed. Using this restrictive approach limits user access creates a separation of duties and increases accountability.

Access: once authenticated and authorised, the employee or user can access company resources.

Manage: managing an access control system involves adding and removing authentication and authorisation of users or systems.

Audit: frequently employed as part of access control to enforce the principle of most limited privilege. Regular audits minimise this risk when there are changes in roles and responsibilities.

Detection of Cybersecurity Incidents

Analysing a system for compromise is exceptionally critical. With the increase in the number of cyber-attacks, no company is immune from attacks regardless of protection. Technological advances in network security have facilitated advanced monitoring and threat detection for analysts. However, these detection tasks cannot be completely automated. Therefore, information and network security should be defended in layers in case one layer fails.

One security tool that companies rely on is IDS. The IDS can detect network intrusions and network misuse by matching known attacks against ongoing network activity. Once the IDS discovers a match to a known type of attack or detects abnormal network activity, it produces alerts detailing the suspicious events.

Once a threat is detected, mitigation efforts must be used to neutralise it before it negatively impacts the organisation. The defensive business programs can ideally stop the majority of known threats. Nonetheless, there are also "unknown" threats that an organisation aims to detect. Since known threats can breach defensive measures, the organisation should seek to detect known and unknown threats. Threat detection requires both human and technical components. The human element includes security analysts who analyse trends, patterns in data, behaviours and determine if anomalous data indicate potential risks or a false alarm. Threat detection technology likewise plays a crucial role in the detection process. However, technology alone is unable to detect all the threats to a network. Instead, a combination of tools serves as a protective layer across the entire network to identify and capture threats before impacting the company.

A robust detection program should employ technologies of:

- **Threat detection:** to collect data from security events across the network, including authentication, network access, and logs from critical systems.
- **Network threat detection**: to understand traffic patterns on the network and monitor traffic within and between trusted networks and the Internet.
- **Endpoint threat detection**: provide detailed information about malicious events on user machines and any behavioural or forensic material to aid in exploring threats. By employing a combination of these techniques, companies increase the likelihood of detecting and mitigating a threat quickly and efficiently.

Spam and Phishing Detection

Spam and phishing detection is a classic example of pattern recognition and aims at reducing the waste of time and potential hazards caused by unwanted emails. Nowadays, unsolicited emails, namely phishing, represent the preferred way attackers gain access to the enterprise network. Spam and phishing detection are increasingly challenging because of the advanced evasion strategies used by hackers to bypass traditional filters. There are different approaches to spam detection. ML techniques are more efficient and scalable than knowledge-based methods. Standard ML algorithms need pre-classified data to train the model or classifier and test the dataset. A dataset is constructed using emails that are classified as spam and regular mails.

Malware Detection

Malware detection is a relevant problem because modern malware can evolve and create variants with the same malicious effects but appear as entirely different executable files. Several IDSs are based on ML techniques because they adapt to new and unknown attacks. Although ML facilitates the safety of various systems, the ML classifiers themselves are vulnerable to malicious attacks. Classifiers separate malicious and benign programs. The trained classifier is a single model that seeks to distinguish between the behaviour of benign and malicious programs. A significant problem faced by these classifiers is that most malware is injected into otherwise harmless programs. For such programs, the execution runs could be either benign or malicious depending on whether the malware injected is triggered, making it difficult to label the program during training.

Respond to Cyber Security Incidents

Planning and preparing for a cybersecurity occurrence is one of the most significant challenges faced by any organisation. A cybersecurity incident requires a rapid response to mitigate any threat to the confidentiality, integrity, and availability of an organisation's information. Cyber incident management helps to reduce risks arising from internal and external threats and helps companies maintain regulatory compliance. An organisation must be prepared to respond to incidents that may originate from different sources such as disgruntled employees, naïf acts, or careless acts from trusted insiders whose actions cause damage by mistake and attacks from cybercriminals. Cyber-attacks' complexity and the increased sophistication of cybercriminals have resulted in cybersecurity incidents becoming popular. As a result, companies need to perform due diligence and respond appropriately to cyber events. A poorly executed response to a cyber incident can cause an organisation significant financial losses, reputational damage, and even business closure.

The response function consists of appropriate activities to take action regarding the detection of cybersecurity incidents. In addition, it supports the ability to contain the impact of a potential cybersecurity incident. Examples of outcome categories within the respond function include:

- Ensure response planning process is executed during and after a security incident

- Manage communications during and after an event
- Conduct analysis to ensure adequate response and support recovery activities
- Perform mitigation activities to prevent the growth of an event and to resolve the incident
- Implement best practices from lessons learned from current and previous detection/response activities

Key Term

Cybersecurity; Cybercrime; Cybersecurity Analytics; Internet of Things (IoT); Bring Your Own Device (BYOD); Machine Learning; Artifical Intelligence; Intelligent Risk Management

Chapter Key Takeaways

- Companies are as secure as their weakest link.
- Big Data stores large quantities of data and further supports analysts in examining, observing, and detecting irregularities within a network.
- Big Data analytics is an appealing approach to prevent cybercrimes and counter cyber-attacks.
- Cybersecurity analytics employs data to detect anomalies, identify vulnerabilities, unusual user behaviour, and other threats.
- Machine learning allows a computer to predict threats and detect anomalies more accurately than relying on security analysts.
- Intrusion Detection Systems (IDS) allow the network to resist external attacks by providing a wall of defence against various attacks and detecting malicious network communications.
- AI-based systems are effective cybersecurity prevention and detection tools. This is because they effectively merge a multiplicity of factors, such as the reputation of the hacker or patterns used to determine how and when the threats may materialise and impact vulnerable targets.
- Employing Artificial Intelligence and Machine Learning (AI-ML) based systems, companies can be proactive in their cyber threats and attacks.
- Bring Your Own Device (BYOD) opens companies to vulnerabilities and increases the complexity of these attacks, often undetected.
- Companies use Big Data analytics to compete with the continuously changing and sophisticated cyber-attacks resulting from increased daily data volumes.
- Most cases of cybersecurity threats are a result of employee-related incidences, also known as insider threats. Cybersecurity measures frequently focus on threats from outside an organisation rather than its employees.
- Examples of Big Data analytics used for security purposes:
  - Network Security
  - Enterprise Events Analytics

- Netflow Monitoring to Identify Botnets
- Advanced Persistent Threats Detection
- Intelligent risk management
- Prevention is the most cost-effective tool a company can employ to guard against an attack. However, in addition to dealing with the internal issues, companies should also assess the external entities such as third-party companies and suppliers.
- Once a threat is detected, mitigation efforts must neutralise it before it negatively impacts the organisation.
- Planning and preparing for a cybersecurity occurrence is one of the most significant challenges faced by any organisation.
- A cybersecurity incident requires a rapid response to mitigate any threat to the confidentiality, integrity, and availability of an organisation's information.

Discussion Questions

1 What is cybersecurity?
2 What is cybersecurity analytics?
3 How does machine learning enhance cybersecurity?
4 What is AI, and how is it helpful in cybersecurity?
5 Give two examples of early adopters of AI and explain how they used AI.
6 Discuss how cybersecurity analytics is used to protect companies from malicious attacks.
7 Identify some of the software defects and discuss how these vulnerabilities can lead to cyber incidents.
8 Explain in detail why malware is increasing in companies.
9 Identify the different types of Trojans and discuss why they are problematic to businesses.
10 Describe a Spam that you are aware of and explain how and why these unsolicited emails are considered dangerous.
11 How are companies using big data analytics to manage the risks of cyber-attacks?
12 Explain how companies are using Big Data analytics to secure networks against cyber-attacks.
13 Discuss the techniques used to detect cyber-attacks.

7   Data Analytics and the Retail Industry

The retail industry is one of the most competitive and fragmented industries. Most companies in the sector are clustered between the low-cost (Walmart) and high-end (Nordstrom). To remain competitive, retail companies face many challenges such as inventory management for in-store and online merchandising, e-commerce fulfilment, supply chain constraints, distribution costs, customer support, and pricing decisions. COVID-19 has highlighted the industry's complexity and challenges as it operates within a brick-and-mortar and online environment. This chapter details how data analytics is used to make the companies in the industry stay competitive and work more efficiently and gain incremental margins, understand competitors' pricing, and avoid over or under-stocking merchandise.

LEARNING OBJECTIVES:

At the end of the chapter, students should be able to:

- Assess the value of Big Data and data analytics in customer analytics in retail
- Know the value of Big Data and data analytics in selecting a store location
- Discuss the value of Big Data and data analytics in supplier selection in the retail industry
- Evaluate the value of Big Data and data analytics in inventory control
- Recognise the importance of Big Data and data analytics in storage assignment and order picking
- Identify the data analytics tools used in the retail industry
- Understand the business value of Big Data analytics for e-commerce firms

The Retail Industry

Retail involves the selling of merchandise directly to customers who intend to use the product. It is a vast sector, ranging from department stores to coffee machines, brick-and-mortar to digital stores.

DOI: 10.4324/9781003129356-7

The retail industry is extensive. It includes giant companies that employ millions of people and generates trillions of dollars per year in sales. For example, in 2019, the US retail industry generated $5.4 trillion in sales.[1] It is estimated that two-thirds of the US Gross Domestic Product (GDP) comes from retail consumption. Worldwide retail sale in 2018 was $23.6 trillion.[2] The retail industry's survival depends on a supply chain that involves manufacturers, wholesalers, and robust transportation and logistical systems. There are different types of retailers – department stores, grocery stores, supermarkets, speciality/outlet retailers (e.g., Victoria's Secret and Nike), convenience retailers, discount retailers (e.g., Family Dollar, Dollar General), and internet/mobile (Amazon, Netflix) retailers. Generally, any business that sells merchandise to an end-user is considered part of the retail industry. The Census Bureau divides retail sales into 13 categories:[3]

- Auto dealers, including auto parts, new, and used vehicle sales
- Non-store retailers, which means online retail sales
- Department stores
- Apparel, such as speciality clothing stores
- Electronics and appliance stores, including big-box retailers like Best Buy
- Food and beverage stores, including grocery and liquor stores
- Building and garden supply stores, such as Lowes and Home Depot
- Sporting goods/hobby stores, like Hobby Lobby and Michael's
- Health/beauty shops, including drugstores
- Furniture stores
- Hospitality and leisure, including hotels, restaurants, and bars
- Gas stations
- Miscellaneous

The list above indicates that retails sell goods and services. Examples of companies selling services include hotels, bars, and restaurants. In addition to the physical brick-and-mortar stores heavily affected by COVID-19 and online retailing, some retailers focus on home delivery (Avon, Casper mattress). In contrast, others rely on TV channels (QVC) and the home shopping network.

Retail Industry and Big Data

Online retailing has changed the industry as consumers' shopping style has quickly changed with COVID-19. Consequently, the demarcation between online and offline is blurring as more retailers adopt a data-first strategy. Big Data is helping businesses understand how customers behave and ensure that they match the right person with the best product. For example, datasets that include demographics and location help retailers understand consumers' behaviour, leading to more targeted solutions that provide value and personalise communications.

Retailers having access to high-quality data, and knowing how to use it, are often successful in delivering high value to their customers. Big Data can identify how customers interact with a specific brand online and offline, allowing retailers to communicate highly contextualised messages. Therefore, Big Data can be used in the retail industry to gain a competitive advantage in a highly competitive market.

Big Data helps retailers answer several questions that are crucial to growing a modern retail business. It also allows them to answer these questions faster than before:

- Who are our customers?
- What motivates them to visit?
- What engages them?
- How do they have behavioural habits outside of the store?
- How can we target them?
  Big Data is used in the retail industry for several purposes, including (see Figure 7.1):
  - To determine product availability
  - Dynamic pricing
  - Identify relevant promotions to customers
  - Increase product demand and determine trends
  - Establish the best time or seasons to offer certain products and services

One of the world's biggest retailers, Walmart, explains five ways it uses Big Data[4]:

- **To Make Walmart Pharmacies More Efficient**. Walmart uses simulations at the pharmacy to determine how many prescriptions are filled

Big Data in The Retail Industry

Figure 7.1 Big Data Usage in the Retail Industry.

in a day and the busiest times during a day or month. This data helps the pharmacy with staff scheduling and reduces the time it takes to fill a prescription.

- **To Improve Store Checkout.** Walmart is testing how to use Big Data to improve the checkout experience. Using predictive analytics, stores can anticipate demand at certain hours and determine how many associates are needed at the counters. In addition, by analysing the data, Walmart can identify the best forms of checkout for each store: self-checkout and facilitated checkout.
- **To manage the Steps of a Supply Chain.** Walmart uses simulations to track the number of steps from the dock to the store. This allows the company to optimise routes to the shipping dock and track the number of times a product gets touched before reaching the customer. The company also uses data to analyse transportation lanes and routes for the company's fleet of trucks. The data helps Walmart keep transportation costs down and schedule driver times.
- **To Optimise Product Assortment**. By analysing customer preferences and shopping patterns, Walmart can accelerate decision-making on stocking shelves and displaying merchandise. Therefore, Big Data provides insight on new items, discontinued products, and which private brands to carry.
- **To Personalise the Shopping Experience**. Big Data allows Walmart to identify a shopper's preferences to develop a consistent and delightful shopping experience. For example, suppose a user is shopping for baby products. In that case, Walmart can use data analytics to personalise mobile rollback deals for parents and help them make better shopping decisions by anticipating their needs.

The Value of Big Data and Data Analytics in Customer Analytics in the Retail Industry

Customer Analytics

One of the biggest challenges to retailers is making an accurate prediction about sales, especially during various festive seasons or holidays such as Thanksgiving, Christmas, Labor Day, New Year. Retailers have to make strategic decisions about sales and all the resources required to meet sales predictions and projections. For example, companies must decide on the number of employees at each store location, the type of product on the shelves, the number of products available, and how to attract customers into their stores or online platforms. Big Data and customer analytics make these predictions a data-driven process.

Customer analytics involves the process of collecting and analysing various types of customer data to understand customer behaviour. Customer analytics is essential as it provides the following benefits, as seen in Figure 7.2.

Figure 7.2 Customer Analytics in the Retail Industry.

- Retailers use this information to understand the market conditions and decide how to attract and satisfy customers.
- It allows retailers to determine the best advertising platform to operate and personalise marketing campaigns.
- It enables faster and better decision-making which allows retailers to create a better experience for customers.
- It helps the sales department to understand customers' buying habits and processes.
- It allows retailers to create real-time and personalise marketing campaigns leading to more significant cost savings and more targeted campaigns.
- It drives innovation and product development which aids retailers in determining which product features are most attractive to the customers. This information is essential for the product manufacturer to make a better product.
- It helps predict customers that are most likely to stop buying the product and identify new ways to keep them as customers.
- It helps to improve productivity and efficiency.

Customer analytics require different types of data to increase the accuracy of predicting customer behaviour. Owing to Big Data, multiple data types can be collected from anywhere the customer interacts with the company. Below are some of the various data types that help retailers create a customer analytics model that provides a deeper insight into customer behaviour.

Loyalty Programs Data. One of the objectives of retailers is customer acquisition. Big Data and new tracking technologies help retailers achieve this objective through models and systems, such as Loyalty Programs which provide valuable consumer data by tracking consumers' interests, behaviour, and location. This kind of data, known as individual-level data analysis, allows for more targeted marketing. In addition, these individualised data provide more detailed information such as credit card information, IP, and email address. This information is captured and stored in a CRM (customer relationship management) system. This kind of system is new to retailing, and it is valuable as it links the customer to the company.

Products Feature Data. Retailers now operate in a data-rich environment where the amount of information available on products is phenomenal compared to 50 years ago. Stock-Keeping Units (SKUs) and Radio Frequency Identification (RFIDs) expand descriptive product information by including product varieties, attributes, categories and sub-categories, and groupings of similar products. For example, all this data allows for better analysis of brand premiums and determining consumer preferences. It is advantageous to retailers as it enables them to adequately inform consumers about the item, especially if it is a newly introduced product in the store.

Location Data. The use of the spatial location of the customer helps retailers with more targeted marketing to either an existing market or a new market. The CRM database and Point of Services (POS) systems also include the consumer's geospatial location, which allows a retailer to determine localised marketing strategies and products based on the target market's specific buying preferences and behaviour.

Bonus Card Data for Household Identification. These are given to consumers and include Loyalty and Bonus cards that allow retailers to aggregate purchase history, demographics, preferences, emails, and even product return history. In addition, they provide a single customer ID that links all the individual's shopping activities online and in the brick-and-mortar store to offer a seamless way for retailers to access the data. Additionally, new data is added each time the customer uses the card, thereby adding to purchase and behaviour patterns, preferences, and propensities – all of which are used for analysis.

Customers' Web-presence Data from Retailer's Site. Retailers' websites and social media platforms offer a wealth of data regarding online consumer history, browsing history, social influence, amongst others. This data can be used to map customers' social graphs. Knowing their social and browsing history, retailers can personalise the marketing campaign for each customer.

Smartphone and Apps Usage Data. Customers who use their smartphones and Apps for browsing provide vast quantities of data for retailers who use geo-location to learn more about them. For example, retailers can learn about customers' impulsive buying behaviour, locations visited, purchase locations, preferences, and how often purchases are made in a particular area.

Environmental Data such as Weather Conditions. The weather also impacts consumer spending, store sales, inventory management, and warehousing. For example, feeds from weather monitoring systems help determine retailers' actions on responding to each store location. For example, environmental data help retailers decide whether or not they need to order more of a particular product and stock the shelves with the item; even shelving positions are determined based on weather forecasts and data feeds. For example, when analysing their scanner data in 2004, Walmart found a significant increase in sales of particular products with each storm warning.[5] Walmart used this data to capitalise on sales highly dependent on anticipation and estimation, two critical factors that allow retailers to use customer analytics effectively.

POS Systems Data. A point of sale (POS) systems collect varying types of data such as varieties of items sold and the prices and the total sales for the day. Most importantly, POS systems gather detailed customer data and the frequency they shop. This kind of data allows retailers to determine the best shopping days of the week and market accordingly to increase sales and profit. A POS is simply a place where customers make payments for the goods or services purchased.

Video Cameras' Data. While initially video cameras were installed to watch customers and prevent theft, many retailers are now utilising the video camera as a tool to analyse consumer behaviour – that is, buying habits and patterns, shopping day preferences, and promotion analysis. It also provides excellent footage of emotional responses.

People Counting Sensors Data. Sensors are a simple way to monitor foot traffic in retail stores. People counting sensors can keep a running count of how many people come into the store on any given day. This data can help companies determine whether retailers should have their business open during certain hours and days.

The Value of Big Data and Data Analytics in Selecting a Store Location

Store Location Analytics

The rise of e-commerce has changed the way the retail industry operates, especially when it comes to the choice of opening a brick-and-mortar store. Even though online shopping continues to proliferate, brick-and-mortar stores sales still outpace e-commerce sales. Most customers still prefer the in-store shopping experience. The biggest questions confronting retailers are when and where to open a store and the best location. Big Data and data analytics are helping retailers to answer these questions. Location analytics uses data from different sources combined with geographical and spatial factors to determine the best location to open a store.

Location analytics help retailers determine whether a store should be opened inside a mall or somewhere easily accessible. It helps eliminate emotion and bias when choosing a location site. Choosing the right location is very important to the success or failure of the store. However, selecting the appropriate location is not straightforward. Businesses must consider space, storage, parking, foot traffic, accessibility, and many other factors. Building an accurate and flexible location analytics model takes into consideration the following data:

- Traffic flow and parking facilities – When retailers are contemplating the location of retail stores, they must consider transportation networks. This is important in metropolitan areas as centrality to shopping areas is a crucial factor to consider.

- Demographic data such as gender, age, occupation, and income – This information will help determine whether the customers in the area can afford certain items such as expensive luxury goods.
- Local population culture – How diverse is the area in terms of ethnicity, religion, and race?
- Macroeconomic factors – What is the purchasing power of the target market?
- Cost of doing business in the area – What is the cost involved in opening a store in the area, how easy or difficult is it to operate a business in the area?
- The presence of competitors – How many other similar stores are in the area, and what is their market share?
- Foot traffic – How many customers enter a given store in the area, how long they remain in the store, and the conversion rate from entry to purchase?

Considering that urban commercial zones have the highest foot traffic of consumers, retailers must use geographical analytics to determine accessible proximity by looking at transportation infrastructure and public transportation and shopping hotspots.

The Value of Big Data and Data Analytics in Supplier Selection in the Retail Industry

Supplier Selection Analytics

While analytics plays a significant role in the demand aspect of business (consumerism), the supply side of companies is also impacted by Big Data. Retailers can use pre-qualification data of suppliers' ratings to determine the overall best supplier to meet their needs. Retailers are dependent on the supply chain of the product they sell. Therefore, the purchasing departments can use Big Data and data analytics for initial screenings of suppliers. Data analytics models help retailers choose suppliers through a pre-selection process. They also help with inventory and order management to facilitate efficient purchasing strategies by analysing supply competition data and availability. Retailers are highly dependent on suppliers to meet consumer demands. Therefore, it is essential to select the right supplier at the onset. In addition, retailers can reduce supply chain and operational problems if data analytics is applied correctly to choose suppliers.

The Value of Big Data and Data Analytics in Inventory Control

Inventory Control Analytics

As online retailing grows, more retailers seek ways to harness efficiency and data analytics provides this, even in segments where it is least expected to impact. For instance, data analytics significantly affects inventory management.

Automating the warehousing system to retrieve RFID-enabled products from storage requires a centralised distribution centre in which smart labels such as RFID tags, automatic identification (auto-id), sensors, wireless communication networks, and indoor warehouse management systems (iWMS) are used. The data collected from these smart labels offer historical information about the product, including how many are available and their location. This data also includes tracking information in real time. This provides an advantage in learning about buying habits, acquiring correct inventory numbers, and providing a shorter response time between warehouse and delivery.

RFIDs play a substantial role in successfully warehousing and identifying sale items for storage and order picking. One main advantage of RFIDs is that it replaces the complexity of SKUs, which may carry one information per item; instead, a single RFID follows the product's entire lifespan – from manufacturing to the sale of the item and beyond.

Shipping Prediction and Customer Purchase Analytics. Omni-channels generate diversified data from multiple sources. One challenge that stands out to retailers is how to get the product to the consumer as fast as possible. Anticipatory shipping is anticipating the sale and shipping the product to the nearest distribution centre, even before the order is made. Therefore, data mining and data analytics are needed to collect data from all channels and analyse it to predict future purchases.

Inventory Replenishment Analytics. Having tight control on inventory management to retrieve and dispatch means that Big Data is also needed for inventory replenishment. The system incorporated must be accurate in processing in real time, reliable in predicting and providing pertinent data, and fast in keeping up with the competitive environment online. In addition, intelligent technologies track the flow from the supply chain to the customer. A break in inventory replenishment may result in increased costs, lost sales, discrepancies in supply and demand, and reduced customer satisfaction. Therefore, business intelligence and data analytics models are needed to provide better collaboration between the business systems. The more retailers are privy to data analytics insights such as customer buying patterns, inventory planning, and replenishment, the more they can improve profitability and competitiveness.

The Value of Big Data and Data Analytics in Storage Assignment and Order Picking

Order Picking Analytics

Order picking is the process of retrieving products from different warehouses to create a custom order. It is one of the first stages in fulfilling a customer's order. The order picking method has to be flawless and accurate to facilitate a smooth shipping and after-sales activity. Order picking accuracy is essential because every time the wrong order is shipped to a customer, it creates additional steps to the sales process such as sales return, updates in stock level, and refunding customer's money. Order picking errors also reduce customer satisfaction, are costly, and lead to losing customers. Therefore, ensuring that the correct product is picked for every order is critical to the success of retailers.

Order picking may seem basic at first sight, but it is not. There are various kinds of order picking systems – packet picking, piece picking, and case picking. The picking process for particular retailers may include batch picking, multi-batch picking, single order picking, and zone picking. Data analytics is making this process more efficient. There is an advantage to deploying data analytics to monitor, track, and secure inventory for big companies with a wide variety of products and to use several supply chains. For example, with its over 200 fulfilment centres and over 1.5 billion inventory items, Amazon uses data analytics to stay abreast of market competition, keeping track of inventory with RFID tagging systems and shipping. In this mix of analysing the technical logistics for inventory purchasing and order picking for dispatch, departments such as Procurement and Warehousing depend heavily on Big Data and data analytics to streamline the process.

Procurement Analytics

The procurement process relies on the supply chain to provide raw materials or finished products that the company will bring to the market. A company may be purchasing from several supply chains and therefore needs Big Data to reveal market trends, customer behaviour, branding trends, and even the procurement patterns of competitors. However, data can become complex when procurement is globalised, and there are thousands of purchases from many suppliers. Because of this, many large and small companies are deploying data analytics tools to make the procurement process efficient and cost-effective.

Distribution Centre Analytics

Before using Big Data to bring a specific order to the storage process, warehousing was done by randomised storage. However, data analytics help bring the ordered item from the warehouse to order picking and shipping functions. In a distribution centre (DC), such as the ones used for Amazon, many products are processed daily to ensure efficiency and quick response time from sale to shipment. As a result, a procedure is necessary. Dedicated storage area zoning in a distribution centre minimises storage assignment problems, improves order picking and operation procedures, and reduces labour costs. Consequently, large companies like Amazon factor dedicated storage area zones when designing their warehouses.

Storage Assignment Analytics

Storage assignment can be a complex matter. Scholars have used mathematical models to increase the efficiency of storage zones. It is projected that an efficient layout can be designed if the order time and the distance required for order picking to fulfil the order manually can be estimated. However, whenever humans are involved in a process, a room must be made for errors and delays. Still, having assigned zoning reduces search time and picking time, and walking distance in batch picking. Big Data and analytics make this process more efficient by predicting where purchase orders are likely to come.

APPLICATION CASE 7.1

Big Data and Data Analysis at Walmart

Walmart, founded in 1945, is one of the largest retail companies in the world. The company operates supercentres, hypermarkets, supermarkets, warehouse clubs, cash and carry stores, and discount stores with membership-only warehouse clubs. In addition, it has several e-commerce websites, such as walmart.com, walmart.ca, walmart.com.mx, flipkart.com, samsclub.com, and mobile commerce applications. The company sells grocery products, health and beauty aids, pet supplies, household chemicals, paper goods, baby products, household products, electronics, etc. Additionally, Walmart offers limited financial services and related products such as money transfers, money orders, prepaid cards, check cashing, and bill payment. The company has more than 11,400 stores and various e-commerce websites in 26 countries.

Walmart's reported revenue in 2020 was $559 billion. It has 2.3 million employees and millions of customers. It is estimated that Walmart collects over 40 petabytes of data from its customers and operations worldwide daily. That is about 40,000,000 Gigabytes (GB) of data a day. In other words, if you have a flash drive that has 1 GB of space, you need 40 million flash drives to handle Walmart data per day. With this amount of data they collect and amount of customers and transactions they execute daily, they need Big Data and data analytics tools to operate efficiently and optimise their product offerings to their retail stores and customers both online and in-store.

Walmart started using Big Data platform a long time ago, but in 2012, the company decided to double its effort to utilise the potential of Big Data. Their primary focus was to integrate their different website into a single database platform. They moved from a ten-node Hadoop cluster that hosts their ten websites to a 250-node Hadoop cluster that consolidated the data on one platform. They continue to invest in Big Data to optimise their operations. In June 2013, Walmart bought a predictive intelligence startup company named Inkiru. The purpose of the purchase, according to Walmart, was to accelerate its analytics capabilities.

The investment in data analytics, using Hadoop, NoSQL technology, and acquiring Inkiru allow Walmart to do many things with the vast amount of data it collects every day. The technology enables both customers and employees to access the data collected in real time for effective uses. Their purpose was to improve their customers' shopping experience and improve its transportation and logistics supply chain around the globe.

The predictive analytic capabilities they have in their platform help them in targeted marketing and merchandising. It improves the personalisation of ads, improves customers' experience on their website, on their mobile device, and in-store. For example, they use Big Data to identify the point of sales pattern for their customers. This pattern helps them customise and personalise their offering for each customer and helps them increase the conversion rate of customers that visit their website or physical stores. They use data analytics also to identify the association between product sales and events. For example, they were able to find that Strawberry pop-tarts' sales increased before a hurricane and which cookies sold more during Halloween. In addition, the data analytics platform helps track down what product is trending on Twitter, local events, and national events. They use this information to position their product offering in each store or geographical location. Data analytics has also helped Walmart find products that can be included in their stores because they are trending on their social media analytics.

Source: Walmart Annual report (10-K SEC): https://stock. walmart.com/investors/financial-information/sec-filings/. *Source*: Walmart Labs Buys Data Analytics And Predictive Intelligence Startup Inkiru: https://techcrunch.com/2013/06/10/walmart-labs-buys-data-analytics-and-predictive-intelligence-startup-inkiru/. *Source*: Project Pro: How Big Data Analysis helped increase Walmarts Sales turnover?: https://www.projectpro.io/article/how-big-data-analysis-helped-increase-walmarts-sales-turnover/109: *Source*: Yahoo Finance: https://finance.yahoo.com/quote/WMT?p=WMT&.tsrc=fin-srch: *Source:* Walmart Company Facts: https://corporate.walmart.com/newsroom/company-facts

E-commerce and the Retail Industry

E-commerce, or electronic commerce, is a broad term used to describe all transactions made over the internet. It includes products bought and sold on online platforms, online auctions, internet banking, and online ticketing. The retail industry has undergone many significant changes over the past two decades. The estimated US retail e-commerce sales for the second quarter of 2021 was \$222.5 billion.[6] This represents an increase of 3.3 percent (±0.7 percent) from the first quarter of 2021. E-commerce sales in the second quarter of 2021 were 13.3 percent of total sales. The internet is identified as the leading cause of the growth of e-commerce retail sales. A decline in in-store sales has coincided with a massive increase in the e-commerce industry and has seen several retailers going out of business. For other retailers, though, the rise of e-commerce and changing consumer habits have led to them evolving and thriving. Meanwhile, the use of retail e-commerce continues to grow, with increasing demand for one-day shipping and voice activation playing a more significant role.

One of the significant changes for e-commerce is the evolution of mobile devices. Issues such as security and hard-to-use e-commerce sites on mobile had previously prevented many consumers from buying through their phones. However, the popularity of e-commerce[7] in the retail industry presents several opportunities:

1 The shift to online shopping allows retailers to leverage additional customer touchpoints across several platforms and services. For example, traditional interaction with consumers was often limited to short-term, in-store exchanges. However, with the popularity of smartphones, retailers can target a broader audience using multi-channel marketing that can reach consumers immediately and continuously by using proprietary apps, email, text messages, and social media. As a result, businesses have unprecedented access to new customers and build closer relationships with existing patrons by engaging them across various media channels.

2 As transactions move to online channels, omni-channel retailers can change their focus from stocking shelves to promoting innovative experiences in physical stores. For example, retailers are investing in features such as automated and mobile checkouts (Zara, Nordstrom) and "magic mirrors" that allow buyers to try on products (Neiman Marcus) digitally to improve the shopping experience. In addition, with less space needed to accommodate inventory, retailers are free to develop creative new uses for real estate and create a brick-and-mortar brand experience.

3 Adding e-commerce channels to traditional brick-and-mortar stores can help a company increase its customer base and revenue generation. The more channels a buyer uses, the more money that customer spends in-store. This is because consumers are learning to combine the distinct benefits of each channel – for example, using online media to browse and in-store channels to test products.

4 E-commerce allows retailers to benefit from Big Data. Historically, customer data were limited, delayed, and sometimes challenging to gather and manage. However, as the number of digital channels increases, large volumes of data are now available on how, when, and why consumers

shop. In addition, Big Data analytics target promotions, track customer movement through physical stores, and shape marketing strategy. As a result, Big Data enables e-commerce retailers to improve decision-making, gain a competitive advantage, enhance their performance, products, and operational processes. It also allows customer behaviour analysis and prompts the discovery of actionable insights.

E-commerce firms are among the fastest groups of Big Data Analytics (BDA) adopters. However, the unprecedented growth in BDA also creates privacy concerns as some consumers may want to protect their privacy.

The Business Value of Big Data Analytics for E-commerce firms

Retailers seek to generate transactional, informational, and strategic benefits from the growth of Big Data. Transactional value improves efficiency and cutting costs, informational value concentrates on real-time decision-making, and strategic importance focuses on gaining competitive advantages. Using BDA in e-commerce, retailers can derive overall business value by serving customer needs, developing new products and services, expanding into new markets, and increasing sales and revenue. In addition to financial gains, Big Data benefits retailers in non-financial parameters such as customer satisfaction, customer retention, or improving business processes. E-commerce retailers can interact with customers more frequently than traditional brick-and-mortar stores. Therefore, there are six tools to enhance business values.[7]

Personalisation

Consumers typically like personalised services or customised products. Buyers want to shop with the same retailer using multi-channels, and that Big Data from these various media can be personalised in real-time. Real-time data analytics enables retailers to offer personalised services comprising unique content and promotions to individuals. In addition, these personalised services allow brands to separate loyal customers from new customers and make promotional offers to attract and retain them.

Dynamic Pricing

Brands must be active and vibrant in today's competitive retail environment to attract new customers while setting a competitive price. For example, Amazon uses Big Data to process competitors' pricing, product sales, customer behaviour, and regional or geographical preferences to establish dynamic pricing.

Customer Service

E-commerce retailers use Big Data to provide fast and reliable customer service. For example, customer grievances communicated through forms in online stores and tweeting allow e-commerce retailers to improve customers' experience when they contact the service centre, resulting in prompt service delivery. Furthermore, retailers can offer innovative after-sales services by providing proactive maintenance or preventive measures before a failure occurs or is detected.

Supply Chain Visibility

When a shopper places an order on an online platform, it is logical to expect companies to track the order while the items are still in transit. In addition, customers expect essential and timely information, such as the exact availability, current status, and location of their orders. However, e-commerce firms often face difficulty addressing customer expectations as various third parties are involved in the supply chain. Therefore, BDA plays a crucial role in collecting multiple information from several parties on multiple products and subsequently precisely advises the expected delivery date to customers.

Security and Fraud Detection

Big Data prevents fraud by identifying relevant insights relating to credit cards, product returns, and identity theft. For example, e-commerce firms can identify fraud in real time by combining transaction data with customers' purchase history, web activities, social media feed, and geospatial location data from mobile apps. For example, Visa has employed a Big Data-enabled fraud management system that inspects 500 different aspects of a transaction. This system has saved the company $2 billion in potential losses annually.

Predictive Analytics

Predictive analytics identifies events before they occur through the use of Big Data. The use of predictive analytics relies on robust data mining. Therefore, predictive analytics helps e-commerce retailers prepare their revenue budgets and recognise future sales patterns from past sales data. This, in turn, allows firms to forecast and determine inventory requirements, thus avoiding product stockouts and losing customers. Increasingly, businesses are using BDA to solve business problems or make decisions and capitalise on the current opportunities of Big Data.

Key Term

Retail Analytics; Store Location Analytics; Inventory Control Analytics; Loyalty Programs Data; Location Data; E-Commerce

Chapter Key Takeaways

- The retail industry's survival depends on a supply chain that involves manufacturers, wholesalers, and a robust transportation and logistical system.
- Customer analytics require different types of data to make predicting customer behaviour more accurate.
- Even though online shopping continues to proliferate, brick-and-mortar stores sales still outpace e-commerce sales.
- Location analytics uses data from different sources combined with geographical and spatial factors to determine the best location to open a store.
- Location analytics help retailers determine whether a store should be opened inside a mall or somewhere easily accessible. In addition, it helps eliminate emotion and bias when choosing a location site.
- Using BDA in e-commerce, retailers can derive overall business value by serving customer needs, developing new products and services, expanding into new markets, and increasing sales and revenue.

Discussion Questions

1 What is the value of Big Data and data analytics in the retail industry?
2 Explain what is customer analytics.
3 Explain at least three benefits of customer analytics in the retail industry.
4 Customer analytics require different types of data to make predicting customer behaviour more accurate. Name five types of those data.
5 What is store location analytics?
6 What kind of data is required to building an accurate and flexible location analytics model?
7 What is the benefit of location analytics in the retail industry?
8 What is order picking analytics?
9 How does order picking analytics enhance the operation of a retail business?
10 Selecting the right supplier is crucial for companies. Discuss in detail how data analytics can assist companies with this decision.
11 Explain how Big Data analytics help companies with inventory control.
12 Discuss how the growth in e-commerce has led to an increase in Big Data in the retail industry.
13 Explain how Big Data analytics is used in e-commerce retailing.

References

1 United States Census, Annual Retail Trade Survey (ARTS), https://www.census.gov/programs-surveys/arts.html
2 The retail market worldwide - Statistics & Facts; https://www.statista.com/statistics/443522/global-retail-sales/

3 US Census Bureau. Monthly Retail Trade, https://www.census.gov/retail/index. html
4 Walmart Corporate, https://corporate.walmart.com/newsroom/innovation/ 20170807/5-ways-walmart-uses-big-data-to-help-customers.
5 Germann, F., Lilien, G.L., Fiedler, L., & Kraus, M. (2014). Do retailers benefit from deploying customer analytics? *Journal of Retailing, 90*(4), 587–593.
6 https://www.census.gov/retail/mrts/www/data/pdf/ec_current.pdf
7 Akter, S. & Wamba, S.F. (2016). Big data analytics in E-commerce: A systematic review and agenda for future research. *Electronic Markets, 26*(2), 173–194.

8 Data Analytics in the Financial Services Industry

As the world economy moves to a digital age, the financial services industry faces many challenges. These challenges include: increased banking regulations from governments, fraud, analysing credit risk and borrowers risk profile, improving financial transactions transparency, making low-risk lending decisions, managing risk exposures, identifying suspicious transactions promptly, and mitigating identity theft. This chapter details how data analytics and Big Data are helping financial institutions to meet these challenges by gaining a deeper understanding of customers' needs and delivering real-time customer experience while increasing investors' return on capital (ROC) and achieving operational efficiency.

LEARNING OBJECTIVES:

At the end of the chapter, students should be able to:

- Understand the financial service industry
- Know the value of data analytics in retail banking
- Understand the importance of data analytics in credit risk analysis
- Assess the value of data analytics in fraud detection
- Identify the significance of data analytics in asset and wealth management

Financial Service Industry

The financial service industry provides financial services to companies and individuals. The word financial service is a broad term that encompasses banking services, investment services, insurance services, amongst others. Investment services provide individual and business access to financial markets such as stocks and bonds. Insurance services protect against death, property loss, or liabilities to individuals and businesses. Many stakeholders and moving parts are within the financial services, including credit card issuers and processors, legacy banks and emerging challengers.

DOI: 10.4324/9781003129356-8

The financial services industry is accelerating its use of digital technology. Paying with cash, participating in in-personal meetings with financial experts, and even using an ATM are all fading features of financial services. With this move to digitisation, consumers can manage their finances from home amid the ongoing coronavirus pandemic. Also, financial institutions and startups are honing their technology and expanding remote services.

There are three general categories of financial services: personal, consumer, and corporate, which constitute the significant players and influencers for companies.

Personal Finance

Personal Finance is an individual's budgeting, saving, and spending of monetary resources. It prepares the individual to meet the requirements of all stages and significant events in life, from buying their first car to retirement planning.

When choosing a bank or other financial institution, an individual typically considers an institution that offers personal financial services, such as financial consultants and the ability to manage personal accounts remotely and take control of their financial health via online platforms and mobile apps.

Consumer Finance

Consumer financing enables customers to make low monthly payments or instalments over a fixed period for goods or services they otherwise could not afford to pay using cash or a credit card. Several stores and businesses are offering consumer financing to assist individuals with purchases. The consumer financial services market comprises significant players, including credit card services, mortgage lenders, and personal and student loan services. Consumer finance solutions help both businesses and consumers. For example, when a business offers financing through a consumer financial services company, it increases the opportunity of generating more sales as customers can make purchases even if they lack funds or credit card bandwidth to cover the purchase immediately.

Corporate Finance

Corporate financing describes a business's financial activities, such as funding sources, capital structure, accounting, and investment decisions on how to increase the company value. It considers how to maximise shareholder value through long- and short-term financial planning and the implementation of different strategies. Corporate finance activities range from capital investment to tax considerations. Key funding sources include:

- Private equity
- Venture capital
- Angel investors

Big Data in Financial Services Sector

Financial markets and technological advancement are related to every aspect of human activity. Big Data technology is an integral part of the financial services sector and will continue to drive future developments and initiatives. These innovations cover various financial businesses such as online peer-to-peer lending, crowd-funding, small and medium-sized enterprises (SME) finance, wealth management and asset management, trading management, cryptocurrency, money/remittance transfer, and mobile payments platforms. These services produce data that are used to:

- make better investment decisions,
- monitor various spending patterns,
- drive trade and investment,
- create tax reform,
- conduct fraud detection and investigation,
- conduct risk analysis,
- promote automation.

Big Data is also vital in providing financial service data to companies like Bloomberg, Reuters, DataStream, which quote financial transaction prices and record millions of daily transactions per second for customer analytics use and regulatory compliance requirements.

Data analytics has changed the face of the financial service industry. The banking sector, in particular, has evolved over the past decade from its traditional paper transactions to a digital age. As consumers' digital footprints grow, new data is added every day, and data analytics is used to understand the trends.

The Value of Data Analytics in Retail Banking

Most banks offer three primary banking services: retail banking, corporate banking/commercial banking, and investment banking. Retail banking, also known as personal banking, refers to the division of a bank that deals directly with individual customers. It serves individuals rather than a corporation. It provides financial services to individuals, including checking accounts, saving accounts, credit cards, mortgages, personal loans, CD, line of credit, and auto loans. In other words, retail banking helps individuals manage their money and, at the same time, extend credit to them.

For several years now, retail banking has expanded its services to include investment services such as retirement planning and brokerage account. In most banks, retail banking is the most extensive portfolio and the most profitable banking services division. For example, in 2019, 48 percent of JP Morgan Chase's revenue comes from its retail banking services, and 49 percent of the profit is attributed to retail banking.[1] Because of the changes in bank regulations, most banks, if not all, offer retail banking services. They range from the largest, JP Morgan Chase, to the smallest local community bank.

Retail banking is changing rapidly, and the digital transformation is leading to more competition in retail banking. Today, individuals have many choices as many non-traditional banks such as private equity firms and Fintech companies offer retail banking services. Data analytics, especially predictive analytics, is becoming the most significant asset for retail banking. It allows banks to assess individual customers' risks and opportunities and address critical issues facing the sector, such as:

1 Which customers are likely profitable?
2 Which customers will likely default on their loans?
3 What is the demographic make-up of customers?
4 How to retain their customers?

Predictive Analytics in Customer Creditworthiness. Predictive analytics is not new to the banking industry in general. These analytics were used in the 1950s to develop what is now known as the Fair Isaac Corporation (FICO) score.[2] This analytic uses various data such as individual credit usage, employment, income, history of paying off loans to develop a single number that can predict the individual future creditworthiness. Most retail banks still use the FICO score as a screening method to determine customer creditworthiness. Retail bankers look for creditworthy and profitable customers and which customers to market which product to. Because of the availability of Big Bata, retail banks are using historical data to construct predictive models that highlight customer financial behaviour. These analytics help the bank to make data-driven decisions on which customers receive a particular loan or bank product.

Analytics and Local Bank Armed Robbery. Big Data and predictive analytics have also been used to predict which banks are most likely to be subjected to armed robbery. Banks can know which branches are most likely to be robbed from various historical data such as bank characteristics, theft, location, and spatial mapping. With this knowledge, a data-driven decision could reduce the risk by adjusting security arrangements and determining which site to open a retail bank branch in. For example, Absa bank in South Africa used predictive analytics to reduce armed robbery by 41% in two years by adjusting security procedures in banks. The analytics predicted a high risk of theft even though bank robbery was decreasing in South Africa.[3]

Delinquency Analytics in Retail Banking. There are always delinquent customers. Companies must avoid the trap of treating each negligent customer the same. Instead, they can use data analytics to identify the different types of delinquency and develop a different strategy to address each group. There are three major types of delinquent customers: habitual, genuine, and intentional one.[4] Using predictive analytics businesses can identify each group and address their issues separately – for example, delinquency, maybe resulting from job loss. Therefore, genuine delinquents should be treated differently as they may recover from any financial challenges they are facing and become very profitable for the bank in the future.

Customer Retention and Engagement. Because of customers' rapid use of technology and the digitisation of transactions, there is less interaction between the local branch office and customers. Instead, there are multiple access points the customer has to the bank, and in each case, data is created. For example, most customers use online deposits, cash apps, and Zelle instead of going into a bank. These access points generate data that the bank can use to analyse and provide service to its customer. Because of these vast amounts of data created every day by customer access to the bank in various means, data analytics has become the primary source of making a decision. Data analytics helps banks make faster and better decisions to help retain their customer base and improve operational efficiency. For example, banks use social media analytics to understand individual customers and identify the potential for cross-selling or offer more bank products and services to these customers.

Data Analytics and Bank Operating Hours. The rise of online banking, mobile banking, phone apps, and financial technology innovation has given retail banking multiple channels to provide products and services to their customers in addition to the traditional physical location. Data analytics is helping retail banks understand customer behaviours and preferences as banking change its payment and services method from a single channel platform to multiple platforms. The migration from the brick-and-mortar banking service to the numerous digital platforms creates more data. It creates an opportunity to understand consumer behaviour and preferences in the different spaces and identifies how a bank can reduce operating costs by closing some branches. Data analytics is helping banks answer questions such as:

1 What are the impacts of closing a bank on the usage of other channels available to the customer?
2 What are the impacts of opening a new branch on the other channels available to customers?
3 Does the presence of a bank branch improve cross-selling of bank products or not?
4 Do customers who use digital banking channels also visit local bank branches? How often?
5 If customers are not visiting banks, how can customer relationships be improved without physically meeting with the customers?

Customer data from offline interaction with the bank through credit or debit transactions or ATMs are very valuable. For example, the data from offline and online interaction with the bank can predict which customer is likely to stop using the bank's product and services and determine which customers have completely stopped using the bank's product or services.

The Value of Data Analytics in Credit Risk Analysis

The vast amount of data and the complexity of financial transactions have made data analytics necessary in credit risk analysis for banking, insurance, wealth, and asset management in the financial service industry. As the types of products and services in the financial service industry continue to increase and the industry embraces new technology to manage their operations, these new products (e.g. Fintech) and services combined with the latest technology present risks that need to be analysed, understood, and monitored. With the vast amount of collected data, these new financial products require a new kind of analytics than the normative approach based on econometrics and statistical techniques that the field of finance has relied upon to understand financial products. Data analytics combined with economic theories provide managers and investors with a more data-driven decision-making process, especially in credit risk analysis.

Most financial products are inherently risky and the higher the expected returns, the higher the risk. However, the large volume of data and the need for real-time decision support make a sophisticated analytics model and approach all but a necessity. Today, besides the traditional markets and financial data such as fundamental and technical indicators used to determine risk and investment opportunities, there is new data such as social responsibility data, social media, and public and investor sentiment data. These data create unknown risks and opportunities for financial institutions that need to be identified and analysed.

Risk Management. Even though managing a financial institution involves many other aspects such as accounting, investment planning, marketing, and other day-to-day operation of the business, risk management has taken a heightened priority. Risk analytics is essential because of the new financial products (cryptocurrencies, crowd-funding, Fintech) and the multiple electronic platforms used to provide these services and products (online transactions and other cloud-based platforms). Financial institutions have also focused on risk management because of strict government regulations imposed on this sector on measuring and reporting their risk exposure in terms of liquidity, market, and credit risk. For example, the first Basel Capital Accord in 1988 and its subsequent five amendments in 1996 require banks to adhere to credit risk, market risk, and a minimum capital requirement.[5]

The Basel Committee on Bank Supervision (BCBS), also known as Basel Accord, is headquartered in Basel, Switzerland, at the Bank for International Settlements. The BCBS was founded in 1974 and has issued regulations on financial institutions concerning market risk, capital risk, and operational risk. The BCBS Accord's primary function is to issue regulations that ensure that financial institutions manage all kinds of threats. They have published a series of international banking regulations known as Basel I, Basel II, and Basel III. Together, the main objective of all three accords is to require financial institutions to manage their exposure to risk by maintaining enough capital on their account that can absorb unexpected losses due to sudden changes in market conditions.[6] Compliance with government regulation on this strict risk management requires a sophisticated data analytics approach.

Data Analytics Approaches in Credit Risk Modelling. Credit risk analytics is a significant focus for financial institutions because these companies provide loans to their customers. The chances of the customers repaying their loans are not always guaranteed. The three main components of credit risk analytics are:

1 Probability of loan default (PD)
2 Loss given default (LGD)
3 Exposure at default (EAD)

That is, the expected loss of a given loan is equal to the Probability of Loan Default (PD) multiplied by both the probability of Loss Given Default (LGD) and Exposure at default (EAD). **That is, expected loss = PD × LGD × EAD.**

Data Analytics and Probability of Loan Default. The Probability of Loan Default (PD) is the likelihood that a borrower cannot make scheduled repayment of a loan over some time. Companies use data analytics to calculate the probability of default for each borrower and assign a credit score. The determination of the default probability is not straightforward because the chances of default are a function of the borrower's characteristics, the economic environment at a certain point in time, and the loan characteristics. Because of data availability such as financial market data, customer personal historical data, social networks, history of delinquencies, corporate data, data analytics has made it easier to identify risky customers before loans are extended to them.

Loss Given Default (LGD) Analytics. A financial institution will likely lose this amount of money when a borrower defaults on the loan. This loss is usually expressed as a percentage of the total credit exposure at the default time. For example, consider Bank of America lends $60,000 to an individual, and that person defaults. Several factors are considered to calculate the loss, such as instalment payment that the borrower may have already made, collateral that the bank may hold, and any amount collected through the court system or collection. In other words, the loss may significantly be less than $60,000. In addition, LGD calculation takes into consideration any amount recovered from the default. For example, if, at the time of default, the outstanding amount is $30,000 and the bank can recover $20,000 through collections or other means, the net loss to the bank will be $10,000. Therefore, the LGD will be 33.3% (That is $10,000/$30,000).

Exposure at Default (EAD) Analytics. The loan amount that the financial institution risks losing at the time a borrower defaults. For example, consider a customer who takes out a loan of $60,000, and if after three years the borrower defaults and the outstanding loan amount at that time is

$30,000, the exposure at default is $30,000. That is, EAD does not consider potential recovery amounts while LGD does.

Determining the amount of LGD and EAD is significant as they are components of credit risk models in financial institutions. Determining credit loss requires analysing historical loan default and other variables. As they analyse credit risk, financial institutions need to predict their exposure to borrowers' default constantly. And in the case of EAD, it changes every month or every time a customer makes a payment that reduces their outstanding loan. Therefore, these types of calculations are made for every customer and loan. In addition, several variables are considered, which require vast volumes of data. That is why data analytics and data analytics tools have become a necessity for financial institutions.

Loan Portfolio Credit Risk and Data Analytics. Credit risk analytics extend far beyond individual borrow or retail banking. First, it is needed to manage loan portfolios. A loan portfolio is a pool of loans that a financial institution owns and manages. For example, a loan portfolio may hold a collection of mortgage loans, commercial loans, and student loans. A loan portfolio is exposed to risk because a large number of borrowers in the pool may default. Therefore, financial institutions need to collect data and analyse them to identify the potential risk exposure. In other words, loan portfolio management and analytics focus on the losses and risks at the portfolio level.

Credit risk analytics is not limited to financial institutions and the issuance of loans to individuals and businesses. It is also essential in venture capital investment, mergers and acquisitions, asset pricing, and various other investments and ventures with some uncertainties. In all of these cases, data analytic tools and approaches have been beneficial and valuable.

Investment Portfolio Management and Data Analytics. Credit risk analytics is not only crucial in loan portfolio management but also critical in investment portfolio management. Investment portfolio management owns and manages a pool of financial assets such as stocks, mutual funds, corporate bonds, government bonds, and currencies, hoping that they will grow over time and return a profit for investors. Thus, the investment could be for the long-term or short-term. Owning and managing an investment portfolio involves two primary issues:

1 Selecting the financial assets to include in the portfolio and determining their risk.
2 Portfolio asset mix or allocation.

Selecting Financial Assets to include in the Portfolio. In constructing a portfolio, the first step is to choose the assets. Selecting the financial assets means determining the profitability, suitability, and risk of these assets. It is a critical and significant step in constructing a portfolio because there are various financial assets from which to choose. Therefore, the portfolio's success depends significantly on the choice and screening of the type of assets.

Multiple issues need to be considered when selecting an asset to be included in the portfolio: market trends, investment environments, fundamentals of each asset, risk, profit potential, and historical data.

Selecting an asset needs both a critical and analytical approach. The judgement approach includes investment preferences and policies for the portfolio manager and investors. The analytics approach, which is the focus in asset screening, identifies and predicts future trends, risks, and opportunities. Data analytics tools such as neural networks, neuro-fuzzy models, and support vector machines have been handy in asset screening. These analytics are used to predict which assets are likely to be profitable and their risk.

Data Analytics and Selecting a Portfolio. Choosing the best portfolio asset mix is the key to a profitable investment portfolio. The portfolio asset mix is the allocation of the percentage of each asset in a portfolio. For example, do you want to have 20 percent of stocks or 10 percent of stocks in your portfolio? The combination of different assets group to make a profitable investment is not a straightforward computation. The Mean-Variance (MV) portfolio selection model is based on a journal paper published in 1952 by Harry Markowitz entitled "Portfolio Selection." This model, often called the Modern Portfolio Theory (MPT), states that portfolio risks can be reduced if an investor selects financial assets with low or negative correlations. Harry Markowitz was later awarded a Nobel Prize in 1990 for his work on portfolio selection.[7] Over the years, there have been various other models added to find a perfect asset mix portfolio. The problem is that establishing an ideal mix of bonds, mutual funds, and stock is challenging and dynamic. Due to the nature of the process, individuals must re-balance their portfolios when the market conditions and investment environment change. To re-balance portfolio and determine the asset mix in a portfolio, portfolio managers have employed data analytics to identify trends that will provide insights on re-balancing the portfolio.

One can safely conclude that integrating data analytics and financial theories allows investors to identify and quantify risk much more quickly than using traditional statistics and econometrics approaches only.

Data Analytics in Fraud Detection and Prevention

Fraud is everywhere in our society, and it occurs when someone or business/entity takes away money or property from someone else without their permission through fraudulent means. Some typical financial frauds are credit card fraud, mortgage fraud, embezzlement, identity theft, and security fraud.

It is estimated that fraud costs individuals, companies, and organisations $2.1 trillion globally per year.[8] Even though fraud has always existed, it has become more sophisticated recently because of technology, and criminals are constantly finding new ways to defraud individuals and companies. Unfortunately, those who commit fraud have also increased. The increasing number of potential fraudsters makes fraud detection and prevention a priority in most organisations. A survey conducted by PricewaterhouseCoopers (PwC) found that employees commit 37 percent of fraud, while 39 percent is committed by customers, vendors, and hackers.[9] In other words, fraud can be executed by employees within a company, individuals outside of the company, professional fraudsters, or collusion with employees and individuals outside the company. There are several access points for fraud in companies, and the internet and the digitisation of transactions have made it even easier. Fraud can be committed through ATM, credit cards, debit cards, internet banking, mobile banking, offline within the bank branch, or online. Companies and financial institutions have also had to deal with sophisticated cyber fraudsters from different parts of the world linked together through social media, emails, and other sources of communication networks.

Fraud Detection Analytics. Banks and financial institutions deploy sophisticated data analytics tools to prevent and detect this vase network of fraud. Big Data analytics enable companies to process and analyse electronic data from different sources faster and make real-time decisions. One significant way analytics allows companies to detect and prevent fraud is by enabling a vast amount of data to be analysed quickly. Data availability from multiple sources such as onsite local bank branch data, online transactions data, social media data, geospatial data, IP address data, telecommunication data makes fraud analytics more efficient and effective. As a result, financial institutions can more readily identify unusual transactions than before the advent of Big Data and data analytics. In addition, the massive amount of unstructured and structured data generated every day by the financial service industry makes data analytics the primary tool for detecting and preventing fraud. Some other ways data analytics is helping detect and prevent fraud are:

- By easily merging and comparing data from different sources to identify suspicious transactions quickly.
- Detecting anomalies and unusual activities. When these anomalies are detected, an authority can focus their attention on the high-risk irregularities and fixing the weakness in the internal control procedures in the organisation.

Fraud detection and prevention are such a significant issue that in 2015, the US government passed a law entitled; Public Law 114–186- Fraud Reduction and Data Analytics Act of 2015.[10] This law seeks to encourage Federal agencies to deploy data analytics to help mitigate fraud risks. Fraud does not only destroy individuals' personal lives but can also affect the profitability and reputation of a company. In addition, customers and investors may be sceptical about doing business with a company that cannot detect and prevent fraud because they do not want their personal information in the hands of fraudsters.

APPLICATION CASE 8.1

Financial Market Analytics at FINRA

The United States Congress authorises the Financial Industry Regulatory Authority (FINRA) to protect investors and safeguard the integrity of the US financial markets. The agency oversees more than 635,000 brokers, processes up to 100 billion transactions a day, and monitors 4,100 securities firms. In addition, they regulate and manage Over-the-counter (OTC) trading for listed and non-listed securities such as NASDAQ, NASDAQ Options Market, NYSE MKT, NYSE, and Chicago Board Options Exchange (CBOE). The US financial market is massive, and it is the lifeline of the US economy, business operations, financing, and the world financial markets. The stock market transactions alone are in the billions of dollars a day. FINRA is responsible for regulating this vast market that involves many players. Its primary responsibility is to ensure that transactions are secure and everyone who participates in the market plays by the rules and complies with every regulation. Additionally, they have to detect and prevent fraud.

Besides monitoring these individuals' trades and transactions, the agency must track daily stock trade, cancellations, orders, and quotes. Stock trade can be in billions in a day. All of these activities are stored most times in different databases. The agency collects a massive amount of data from various exchanges and securities. They investigate any fluctuations of the stock market or the stock price of a particular company, especially if it happens before a significant event in the company, such as stock split, earnings announcements, or merger and acquisition deal. They look for unusual events in the movements of the financial system and stock market.

But most of their activities often takes place after the event, more like auditing a past event. While it has been effective in catching and prosecuting violators of rule and regulation – securities fraud, it would like to take care of some of these issues in real time. The agency wants to integrate these massive amounts of data into one place for easy analytics. They had an in-house platform that was proving to be insufficient. So, they decide to invest in a cloud-based Big Data platform for flexibility and space. The cloud-based platform was Amazon Web Service (AWS) and Cloudera, which provide a Hybrid Data Platform. They also use open-source data analytics tools such as Presto, Hbase, Hive, and Apache Hadoop to make the platform efficient and less costly. Integrating AWS, Cloudera Hybrid Data Platform, Hadoop, Hbase was a technical challenge, but it was effective and cost-efficient. Hadoop was used primarily for surveillance analytics to identify unusual patterns

(Continued)

and analyse trade relationships between those unusual trade patterns over some time.

The capabilities of Hadoop reduce queries and response time from hours to a few minutes. This is very important if you consider the billions of financial transactions executed in a day. In November 2017, FINRA's Vincent Saulys and David Yacono, senior directors at FINRA's cybersecurity and technology, were speakers at an AWS re-INVENT conference. They explained how their embrace of data analytics and cloud computing using AWS and other analytics tools has helped make their work at FINRA more effective for their data scientists and users.

These analytics tools were used to validate and monitor transactions in the National Market System (NMS) and for equity markets' OTC transactions such as NASDAQ. Together, this platform and the analytics tools are used to detect and prevent fraud, enforce compliance with financial market regulations, and avoid market manipulation by rogue agents.

The Big Data platform deployed by FINRA has paid many dividends. FINRA can monitor the billion of day-to-day transactions taking place in the US financial markets in real time. These capabilities enable them to detect unusual transactions quickly and prevent any adverse effects that might disrupt the financial system. Analytics that used to last for hours now can be completed in seconds. And the agency was also able to save millions of dollars in operating costs because of the effectiveness of the analytic data platform they have set up. The analytics can give them alerts on specific issues and areas to look at in the market instead of guessing. This specificity of alerts allows them to focus their resources on where it matters most and leads to cost savings in operations.

Their investment in data analytics gives them a wide range of options to monitor the market over the years. In 2020, they brought in 808 disciplinary actions against registered brokers, prosecuted more than 970 fraud and insider trading cases, and ordered about $25.2 million in restitution to investors. In addition, they believe in technology and Big Data so much that they sponsor open-source software development and Big Data analytics projects. They are also encouraging knowledge sharing and collaboration in technology and data analytics.

Source: Financial Industry Regulatory Authority: https://www. finra.org/#/: *Source*: FINR Technology, November 2017. How FINRA Secures Its Big Data and Data Science Platform on AWS: https://technology.finra.org/articles/video/secure-data-science-platfrom-aws.html: *Source*: Stock Market Analytics: Tracking Billions of Trades, Daily. https://www.rtinsights.com/stock-market-analytics-tracking-billions-of-trades-daily/: *Source*: Using the Cloud to Improve Analytics: https://technology.finra.org/articles/using-cloud-to-improve-our-data-science.html

The Value of Data Analytics in Asset and Wealth Management

Most financial institutions manage the assets of wealthy clients. Asset or wealth management is the process of handling clients' money. Clients include individuals, small businesses, not-for-profit organisations, or large companies. Managing wealth involves identifying the clients' goals and achieving those goals by buying stocks, bonds, and other financial assets to increase the client's wealth. Assets managers are also called institutional wealth managers, financial advisors, registered investment advisors (RIAs), and wealth managers. The terms asset and wealth management are interchangeable in this book.

Over the past several years, asset and wealth management has grown because people are becoming wealthier, and the number of millionaires worldwide is multiplying. Another reason is that data analytics and artificial intelligence have transformed this sector into a very efficient and profitable venture. However, the industry faces issues such as integrating new technologies, complying with new regulations, obtaining data, and choosing the best investment options.

Therefore, most asset management units of financial institutions are deploying advanced analytics to improve investment performance and operating models. As the number of millionaires increase, the competition to win these new clients also increases. Asset and wealth managers seek the best ways to capture a share of these new millionaires to manage their wealth. Predictive analytics especially has moved the industry to a more foresight paradigm than an insight paradigm. In other words, to succeed in this sector, the asset manager needs to predict asset performance. To stay ahead of the game, asset and wealth managers are using Big Data and data analytics tools in the following way:

- Acquiring new clients
- Engaging and maintaining good client relationships
- Improving operational efficiency and flexibility
- Improving performance management using people analytics
- Improving productivity and reduce systematic bias

Acquiring new clients analytics. Assets and wealth managers use data analytics to identify potential new customers, generate leads, and win new customers. Using predictive analytics, they use both external and internal data to create a comprehensive customer profile. Therefore, as the demographic of wealthy individuals changes from the older to the younger generation, asset managers need to understand how to attract and serve these two seemingly distinct groups. Data analytics is helping to identify what these clients value the most and pinpoint growth opportunities that appeal to both older and younger wealthy clients. With such information, wealth managers can target these different groups with personalised messages to win their business. Predictive analytics also help asset managers identify where potential customers are most likely to live, demographics, and values. By linking external and internal data, and connecting them with recent information, personal events, social media data, media posting by potential clients, data analytics can help asset managers accurately predict the investing values of potential customers. Wealth managers can provide real-time personalised messaging to attract these clients to their services from the information gathered. In other words, the analytics helps provide messaging that influences a potential client's decision-making process.

Engaging and Maintaining Good Client Relationship Analytics. Wealth and asset management require a high level of trust. Therefore, understanding and engaging their clients is critical for wealth and asset managers to maintain trust and business relationships. To engage and understand their clients effectively, assets managers use data analytics to determine the ideal counsel for each client to help maintain a positive and productive relationship. Predictive analytics provides data-driven insight on the best way to interact with existing clients and what kind of advice to offer them. For example, the asset manager can gather social media data on their clients' interests, current satisfaction regarding their investment, and risk tolerance by using data analytics tools. With such information, they can engage their client constructively. Therefore, wealth managers can use data analytics to assess and compare clients' optimal investment positions and risk tolerance to determine investment approaches. These practices are crucial, especially for older investors whose investment goals and risk tolerance change with time. For example, if older investors are thinking of retiring, they may be more interested in succession planning and how their wealth may be used to support loved ones in the long run and, therefore, may have a low risk tolerance.

In contrast, younger clients may focus on generating wealth and may be more willing to take risks. Therefore, predictive analytics is necessary for asset and wealth managers to understand what each client values the most and determine the best way to engage each client to maintain a good business and profitable relationship. By regularly collecting data on each client and analysing them, asset managers will identify behaviours and patterns that can influence decision-making and nurture the relationship with a high degree of flexibility and foresight. As a result, data analytics is helping asset managers to make quick and reliable decisions for each client.

Data Analytics Improves Operational Efficiency and Flexibility. Asset and wealth managers are using data analytics tools to improve productivity in their operations. For example, using data analytics tools such as Natural Language Processing allows asset managers to collect and analyse voice, text, and other unstructured data more quickly. Collecting and analysing data of different types from multiple sources enhances operational efficiency in regulatory compliance and risk assessment of potential investment. Consequently, data analytics and data analytics tools reduce the labour-intensive process of collecting, compiling, cleaning, and processing a large amount of information. With the ability to quickly process large quantities of data, asset managers and their research teams can quickly access and analyse changes in public filings and investors' sentiment and re-align their investment approach to market conditions and clients' shifting sentiments. These are very important since at the core of asset and wealth management is the client. Data analytics provides asset and wealth managers with the necessary tools to manage their client assets effectively and reliably in an increasingly complex market environment.

Improve Performance Management through People Analytics. Data analytics has also helped asset managers determine the high performer in their teams and what makes some asset managers perform better than others. By selecting the high performers and their characteristics, executives in the asset and wealth management sector can use this information to recruit, retain, and effectively train and manage current asset and wealth managers who are not performing to expectations. In other words, data analytics is used to improve client wealth and the professional development of asset and wealth managers. People analytics is simply using employees data to determine high-performing employees. Using employees' social networks, their relationships with others, predictive analytics can identify which employee is most likely to be efficient and innovative.

Data Analytics Improves Productivity and Reduces Systematic Bias. Data analytics and predictive algorithms have significantly improved asset managers' productivity by generating actionable client insights and identifying specific products for each client. It also creates opportunities to cross-sell products to a group of clients based on the predictive algorithms results. Systematic bias has long been a problem in making an investment decision for asset and wealth managers, in particular, and investors in general. Data analytics reduce or eliminate this bias because it allows an analyst to put together a vast amount of data from different sources, eliminating human intuition most often crowded by bias. This allows asset managers to make operational improvements based on data.

Key Term

Financial Service Industry; Retail Banking; Fintech; FICO Score; Customer Credit Worthiness; Loan Portfolio; Probability of Loan Default (PD); Loss Given Default (LGD); Exposure At Default (EAD); Fraud Detection Analytics

Chapter Key Takeaways

- The financial service industry provides financial services to companies and individuals. The word financial service is a broad term that encompasses banking services, investment services, insurance services.

- Data analytics and Big Data are changing the face of the financial service industry. The industry, and the banking sector, in particular, have evolved over the past decade from traditional paper transactions to a digital age.
- Data analytics, especially predictive analytics, is becoming the most significant asset for retail banking. It allows banks to assess individual customers' risks and opportunities and address critical issues facing the sector.
- Because of the availability of Big Data, retail banks are using historical data to construct predictive models that highlight customer financial behaviour. These analytics helps the bank to make a data-driven decision on which customers receive a particular loan or bank product.
- Big Data and predictive analytics have also been used to predict which banks are most likely to be subjected to armed robbery.
- Data analytics helps banks make faster and better decisions to help retain their customer base and improve operational efficiency.
- The vast amount of data and the complexity of financial transactions have made data analytics necessary in credit risk analysis for banking, insurance, wealth, and asset management in the financial service industry.
- Data analytics combined with financial theories provide managers and investors with a more data-driven decision-making process, especially in credit risk analysis.
- Data analytics tools such as neural networks, neuro-fuzzy models, support vector machines have been helpful in asset screening. These analytics are used to predict which assets are likely to be profitable and their accompanying risk.
- The massive amount of structured and unstructured transactions data generated by the financial service industry makes data analytics the primary tool for detecting and preventing fraud.
- Asset and wealth managers use data analytics to identify potential new customers, generate leads, and win new customers.

Discussion Questions

1 What does the financial services industry provide to individuals and companies?
2 What is retail banking? Give examples of retail banking services.
3 Explain how retail banks use FICO scores.
4 Explain how data analytics is used to prevent an armed bank robbery.
5 How is data analytics helping banks manage their opening hours?
6 What are the three components of credit analytics? Please explain each of them.
7 What is a loan portfolio? What is the value of data analytics in loan portfolio management?

8   What is an investment portfolio?
9   How does data analytics aid in selecting an investment portfolio?
10 Explain how data analytics is used to prevent and detect fraud.

References

1 JP Morgan chase (2019). Financial statement.
2 Fico.com
3 Lamont, J. (2005). Predictive analytics: An asset to retail banking worldwide. *KM World, 10,* 16. See also www.absa.co.za/about-us/absa-bank/
4 Budale, D. & Mane, D. (2013). Predictive analytics in retail banking. *International Journal of Engineering and Advanced Technology, 2*(5), 508–510.
5 https://www.bis.org/publ/bcbs04a.htm
6 History of the Basel Committee (bis.org), https://www.bis.org/bcbs/history.htm
7 https://www.nobelprize.org/prizes/economic-sciences/1990/press-release/
8 Fighting Fraud with Analytics – Vitamin D Blog | Deloitte US; https://www2.deloitte.com/us/en/pages/deloitte-analytics/articles/fighting-fraud-with-analytics.htm
9 PwC's Global Economic Crime and Fraud Survey 2020, https://www.pwc.com/gx/en/services/forensics/economic-crime-survey.html
10 Fraud Reduction and Data Analytics Act of 2015, https://www.govinfo.gov/app/details/PLAW-114publ186#:~:text=An%20act%20to%20improve%20Federal,to%20fraud%2C%20including%20improper%20payments.

9 Data Analytics in the Sports Industry

The amount of data available within the sports industry because of technological advancements has grown exponentially. This explosion of data is due to advances in Big Data and sports science. These advances in sport science and data analytics positively affect training routines, nutritional regimens, and improve medical staff and trainers' reporting. With increased computing power and reduced storage costs, historical data about the games are employed to provide unique summaries and indexes that teams utilise to their advantage. The sports industry uses sports analysis to increase revenue, improve player performance and team results, prevent injury, and enhance the fan's experience. In addition, sports data analytics are used for a competitive advantage. This chapter details how data analytics benefits many individuals, including coaches, players, administrators, agents, scouts, marketers, medical personnel, and the analytics staff.

LEARNING OBJECTIVES:

At the end of the chapter, students should be able to:

- Understand Big Data in the sports industry
- Know the value of Big Data and Data Analytics in Team Performance, Team Evaluation, Game Tactics, and Player Efficiency
- Develop an understanding of the value of Big Data and Data Analytics in Fan Engagement and Tickets Sales
- Analyse the significance of Big Data and Data Analytics in Player Fitness and Safety, Injury and Health Assessment, Nutrition to Maximise Fitness, and Exercise

The Sporting Industry

Sporting events are an integral part of society. In the United States, the five major team sports are baseball, basketball, football, hockey, and soccer. Professional teams are divided into leagues and divisions consisting of administrators and other employees involved in scheduling games and tournament

DOI: 10.4324/9781003129356-9

play, reviewing and changing policies and procedures, and hiring league personnel such as umpires, coaches, referees, among other duties. Other staff members work directly with athletes or are involved in officiating, sales, concessions, and other game-day activities. In addition, many individual sports exist, including tennis, golf, boxing, wrestling, horseracing, and race car driving.

A wide variety of other industries are also involved in sports. These include companies responsible for:

- design, manufacture, and sales of sporting goods and equipment;
- sports technology and the development of advanced equipment and sports facilities;
- publishing books and magazines regarding sports-related topics and subjects;
- advertising and marketing of sporting events;
- the design of clothes and fabric of athletic products;
- broadcasting and publishing games and events to fans and a broader audience.

Sports medicine is another significant area in the industry. It employs sports doctors and surgeons specialising in injuries particular to athletes. In addition, more teams and athletes are using massage and physical therapists, chiropractors and kinesiologists, sports nutritionists, and skilled sports trainers to assist with players' well-being.

Big Data in the Sports Industry

With Big Data, sporting events are no longer just about the physical games, but considerations are given to the numbers associated with each event. Team sports such as baseball, American football, soccer, basketball, and digital games such as fantasy sports depend on Big Data to enhance the efficiency of its players and work towards predicting future performances. In addition, managers and coaches use historical data, scorekeeping, and forecasting to determine algorithmic performance or players statistics. As a result, Big Data is an integral part and parcel of the sports industry.

The collective knowledge of player statistics, their abilities, and complete performance skills are the components that promote the results to fans and how the game is experienced. Big Data has changed the sports sector by highlighting statistical data in the following areas:

- **Creating better sporting strategies**
  Developing strategies is an integral part of any sports event. Professional athletes and teams rely on these strategies to compete and win against their opponents. Big Data is used to create winning strategies to help individual athletes and the team as a whole. It allows coaches to construct

hyper-personalised athlete tactics for every game the team plays. Therefore, the team's tactics are unpredictable yet effective in winning.

- **Improving college athletes recruitment decisions**
  Big Data helps colleges and universities discover upcoming athletic stars. These institutions use Big Data to track and recruit potential athletes by offering them scholarships related to sports. One such example is the University of Virginia that uses Big Data to determine the probability of a football player entering the NFL or attending their university. Therefore, recruiters can know where to invest their efforts and time. Having successful athletes also enhance the reputation of the university.
- **Promoting fantasy sports**
  Big Data allows broadcasters and sports officials to increase fan engagement to increase revenue.

  Fantasy sports is a quick and profitable way to increase fan engagement across any sport. These sports allow individuals to build their virtual professional franchise based on real athletes. For example, fantasy football accounts for 25 million active participants, mainly found in the US. In addition, many fantasy sports leagues are designed around Big Data analytics to help participants build a fantasy team using detailed real-time data.

Data analytics help teams analyse position variations, playing positions, running patterns, sprint distances, physical performance parameters, movement patterns for professional athletes, and tracking data during competitive games to understand overall the performance management of a professional team. Teams use analytics to improve tactical training, optimise player performance, minimise the risk of injury, and ensure the team's overall well-being. Sports team management can be complex, but the varying analytical tools used for performance analysis in professional sports help teams and coaches to navigate the process more efficiently. It has helped teams manage player fatigue, scout for new players, injuries, provide pre-game analytics and post-game analysis.

Sport Analytics

The sports market is a billion-dollar industry. Many analysts believed the industry was worth over $620 billion as of 2020. According to Markets and Markets Research Private Ltd, the sports analytics market will grow to about $5.2 billion by 2024.[1] Sports analytics uses relevant and historical data to provide a competitive advantage to a team or individual for a sporting event. Sports Analytics analyses sports data to enhance decision-making in all aspects of the sport. The advent of technology in sports has impacted various aspects of the athlete's lifestyle, including training, scouting, talent screening, and the entire sports ecosystem. As in a general business ecosystem, the sports ecosystem includes a network of organisations or stakeholders involved in scheduling the time and place for a particular sporting event. The sports ecosystem has many stakeholders such as players, fans, sporting arenas, municipalities, TV, and broadcasters. Each of these entities is affected by the other. Hence, sport analytics is helping stakeholders work together more efficiently. For example, data analytics help determine profitable concession stand items in a stadium and predict attendance estimation, thus impacting related products and services such as catering, security, parking congestion, and crowd control.

Value of Data Analytics in Sport

Data analytics tools have given coaches insight into improving athletes, motion, skills, speed, agility, strength, endurance, flexibility, and preventing injury. Teams can engage fans, streamline operations, create an efficient exercise routine, monitor athlete load management, wellness data, fitness data, and player and team statistics. In addition, teams can track and monitor player talent, marketing data, team management process, and recruitment process of new talent. Therefore, it is helping sports organisations recruit high-quality athletes. In addition, it provides coaches real-time data that help them create better game plans and analyse opponents' tactics more efficiently.

The Value of Big Data and Data Analytics in Team Performance, Team Evaluation, Game Tactics, and Player Efficiency

Until recently, teams used observational data to analyse team tactics. However, data analytics has driven teams to use tactical analysis with more data. Today, tactical analysis frequently occurs to strengthen team strategy and improve the team's physiological performance and behaviour. Even though most sports are team games, individual contribution is significant. Therefore, player evaluation is key to team evaluation and performance. This section looks at various data analytics tools in sports team evaluation, player evaluation, and data analytics metrics in basketball and soccer.

Data Analytics Tools in Sports

Spatial Analytic in Sport. Reports the movements of teams, players, and tactical performance within the playing areas using GPS data. Coaches can tap into this kind of data to assess tactical and defensive patterns and further strategise on developing a more accurate ball-and-player tracking approach. Tracking the surface coverage of players helps predict their next possible move. This valuable data is also used in evaluating the playing pattern of the opposing team.

3D Video Analytics. Teams use 3D depth camera data to analyse detailed moves, shots, and even the location of players on the court. With the help of massive data generated by wearable devices such as wristbands for athletes, smart clothing, optical tracking device, and tagging, data analytics gives teams and coaches a unique vantage point in analysing their players' movement and performance during games.

Player Tracking Analytics Tool. A new type of data, known as player tracking data, is used to track player's performance. It is numerical, and it counts the player's number of contributions to the game. For example, in basketball, the five (5) statistical factors are points, rebounds, assists, steals, and blocks. These data are foundational to basketball, and the player's performance can now be quantifiable. Because of this measurable data, a player's data can be broken down into different categories: the number of dribbles before a shot, shooting percentage and proximity, and rebound rate and location. Such detailed data helps improve the player's tactical strategy and performance on the court. The National Basketball Association (NBA) introduced this player tracking data system in the 2013–2014 season.[2]

Today, most sports teams deploy a data analytics system that integrates various technologies from numerous sources to form a combined data analysis that yields high-performance data for monitoring performance and making decisions. These systems pull multiple data from different sources, such as event location, heart rate, match, and event data. This process enhances communication between the coach and the team and the entire team ecosystem. The benefits of such integration (of all the data) are primarily to reduce data duplication, provide a more streamlined process to avoid confusion from an overwhelming amount of data, and optimise the team's decision-making process.

Player and Team Evaluation Analytics

The selection process of players is now subjected to analytics. Consequently, coaches are not using intuition to select players; but evaluate players by looking at the player metrics. These metrics include analysing how players perform under pressure during tight games and players' behaviour. Using past performance, data has proven to be a rich source in performance prediction. Knowing how each player performs brings an advantage to forecasting and better decision-making. Therefore, data gathered from devices such as SportsVU cameras, wearable devices, smart clothing, and Electronic Performance and Tracking Systems (EPTS) have all being beneficial in analysing player efficiency.

Performance Metrics in Major Sports – Basketball and Soccer

A player's performance is dependent on many variables, and no two players' evaluations will produce the same results because the variables differ. The variables, such as emotion, past performance results, and injury, impact future performance. The analytics can determine possible future selection for a team or whether a player is benched for an upcoming game. Analytical evaluation can also resolve the team's line-up for the season. As technology improves and integrated solutions are developed and combined, the metrics become more advanced, including player tendencies and behavioural metrics. Advanced analytics can enhance performance, which leads to successful games.

Basketball

Data analytics has revolutionised the game of basketball. In basketball and sports in general, teams can use analytics to make crucial decisions during or after the game. Sports analytics help quantify the game's various elements to provide information on the strategy, play tactics, style, and team performance. It can also help improve player efficiency by evaluating player value, defensive ability, and shots.

Basketball Player Analytics

Basketball analytic metrics fall into four main categories, offensive, defensive, overall team performance, and advanced rating. The basic analytics are points, rebounds, assists, and shooting percentages in each distance. Therefore, team selection and rotation of players are made using analytical metrics, and these actions are necessary to improve the players' performance on the court.

Plus/Minus (+/−or PM) measures a player's impact in a game (quality and contribution). It is calculated as the difference in points that a team scores versus the opponent's scored points.

Performance Index Rating (PIR) is used in European Basketball leagues, giving a view of the player's total performance. It is calculated as: PIR = (Points + Rebounds + Assists + Steals + Blocks + Fouls Drawn) − (Missed Field Goals + Missed Free Throws + Turnovers + Shots Rejected + Fouls Committed). Its initial use was to help select MVP awards in the Euroleague.

Game Score (GmSc) gives attention to any statistical detail of the player's box score. It is an extension of the Player Efficiency Rating. It uses every statistic listed on a player's box score to calculate their total value in the game. The higher the number, the better.[3]

Assist to Turnover Ratio (AST/TO). An assist occurs when a player passes the ball to a teammate, who then scores a basket. A turnover takes place when a player loses possession of the ball to the opposite team. A player who creates more assists and fewer turnovers is said to be efficient.

Assist Ratio (AST). This measures how frequently a team uses assists to score a basket. A team with a high assist ratio is more likely to score and win a game. Additionally, a team with a high assist ratio indicates trust among the players and will most likely win many games.

Net Rating (NetRtg) is used in the NBA for counting a team's point differential per 100 possessions. It refers to the offensive (OffRtg) and defensive (DefRtg) rating of a team. A team with a higher rating usually wins the game.

Player Efficiency Rating (PER) measures the player efficiency per minute. PER sums up all the positive actions of players, deducts the adverse events, and returns a per-minute rating of a player's performance.

Win Shares (WS) estimates the number of wins each player contributes to the team's overall success in the season.

The Usage Rate (USG) counts the percentage of player engagement during the time played.

REB% calculates the percentage of rebounds that a player takes when on the court.

Points Per Possession (PPP) measures the scoring efficiency while a player has the ball.

Turn Over (TOV%). It is an analytics metric that focuses on the percentage rate that a player makes mistakes over time while on the court.

The highest individual ratings on these metrics usually win the Most Valuable Player (MVP) award.

APPLICATION CASE 9.1

National Basketball Association (NBA) Most Valuable Player Award (MVP) is Data Analytics-Driven

2020–2021 MVP: Nikola Jokic

The Serbian centre, Nikola Jokic, who plays for the Denver Nuggets, had high scores in most basketball analytics in the 2020–2021 season and won the MVP award. He was not only the first member of the Denver Nuggets to win the MVP award, but he was also the lowest-drafted player to win the award. Nikola is the first player from Serbia to win the NBA MVP award. Even though the award is voted by a global panel of 100 broadcasters and sportswriters, data analytics primarily influences the votes. He won because he led in most of the NBA analytics collected.

Nikola averages 26.4 points per game (PPG), 8. 4 assists per game (AST), 10.9 rebounds per game (REB%), and 1.32 steals per game (STL%). His field goal percentage was 56.6 percent, and free throws were 86.8 percent. He led the NBA in double-doubles and was second in triple-doubles. His player efficiency rating (PER) was 31.36, the highest in the league in the 2020–2021 season.

2019–2020 MVP: Giannis Antetokounmpo

Milwaukee's Giannis Antetokounmpo wins the 2019–2020 NBA Most Valuable Player Award. Giannis, a native of Greece, won because he led in most of the basketball analytics in the 2019–2020 NBA season. Giannis Averages 29.6 points per game (PPG), 5.8 assists per game (AST), 13.7 rebounds per game, 1.02 blocks per game, and 1.04 steals. Giannis' field goal percentage was 54.7 percent. He helps his team lead the league net rating (NetRtg), used in the NBA to count a team's point differential per 100 possessions. It refers to the offensive (OffRtg) and defensive (DefRtg) rating of a team. A team with a higher rating usually wins the game. Giannis' player efficiency rating (PER) was 31.9, the highest ever in the league. As a result, Giannis ended up winning the MVP award by a wide margin. This happens in most seasons in the NBA since sports analytics has become the centre of decision-making in sports. Therefore, the MVP Award goes to the individuals who led in the league's data analytics.

Source: NBA.com and NBA.com/starts

Soccer (Football)

Soccer is an invasive sport. One team must invade the other's space to direct the ball to the target. The other team must prevent this by reclaiming their invaded space, protecting the target (the goal post), and regaining possession of the ball. Soccer is a team sport and requires the players' cooperation and team spirit to be successful. Before data analytics, technical and tactical decisions were made based on a coach's observation. Intuition and a non-scientific approach work at some point, but it is less effective and subjective. Data analytics has reduced the need for one person's opinion and moved to a more data-driven approach to tactical decisions in a game. Performance analysis software has been extended to other sporting arenas such as soccer. Soccer analytics uses digital video footage, semi-automated computer tracking systems, and global positioning systems (GPS) to use quantitative techniques to analyse each player. In the past, the analysis was carried out by the coach watching hours of video footage to evaluate each player's performance. The quantitative analysis has become more integrated into evaluating professional soccer players, and soccer clubs employ performance analysts to monitor the players' pre- and post-match training. Data analytics has changed the dynamics of ball sports, and it has done the same for soccer. GPS is also used to track the movement of soccer players during a game, and it has helped football clubs and academies improve training and future matches.

Soccer Tactic Analytics

In pre-game preparations, it is necessary to strategise and agree upon the tactics to be used within the game. Team strategy involves the decisions a team makes on how to play in the next game. Team tactic consists of looking at the approach of the two groups, the results of the teams' interaction in past games, and making new decisions for real-time play. Therefore, the past strategy impacts real-time play. Team tactics include offensive and defensive formations and positioning decisions for both the individual and the group players. A coach must consider the play pattern of both the offensive and defensive teams, the weather, the fans in the stadium, prior decisions, and real-time situations. Although there are several variables coaches have to consider, sports data analytics provide the valuable data they need to make crucial decisions that will significantly impact their teams.

Soccer Playing Styles Analytics

Sports data analytics measure playing styles such as offensive and defensive styles, long and short passing sequences, and tactics such as counterattacks. Below are eight playing styles in soccer. Analytics involves field positions of each player, offensive and defensive play tactics and passing sequences, and so on.

1 **Direct Play (DP).** The team aims to get the ball directly to the goal with a series of passes and indirect and direct kicks.
2 **Counterattack strategy** refers to the team's motive to regaining possession of the ball through dribbles and direct kicks.
3 **Maintenance (MA)**. The team maintains possession of the ball for more than 10 seconds. This is a defensive tactic.
4 **Build Up (UP)** is the number of controlled ball possessions while looking for an open attack, which makes this style of play pretty standard.
5 **Sustained Threat (ST)**, 6 seconds spent attacking a third of the pitch, is the requirement for this style of play.
6 **Fast Tempo (FT)** refers to the speed of the game. It includes a fast pass or dribble (in less than 2 seconds) from one player to the next.
7 **Crossing (Cr)** happens when the ball is kicked in the open field with the hopes that a teammate rescues it.
8 **High Press (HP)** refers to attack play to recapture the ball with interceptions, header, tackles, and blocks. The opposition must take possession for more than 10 seconds.

The Value of Big Data and Data Analytics in Fan Engagement and Tickets Sales

Sport is a game of fans. For example, it is estimated that soccer has 4 billion fans, cricket 2.5 billion fans, and basketball 805 million.[4] Therefore, fan engagement is paramount in sports. This section looks at how data analytics is

APPLICATION CASE 9.2

Injury and performance analytics can help teams win games

In the 2015–2016 football/soccer season, not Manchester United, not Chelsea, not Arsenal, not Liverpool, but little-known Leicester City football club won the English Premier League title. The chances of that happening were remote because they are not a rich club to buy the most talented players, nor are they the most famous club to attract even the second-tier gifted players. The odds for them to win the title was 5000-1. In statistics, it means zero chance; but they did win the title. How did they do that? Performance analytics.

The team integrated sports analytics, fitness, safety, workload, and playing tactics in their decision-making process. Instead of relying on general football statistics such as possession or shots on target, they created their internal metrics. The team builds in-house algorithms that focus on performance improvement and injury reduction analytics. Their objective was an optimal performance for each player because they do not have the star players that other teams have. Therefore, they pay attention to player workload and collect data on gym time, training, games played, medical, and conditioning. The team gives players 48 hours of rest after every game, and the players also have one day off during the week. The team has a group of doctors and analysts to monitor each player's workload and metrics. The team's primary focus is to get to that optimal load for each player to perform at their best in every game. They use GPS systems and heart-rate monitors, and players are asked to complete daily questionnaires on their mental and physical well-being.

The club's focus on injury and performance analytics gives them a better understanding of the factors that affect their players' optimal performance level. Moreover, since the club is not one of the wealthiest clubs able to buy more players, preventing injures enables them to use all their players and reduce the workload for each player. In the end, integration of sports analytics, football tactics, injury analytics, and performance analytics made Leicester beat all the odds and win the highest prize in English football, the English Premier League title.

Source: SD. Times, a Monthly Software magazine: *How sports performance analytics can help technology organisations win the game.* https://sdtimes.com/analy/how-sports-performance-analytics-can-help-technology-organizations-win-the-game/

used to help fan engagement and improve ticket sales. Data analytics can help to drive fan engagement by enhancing the game experience. The benefit of this is fan retention, improved participation and attendance, and increased opportunities for sponsorship.

Data Analytics Enhance Fan Engagement

Technology has advanced so much that the digital engagement of sports fans can be detected or encouraged. Sports marketers use social media to promote games, market tickets, drive momentum, and connect with fans. Data from each fan or customer provides a wealth of information on how involved people are, from university varsity games to major league and professional sports. Sports analysts use this data to understand what motivates fans and how to better serve them and engage them during games and after games that will drive fan engagements and ultimately sell more tickets or increase fans' attendance in games and predict ticket sales.

Fan Engagement Tools

Nowadays, digitally oriented stadiums offer digital ticketing and biometric stadium entry systems, where fans are more engaged in live events. Thus, marketers too can garner valuable data, for example, the kind of fans (age group, demographics) and percentage of fans present. This gives sponsors an overview to improve their advertising opportunities. Nowadays, live streaming makes it possible for marketers to engage with fans in real time. Furthermore, live streaming on a Jumbotron presents more potential for the fans to interact with the team and each other. As a result, live promotions and live announcements of the winners provide the fans with a more in-depth game experience.

Live Game Fan Engagement Analytics

No longer do marketers have to wait for an event to be over to access the data. Live data is considered rich data because it provides access to live stream data in real time. Now, sports teams can engage fans directly in real time, thereby boosting fan retention and revenue. Therefore, marketers can use this foundation to offer concession stand items by providing revenue-enhancing ideas such as in-game features. Also, with this kind of engagement and participation, marketers have access to attendees' profiles, thereby allowing them to offer more targeted marketing. For example, suppose the data shows increased attendance in a specific location. In that case, marketers can offer discounts on early ticket purchases to the next game in the same place to encourage repeat ticket sales. Integrated data can also target people who do not attend games frequently, mainly because their data was already captured from previous game attendance. This group of attendees can be encouraged to buy tickets from more tailored promotions that provide rewarding incentives.

Live Game Fan Engagement Data Expand Sponsorship Opportunities. Big Data can help marketers to become more creative in offering customised marketing since it integrates engagement data and profile data. Therefore, marketers understand their target market and what makes them engage with sports. In addition, having access to Big Data gives sponsors the chance to broaden their offers outside of the game, such as hotel loyalty programs, credits, or rewards for concession stand items. This action is known as cross-selling, and it allows marketers to sell a wider variety of products and services. Finally, Big Data can get personal. Sponsors can now know the fans filling the stadiums and where they are sitting. Digital ticketing and biometric systems now make this possible. Why is this important? The more marketers "know" the customers, the more likely they are to fulfil their needs.

Fan Profiles Analytics

The profile gives insight into the customer's behaviour, whether they are longtime fans and have attended most games. Marketers can use this information to reward loyal fans with seasonal passes and discounts. From past data, marketers can also identify those fans who are irregular in their game attendance and customise their marketing with incentives to encourage increased attendance.

Analytics integrated from various sources can reveal the non-attending demographics. For example, analytics reveals loyal customers and fans. However, it also shows groups not yet in the database. In other words, it can indicate a section of the market that has never attended any of the team's games. Therefore, these individuals may be reached by taking a different approach. For example, their interest could be piqued by tapping into their other interests, such as offering discounts through a favourite online store, like Amazon.

Data analytics can also provide knowledge of fan's affiliation. Marketers no longer have to guess a fan's affiliation to a local team. This information is all provided in the database. Now professional teams can reach out to local groups to broaden fan engagement and build relationships on a regional or local level. One example of this kind of team/community interaction is launching a friendly competition between the professional and the local teams. This public relation interaction builds and deepens relationships, increases the team's popularity, and boosts ticket sales.

Opportunities for customisation. Tailor-made sponsorships (lower ticket prices) and team sponsor agreements are more likely to occur when fans actively engage with the team. Sponsors are more motivated to provide fan incentives, especially when they understand the fanbase. Such incentives drive more traffic, make it a win-win for all parties involved. Sponsors can sectionalise incentives depending on the kind of rich data collected from the fanbase profiles. Sectionalising helps determine the rewards that would best suit a seasoned ticket-holder versus the occasional attendee. Teams can also streamline their loyalty programs to encourage more prolonged fan engagement. Of course, integrated data from different data sources helps to make all this possible.

Fan Engagement Measurement Analytics

Fan engagement is real and can be measured. Studies indicate that a team's identification, performance, and ticket purchase intention exist in a sequential relationship.[5] It suggests that fan engagement is specific and measurable. Fan engagement constitutes behaviour, and this behaviour may be interactive, spontaneous, and even non-transactional. While the behaviour is powerful enough to lead to a purchase, it should be noted that such behaviour could also influence others through referrals and recommendations. As a result, fan or customer engagement is a decisive marketing advantage for marketers to gain an edge over competitors and boost sales.

The Commercial Value of Engaged Fans

Fan engagement can drive a brand. While the brand personality can push the target market to purchase tickets and merchandise, fan engagement can also influence its rise and fall. Sports clubs help to promote fan engagement, as fans are allowed to meet and interact with members of their favourite team's sports club. The more engaged a fan, the more likely they will attend special team events, and loyal fans will commit both finances and effort to a sports club affiliated with their favourite team.[6] The link to consumers' loyalty and purchase behaviour is value. The product or service must align with the consumer's values. Therefore, the more valuable the product, the more consumers will interact with the product or service.

The Value of Big Data and Data Analytics in Player Fitness and Safety

Player fitness, safety, and injury are mostly data-driven in today's sport environment. Big Data and data analytics are helping sports teams monitor players' body functions during training and games and understand the limits of their athletes. Injuries are inevitable in sports, and they negatively impact the team because they are costly and affect participation and team performance. In addition, some injuries are career-ending for athletes and affect their quality of life and economic well-being. But because of Big Data and data analytics tools in conjunction with sensors and wearables devices, it is possible to improve the safety of players by identifying injury risks during training and games.

Injury Prediction and Prevention Analytics

Sports teams look for information that may indicate athletes' risk of injury and conditions most likely to result in an injury. Injury prediction and prevention are essential for both the team and the athletes. Injuries can have severe consequences on the team and individual performance. It may have far-reaching implications such as losing a competition, ticket sales, athletes' medical expenses, injury recovery time, and sponsorship for both the team and athletes. For athletes, preventing injuries is very important as it lengthens their playing career and increases their chances of making more money. Therefore, accurate injury prediction is vital for both players and teams. Recently, athletes suffering from concussions have become a primary concern, especially when the athlete or the relevant stakeholders disclose the injury and it is dismissed. Therefore, data analytics is an effective weapon for tracking the number of incidents in a particular period.

Big Data and data analytics tools have been crucial in providing insights into when conditions that may increase the chances of injury are present. Injury prediction and preventions analytics involve collecting a vast amount of data such as game load, training workload, nutrition, sleep, injury recovery time, exertion, strains, neuromuscular data, body muscles, speed, and reaction time. Data analytics tools use this data to determine the potential for injury. This information is used to adjust the athletes' training workload, playing time, and other adjustments to keep the athletes in good playing shape.

Types of Data Collected for Injury Analytics

Teams collect the following data from their athletes, broad jumps, vertical jumps, pushups, pullups, 5-yard sprint, pro-agility shuttle, L-drill, arm measurement, body fat percentage, neck measurement, measure squat, 20-yard sprint. Data on general athletic movement collected are running and jumping. In addition, daily wellness data questionnaires are given to athletes to collect information such as strength valuation and kneeling med ball toss. Other data collected are height, body weight, body composition, speed-strength, flexibility on sit and reach, absolute strength, push jerk, explosive power, acceleration on a 5-yard sprint.

Tools Used To Collect Data

There are varieties of tools used to collect data from athletes' day-to-day sporting activities. They include Body Composition Tracking System (BOD POD), NordBord, which measures and monitors athletes' hamstring strength and imbalance. GPS systems have proven effective in gathering valuable data in sports such as rugby, hockey, and soccer. GPS is instrumental in revealing the player's impact against objects and surfaces. As a result, it tracks each player's geographic location in proximity to others. Player tracking is essential because it helps identify whether players are adhering to the training routine or program. Trojan Strength Rating (TSR) is a pound-for-pound strength rating. Wellness questionnaires are uses to keep track of stress, nutrition, and sleep. Functional Movement Screen (FMS) measures shoulder mobility, hurdle steps, in-line lunge, deep squat, trunk stability pushup, and active straight leg raise. Other devices are heart-rate monitors, biofeedback devices, blood pressure monitors, velocity-based training devices, muscle lab, vertical jump pads, handheld timing, and athletic management software.

Use of Data Collected

The data collected and the result of the analytics is used for various purpose. Sometimes it is used for motivating the athlete as most players are more engaged when they know their performance target. In other words, the data create an atmosphere of expectation for the athletes and then a commitment to succeed. The insight from the data may make an individual athlete changes their lifestyle and training effort to improve their performance. The analytics results also help coaches customise training routines for individual athletes based on their capabilities and set up team protocols on training, recovery, and rest. The data is also used for a year-to-year comparison of player and team performance, identifying strengths and weaknesses for the team and players, and whether the training routine adds value to the athlete's performance and wellness.

The insight from data analytics also informs coaches on player fatigue during games and practice. The aim is to keep the players fresh before a match. Data analytics helps determine athletes' capabilities, and sport managers use this information to get the best out of an athlete without exposure to injury. The data collected and analysed provides coaches with a better understanding of their players' physical and mental condition daily. Coaches use this information for team selection, motivation, tactical decisions, and team competitions.

Key Term

Sports Analytics; Spatial Analytic in Sports; Player Tracking Analytics Tool; Performance Index Rating (PIR); Assist to Turnover Ratio (AST/TO); Player Efficiency Rating (PER); Fan Engagement Analytics; Injury Prediction and Prevention Analytics

Chapter Key Takeaways

- These advances in sport science and data analytics positively impact training routines, nutritional regimens, and improved medical staff and trainers' reporting.
- The advent of technology in sports has impacted various aspects of the athlete's lifestyle, including training, scouting, talent screening, and the entire sports ecosystem.
- Data analytics tools have given coaches insight into improving athletes, motion, skills, speed, agility, strength, endurance, flexibility, and preventing injury.
- Until recently team used observational data to analyse team tactics. However, data analytics has driven teams to use tactical analysis with more data.

- The selection process of team players is now subjected to analytics. Today, coaches are not just using intuition to select players; they evaluate players by looking at the player metrics.
- Data analytics has reduced the subjective opinion of often one man to a more data-driven approach to tactical decisions in a game.
- Sports analysts use Big Data to understand what motivates fans, serve them better, and engage them during and after games.
- Analytics reveals the loyal customers and fans. It also shows which group is not yet in the database. In other words, it can indicate a section of the market that has never attended any of the team's games.
- Fan engagement can drive a brand. While the brand personality drives the target market to purchase, fan engagement can also influence their rise and fall.

Discussion Questions

1 What is sports analytics?
2 What is the value of data analytics in sport?
3 List and explain at least three use of data analytics in sport.
4 How is spatial analytics used in sports?
5 List and explain two data analytics tools used in sports.
6 List and explain six basketball analytics used to measure player performance.
7 List and explain five soccer-playing styles.
8 What do you understand by fan engagement analytics?
9 How does live game fan engagement analytics enhance team sponsorship?
10 What is the commercial value of fan engagement in sports?
11 How has data analytics helps in the injury prevention of athletes?
12 What are some of the tools used to collect data from athletes' day-to-day sporting activities?

References

1 Sports Analytics Market, https://www.marketsandmarkets.com/Market-Reports/sports-analytics-market-35276513.html
2 Skinner, B. & Guy, S.J. (2015). A method for using player tracking data in basketball to learn player skills and predict team performance. *PloS one, 10*(9), e0136393.
3 Captain Calculator, https://captaincalculator.com/sports/basketball/game-score-calculator/ and https://captaincalculator.com/sports/basketball/
4 https://www.worldatlas.com/articles/what-are-the-most-popular-sports-in-the-world.html)
5 Yoshida, M., Gordon, B., Nakazawa, M., & Biscaia, R. (2014). Conceptualisation and measurement of fan engagement: Empirical evidence from a professional sports context. *Journal of Sport Management, 28*(4), 399–417.
6 Nalbantis, G., Pawlowski, T., & Coates, D. (2017). The fans' perception of competitive balance and its impact on willingness-to-pay for a single game. *Journal of Sports Economics, 18*(5), 479–505.

10 Data Analytics in the Accounting Industry

The role of accountants in both industry and public practice has expanded tremendously in this data-driven economy. They have to deal with internally generated accounting and finance data and the entire enterprise's internal and external operational and transactional data. All this data needs analysis to discover new insights into business risks and assist business managers in decision-making. The role of accountants, auditors, finance and tax professionals in a company is to understand the entire enterprise business process and ensure that all transactions are captured and recorded accurately, and that controls exist to detect risk. This chapter details how data analytics is helping auditors shift from sample-based model auditing to continuous monitoring/auditing. Tax professionals quickly analyse complex tax scenarios related to investment decisions. Accountants use financial and non-financial data to identify valuable insights within the company's financial data to improve operational efficiency and risk management.

LEARNING OBJECTIVES:

At the end of the chapter, students should be able to:

- Have a basic understanding of accounting and its role in business
- Know the value and role of data analytics in financial statement reporting
- Identify the value and role of data analytics in internal and external auditing
- Understand the importance and role of data analytics in Taxation

Accounting and Its Role in Business

Accounting is often referred to as the "language of business." It is primarily true as the objective of most businesses is to make a profit. However, the word profit is an accounting terminology. To make a profit, companies need to determine the cost of their products or services and determine how much they will charge customers for them. Thus, the profit is the difference

DOI: 10.4324/9781003129356-10

between the price charged to customers for products or services and the cost associated with producing these products and services. That is to say, in its simplest form, accounting is the process of recording business transactions and finding out if the business is profitable or not. Thus, accounting helps companies maintain accurate records of their day-to-day business transactions. These business records are summarised into three main reports – Profit and Loss Statement or Income Statement, Balance Sheet, and the Cash Flow Statement. Together, these three statements give an overview of the activities and financial viability of a business. In other words, accounting is comparable to an information system that provides information about a company's financial status to stakeholders.

However, preparing records or financial statements is governed by laws and standards to maintain the integrity of the information provided to the users of the financial statements. These laws and standards are referred to as Generally Accepted Accounting Principles (GAAP). In the United States, the Financial Accounting Standard Board (FASB) is primarily responsible for developing those laws. In contrast, the International Accounting Standards Board (IASB) sets regulations for countries outside the US. Regardless of the size of the business, each company's financial statements should follow GAAP to be counted as reliable and valuable. To validate the reliability of financial information reported by a business, most often an audit is required. **Auditing** is a branch of accounting that ensures that GAAP is followed in preparing a company's financial statement and that all the activities included in the reporting are accurate. As stated before, accounting and accountants provide three significant roles to business – financial statement reporting, auditing, and tax planning.

The Value and Role of Data Analytics in Financial Statement Reporting

Financial statement reporting is the process of preparing the day-to-day business activities of a company into three primary statements – Income Statement, Balance Sheet, and Cash Flow Statements. These statements can be prepared monthly, quarterly, or annually. The process of preparing these statements can be extremely tedious and time-consuming, especially for large and publicly traded companies. For example, the process of financial statement reporting for a company like Amazon with millions of customers and vendors, worth over a trillion dollars, and involving millions of business transactions each day, can be a headache. Preparing financial statements for such companies requires a tremendous amount of time and care to ensure accuracy. In addition, financial statements reporting involves summarising vast amounts of business transactions data into different account groups such as income, account receivables, accounts payable, and assets. An efficient and accurate process of doing this is necessary for the usefulness and reliability of the financial statements.

Over the years, accounting standards and accountants focused on ensuring that the data generated is useful and reliable. While the usefulness and reliability of information are very important, equally valuable today is how to leverage this data more efficiently and effectively to add value to the organisation. Big Data and data analytics tools have provided a platform for accountants to process and convert this data into actionable insights to facilitate decision-making processes that add value to the company. This data analysis needs to be timely and relevant to ensure action is taken to achieve companies' goals.

The account groups and accounting functions are broad but below are some areas where data analytics can be most helpful in the financial reporting process.

- Revenue recognition
- Accounts receivable
- Accounts payable
- Financial statement analysis

Revenue Recognition and Data Analytics

The revenue recognition principle, one of the GAAP, identifies the conditions in which a specific revenue can be recognised and recorded in a company's books. The revenue recognition principle determines when and how revenue is recognised based on the type of revenue and the transaction. In most cases, revenue is only recognised when a particular event has occurred. For example, in the retail industry, revenue is recognised when a product is sold, and the customer has possession of the product. However, recognising revenue is not always that straightforward when services are performed, when a client contract is involved, and when it takes a long time to produce a product or perform a service. As a result, revenue recognition can be complicated and need careful consideration since revenue is the key to a business. Companies should avoid over-recognised or under-recognised revenue so as not to be accused of misstatement or misleading investors.

The guidelines surrounding accurate revenue recognition are not new but keep evolving as the FASB releases new standards. It usually takes time and money to implement some procedures depending on the complexity of transactions and contracts. For example, the new revenue recognition standard, Accounting Standard Codification (ASC) 606, jointly developed by the FASB and the IASB, outlines a five-step process to recognise revenue for all business that enters into contracts with customers to provide goods or services.[1] The five- step process is:

1 **Identification of contracts and the clients.** Contract identification can be time-consuming for a large company with many contracts and clients and lacks a central repository to keep all these contracts. Even if

they have a central location to store the contracts, new agreements need to be updated, old ones removed, and all modifications must be monitored and updated. In addition, it is sometimes difficult to identify the actual client if the contract involves multiple parties.

2 **Determine what needs to be done for each client**. The services that need to be provided for each client need to be accurately identified and segregated. Additionally, the company performing the service must note the date the service is conducted to avoid a breach of contract. Finally, it should be determined if the services need to be completed over time or as a one-time service obligation.

3 **Determine the price.** The client's service cost needs to be accurately determined for each service component stated in the contract. In addition, other variables such as discounts, non-cash considerations need to be considered in determining the price. Also, any changes in price or performance obligation must be updated immediately.

4 **Allocate transaction price**. Some contracts have more than one service component that the client needs to provide and have a different fee structure. For example, some contracts have both a fee and commission component if specific deliverables are met. Therefore, the price for each performance obligation needs to be determined and allocated separately.

5 **Recognise revenue.** Revenue will only be recognised when services are performed, and all performance obligations stated in the contract are satisfied. In most case, revenue is recognised over time as each performance obligations are met.

The process of recognising revenue can be complex, time-consuming, and labour-intensive. Moreover, there is no space for errors. Hence, data analytics and data analytics tools are making a difference in the revenue recognition process.

Data analytics provides the financial reporting process to integrate these five-step processes into a practical approach that reduces the chance of errors and recognises revenue more efficiently and accurately. Data analytics provide contract analytics platforms that integrate, organise, and categorise contracts by performance, prices, date, clients, due dates, and when revenue should be recognised. One of the greatest fears every quarter-end closing for accountants is failing to recognise revenue due to unavailable contract information, especially when a new contract is signed or an old contract is renewed with new revenue streams. Data analytics tools can track contracts and addendums immediately after a contract process is initiated. Also, companies use analytics tools or machine learning tools such as optical recognition software, scanners, PDF to match source documents and review client contracts more effectively.

Accounts Receivable Analytics

Accounts receivable is simply the amount of money a customer owes a company. Most often, companies have a long list of customers owing money.

This list includes the amount of money, the due date, and the terms of the receivable. As usual, not all customers will pay their bills on time. Therefore, companies have to find a way to collect outstanding money. Big Data and data analytics have been beneficial in this area. For example, companies use data analytics to analyse customers' payment patterns and when specific customers usually pay their bills. With this information, if a customer who typically pays a debt at a particular time of the month fails to pay, data analytics will highlight that customer and alert the account receivable personnel to follow up. It allows companies to stay updated on the cash collection process and resolve potential account receivable issues ahead of time. It makes the company's cash flow predictable, and management will know when and if another source of cash is needed.

Data analytics tools detect customers' payment patterns and identify customers who routinely pay their bills late. This helps the company decide whether to reduce the credit amount or reduce the credit term of those customers or discontinue doing business with them. In addition, these will highlight customers with continued late payment and flag this as a warning sign of the financial difficulty the customer is experiencing and which may ultimately lead to bankruptcy. Therefore, a data analytics warning system may reduce a company's exposure to customers heading to bankruptcy.

Cash Collection Predictability. Big Data and data analytics provide the account and finance department with the ability to predict customer payments. The department can decide which customers to focus on and which collection actions to take with this information. This will improve the predictivity of cash collection and the company's cash flow.

Customer Creditworthiness Internal Analytics. Data analytics allow companies to analyse, predict, and monitor customers' creditworthiness by creating an internal credit scoring system based on past payment history. This information enables the accounting and finance department to identify trends in customers' creditworthiness, payments, and reducing or extending credit terms.

Customer Creditworthiness External Analytics. Because of Big Data, companies can also follow and collect customer information on social media. The collected data is used to determine if there is any change in the customer's day-to-day business operation that will indicate a shift in creditworthiness, credit risk factor, or customer industry that may show potential financial difficulties.

Delinquency Risk Analytics. Companies use data analytics to evaluate their account receivables and customer payment patterns to identify those at risk of delinquency. This predictive analysis on the potential negligence of customers helps companies make data-driven decisions on how best to engage with customers.

Cash And Working Capital Management. Through data analytics on account receivables, companies will be able to determine present and future cash flow. This information helps them decide how much cash is needed now to maintain the daily operation of the business. Additionally, it will help the company determine how much money is required for the future and whether to raise additional funds because of customers' potential late payments or delinquency.

Data analytics significantly impact a company's cash flow and working capital management because it can improve the cash collection process, reduce late payments, and enhance a better understanding of customers' creditworthiness and payment pattern. Data analytics, especially predictive analytics, will strengthen a company's ability to forecast cash collection by identifying receivables that are likely to be paid late and at risk of not being paid. Predictive analytics will also identify potential changes in customer creditworthiness and trigger an alert so that company personnel can take proactive steps before it is too late.

Accounts Payable Analytics

Accounts payable (AP) represent the amount of money a company has to pay to its creditors or suppliers within a short-term period. The management of AP is very important in a company because the increase and decrease impact a company's cash flow management and creditworthiness. For example, if AP increases, a company is buying more goods or services on credit. If it decreases, the company is paying its debt faster than it is taking on new credit. Each of these scenarios has working capital management implications.

Most companies, if not all, have a vendor master database. The database lists all vendors or suppliers that a company has approved to purchase goods or services. It is from this database that most AP transactions usually originate. Big Data and data analytics have allowed companies to collect comprehensive information about vendors and enhanced the data analysis inside the vendor master database to ensure that each vendor has been validated and is a legitimate business. For example, data analysis will highlight the status of days payable outstanding against the benchmark and how many invoices are processed per day and month. This analysis is vital for cash management purposes, especially on the issue of how to control cash flow and at the same time maintain a good relationship with vendors.

AP Metrics And Data Analytics. Big Data and data analytics can significantly improve the AP function by developing analytics for the entire payable process. As a result, the AP process will work smoothly and add value to the cash flow management with well-defined metrics and analytics. Some of the questions data analytics will answer in the AP process are:

1 What is the composition of the payable by age (bucket analysis) and the Top 20 vendors in each age category?
2 Are prompt payments eliminated while at the same reduce late payment penalties?
3 What is the maximum cash flow for renegotiating terms of payments?

4   Are companies capitalising on discounts by analysing the impact of invoice payments at par versus paid after the due date?

Remove Inefficiencies in the Payables Workflow Process. Data analytics can help identify and remove inefficiencies in the AP workflow process. Some of the issues data analytics will address are:

1   The loss of discount as a percentage of purchases.
2   Delayed payment and the reason for the delay.
3   The number of invoices the company processed per day or week.
4   Appropriate attention should be given to large cash items.
5   The percentage of duplicate payments of invoices and how to prevent these duplications.
6   Number of electronic payments versus manual payment invoices.

Because of Big Data and data analytics tools, companies can efficiently control accounts payable, manage cash outflow, and maintain a good relationship with their suppliers and creditors.

APPLICATION CASE 10.1 (ACCOUNT PAYABLES ANALYTICS)

Purple Speeds Invoice Processing Time by 63%

About Purple

Purple is an innovative comfort product company that designs and manufactures products to improve people's lives. It designs and manufactures a range of comfort products, including mattresses, pillows, and cushions, using its patented Hyper–Elastic Polymer® material designed to improve comfort.

Challenge

Purple, the Utah-based company that kickstarted the mattress revolution in 2013, is known for creating the "World's First No-Pressure Mattress." To do so and continue delighting the 42,000+ customers that have left verified reviews of their products, they work with about 1,350 vendors.

As Peter Taylor, Corporate Controller at Purple, says, "Our A/P inbox was like a giant black hole. We would request that our vendors send invoices to a Purple A/P email inbox that was managed by an A/P clerk and an A/P supervisor."

> We did weekly pay runs that took our two resources nearly two full days to draft the list of vendors we needed to pay that week as

they manually searched through Outlook to determine which bills needed to be paid.

We needed an A/P automation platform that would provide full control of the invoice lifecycle, allow us to centralise communications and collaboration on each invoice so we could better manage the process, reduce our backlog, and easily track all invoices to keep auditors happy.

Solution

We initially tried to implement Concur Invoice, as we were already using their expense tool. But my team was reluctant to use the tool, as it required a professional services engagement to implement it. Months later, we hadn't made a dent in our invoice backlog.

"The functionality didn't work well with our system, especially for invoices that go through PO, which is 65% of our volume," says Peter.

During this time, Peter received a marketing email from Stampli, and after determining Concur was not the right solution, he began a free trial.

Bottom Line

Before implementing Stampli, Peter considered adding a third A/P employee but found he didn't need to. As a result, purple now has 90+ people using Stampli, most of whom are approvers, who got up and running quickly.

The workforce productivity optimisation has been, in my mind, the best because I like my team doing things that add value to our business, like expanding vendor relationships and delivering goodwill via our modernised A/P workflow to the rest of our organisation,

says Peter.

We see a reduction in OPEX with Stampli. Not only have we reduced invoice backlog by at least 50% in the first few months, but we've eliminated paying duplicate invoices. That's something that seemed to happen more often than not,

says Peter.

Because Stampli is cloud-based, power and general users have anytime/anywhere mobile access, so if they're working remotely, invoice processing is still lightning fast. Before, only 25% of invoices were adequately documented in Oracle NetSuite, and they didn't have an

(*Continued*)

established purchasing policy. According to Peter, "When it came to mapping approvers to invoices, it was done by tribal knowledge our AP clerk had, as they knew who in our organisation had a relationship with a specific vendor."

Peter says, "With Stampli, 100% of our invoices are appropriately documented. With automation, approvals based on amounts or purchase type are all embedded into the application. We've eliminated gaps with a tool that helps track our workflow and approvals throughout the entire lifecycle". As a publicly traded company, Purple's procure to pay (P2P) process is highly regulated, and they have SOX and other regulatory compliance requirements. With Stampli, Peter says, "The audit process has become self-service, as we can send an invoice URL to the auditors, and they can quickly find what they need"

> With Stampli, we have reduced the time to process invoices from eight days to three days. One of the areas in which we've saved the most time is getting invoices into the system. The second area in which we've dramatically reduced time is in getting approvals,

says Peter.

The previous process took their A/P team too much time to decide who the approvers should be. "Using Stampli to automate data entry and leveraging artificial intelligence (AI) and optical character recognition to apply GL codes has been great. It's helping us route invoices to the correct approvers much faster."

Source: Stampli, an AP automation company: *Purple Speeds Invoice Processing Time by 63% with Stampli*, https://www.stampli. com/purple/. Used by permission from Stampli.

Financial Statement Analytics

Financial statements analysis is the process of analysing a company's financial statements to understand its position and health and decide where it is headed. Financial statement analysis is used by two major parties, internal stakeholders and external stakeholders. External stakeholders such as investors, auditors, analysts, suppliers, creditors, and government entities are interested in knowing the company's overall health and prospects. Internal stakeholders such as management and employees are interested in understanding the strength and weaknesses of the company, its operational efficiency compared to its competitors.

There are three primary financial statements:

1 **Income Statement**: the Income Statement summarises a company's income and expenses at a point in time, monthly, quarterly, or yearly. In addition, the income statement shows the net profit or net loss of a company. The income statement has multiple names, including Profit and

Loss statement (P&L), Statement of Financial Performance, and Statement of Operation.

2 **Balance Sheet**: A Balance Sheet provides a condensed picture of the business's assets, liabilities, and equity at a given point in time. It shows the financial worth of a company in terms of book value.

3 **Statement of Cash Flows** provides an overview of a company's cash flow and provides information about two main questions:
    a   Where is the cash coming from?
    b   Where is it going?

These statements are interconnected and provide different views of a company's activities and performance.

Data Analytics Techniques

Because of the availability of Big Data and data analytics tools, four basic data analytics techniques are used to analyse financial statements; sentiment and text mining analytics, horizontal analysis, vertical analysis, and ratio analysis.

Sentiment and Text Mining Analytics. Big Data and data analytics tools allow internal and external users of financial statements the opportunity to know the public sentiment of a company through sentiment analysis. By having an idea of how the public, suppliers, investors, and other stakeholders view the company, management will make a better data-driven decision to respond to external factors. For example, companies can now use text mining from social media posting and read all the sentiments expressed by the public about the company's product and services. Likewise, analysts, investors, suppliers, and other users of financial statements can use the company's financial statements, the Security and Exchange (SEC) filings such as annual reports (10-K), and quarterly reports (10-Q), to extract words that might indicate where the company is heading. For example, text mining and sentiment analytics might identify the company's direction or indicate a problem. Also, investors are using text mining and sentiment analysis to predict the direction of a company's stock market and industry in general.[2]

Horizontal Analysis compares historical data over a period such as monthly, quarterly, yearly, or several years. It is used to detect trends in accounting numbers over time for an individual company. It enables the analysis of line items in the financial statements across two or more periods. It also allows the comparability of financial statements of different companies across time. Finally, both internal and external users of financial statements use it to identify the growth patterns of a company.

A Vertical Analysis is also known as a common-size financial statement analysis. It displays each line item as a percentage of a base figure within the financial statement. For example, the balance sheet can be stated as a percentage of total assets and the income statement as a percentage of sales. It enables users to quickly identify trends in financial statements and compare them with other companies.

Ratio Analysis uses specific financial ratios to understand the state of a company's profitability, liquidity, operational efficiency, and solvency. For example, a deeper analysis of the balance sheet using liquidity ratios such as current ratio, quick ratio, and cash ratio will indicate whether the company can pay its bills in the short term. Likewise, an analysis using financial leverage ratios such as debt to equity ratio, long-term debt ratio, and equity multiplier will indicate whether the company can meet its long-term obligations – that is, can the company survive a little longer?

Data Analytics and Financial Statements. Because of Big Data and eXtensible Business Reporting Language (XBRL), users of financial statements can quickly and efficiently gain access to financial statement data of all publicly traded companies in the US. One of the most critical tools for Big Data and data analytics in the accounting industry is joining data from multiple sources into one database. The ability to merge both structured and unstructured data enables accounting users to extract data, summarise, analyse, identify anomalies and misrepresentations, track exceptions, and perform variance analysis, which will not be possible if data is in different places. In addition, data imports, extractions, and analysis for month-end and quarter-end close and variance analysis helps in financial statement analysis. With the availability of data analytics tools such as PDF converters, drag-and-drop abilities, and Open Database Connectivity (ODBC), data analytics saves hundreds of hours of work and, at the same time, ensures more efficient and effective analysis.

Big Data and data analytics have enabled the accounting reporting aspect to be very efficient and value-adding to the operation of a business. It has made the revenue recognition process and compliance more efficient and accurate. Financial statement analytics such as sentiment analytics, horizontal, vertical, and ratio analysis have become more efficient in predicting a company's future performance because data analytics tools allow for data centralisation from various sources. Sentiment and text analytics help companies understand the public opinion of its product and services. Accounts receivables, accounts payable, and the management of the company's cash flow and working capital, in general, has become more efficient and predictable because of Big Data and data analytics.

The Value of Data Analytics in Internal and External Auditing

Audit Analytics. Auditing is simply the verification and examination of a company's financial statements. Data analytics has a dramatic impact on the auditing profession. Most auditing firms, internal auditors, and the American Institute of Certified Accountants (AICPA) embrace its prospect and potential to enhance audit quality. Data analytics tools can help produce high-quality audit evidence by efficiently and accurately identifying unusual transactions associated with fraud.

Additionally, it makes the audit process more efficient by eliminating non-value-added or repetitive tasks in the audit process. The value of data analytics in the auditing process has been well known by many organisations for many years. Still, the problem has been for companies to embrace and invest in the technology needed to utilise its value entirely. As the advent of cloud computing becomes widespread, the digitisation of transactions a common occurrence, and the business environment becoming complex and fast-paced, it becomes self-evident that companies have to invest in technology and personnel to take advantage of the infinite value of data analytics.

With the desire to add value to the auditing function and the availability of Big Data, the job of the accounting and auditing profession is no longer limited to detecting errors, fraud, risk, and misstatements. Instead, the focus is on analysing data to enhance data-driven decision-making by management. As a result, the auditing process becomes a partner in helping companies improve operational efficiency and reduce waste in the day-to-day operation of the business.

Data analytics has expanded audit capabilities because auditors can now analyse a complete database rather than just a sample of data used in the traditional auditing process. Because of these expanded capabilities, auditors are now better positioned to understand and assess entire business risk and improve internal controls in the organisation as a whole. Therefore, auditing analytics can help in the following:

- Continuous auditing and monitoring
- Audit Sampling and population testing
- Compliance

Data Analytics and Continuous Auditing

Internal and external auditing is based on testing the company's risk, review policies, procedures, and approvals that often take place weeks or months after the transaction has occurred. This process is backwards-looking and sometimes too late to mitigate or address a serious issue that exposes a company to potential liability. **Continuous auditing** is the process of using data analytics to constantly evaluate and monitor a company's accounting practice, transactions, compliance, and internal controls on an ongoing basis. Because of Big Data, auditors have real-time access to a vast amount of data that can be used to automate the audit process and can automatically perform a particular audit process. These include matching transactions and invoices at a specific time or day and alert the internal control audit staff when exceptions or errors are detected[3].

Continuous auditing can be used for the entire organisation or specific transactions such as travel and entertainment expenses, AP processing, and regulatory compliance.

Data Analytics and Audit Sampling

According to Auditing Standard 2315 (AS 2315), Audit sampling applies an audit procedure to less than 100 percent of the items within an account balance or class of transactions to evaluate some characteristic of the balance or class.[4] Various statistical methods are used for audit samplings, such as systematic sampling, random sampling, stratified sampling, and block sampling. However, regardless of the method used, it should produce an equal probability that each item in the database could be selected. Because the audit data is so unstructured and sometimes challenging to use, the AICPA's **Audit Data Standards (ADS)** tries to standardise the data format provided to auditors to perform their audit tasks. Even though it is just a recommendation, the standard provides examples of how the tables and fields can be included in the data. ADS aims to reduce the time taken by an auditor to convert data into a structured and usable format. However, it is voluntary, and companies are not required to implement it.[5]

The availability of Big Data and data analytics has made testing an organisation's data more efficient and cost-effective. Previously, testing and data analysis was limited to the structured data that is available to auditors. Today, however, because of the vast amount of data that auditors can access and the availability of data analytics tools, sampling and testing can use the company's entire dataset instead of just relying on a sample of data.

Data analytics allow auditors to combine structure and unstructured data, summarise the data, break it down into different buckets, analyse and test to identify errors and anomalies. These practices have increased the efficiencies and yielded more value to the organisation than the traditional audit process that depends solely on structured data and sample base sampling.

Because of audit analytics, auditors today can test 100 percent of a company's transactions to identify trends and assess risk. As a result, data analytics has enabled auditors to detect fraud more efficiently at a meagre cost. Additionally, it has allowed auditors to use external data such as industry, macroeconomic, and non-financial data to widen the scope of risk analysis and provide real-time advice to companies to make a strategic decision about business operations.

Data Analytics and Compliance

Compliance is the necessary steps a company takes to comply with the relevant laws required in the day-to-day operation of their business. Due to the ever-changing regulatory environments and expectations by governments, industry standards, the Department of Justice, accounting standards, environmental bodies, and privacy issues, companies use a tremendous amount of time and resources to document and meet the compliance requirements for these agencies. As a result, most companies use compliance analytics via data analytics tools to streamline the compliance process and make it more efficient. **Compliance analytics** involves collecting relevant data and mining it for patterns, discrepancies, and anomalies. It enables companies to detect and avoid potentially harmful transactions before employees, third parties, or unauthorised personnel can access them. Likewise, it helps companies identify concerns proactively, take corrective action, and self-report to regulators on a timely basis. In the past, companies became aware of non-compliant issues after they took place, or an external agency audit identified the problems. However, this method has been costly as the fines and penalties levied to the non-compliant organisation are often prohibitive.

Non-compliance can lead to many issues, including damage to a company's or brand reputation, financial losses, loss of license to do business in a particular area, and heavy penalties from regulatory bodies such as the FDA, DOJ, SEC, and FinCEN. For example, the US Financial Crime NetWork (FinCEN) has brought enforcement action for violations of the reporting, recordkeeping, or other requirements of the Bank Secrecy Act (BSA) against Capital One bank for compliance issues. On January 15, 2021, the bank was fined $390 million for failing to

> implement and maintain an effective AML (anti-money laundering) program to guard against money laundering through the Check Cashing Group (CCG). In addition, for failing to accurately and timely report suspicious transactions relating to the CCG (check cashing group), and negligently failed to timely report transactions involving currency in amounts greater than $10,000.[5]

Therefore, many companies are deploying compliance analytics to identify non-compliance issues before regulators notice or damage happens. The availability of Big Data and data analytics tools allow companies and organisations to identify or address potential compliance violations before they occur and meet the compliance requirement mandated by different agencies. As the source and volume of data increase, companies are building compliance programs driven by analytics.

The Value and Role of Data Analytics in Taxation

There are about 12 different types of taxes that individuals or corporations[6] have to deal with:

- individual income taxes,
- corporate income taxes,
- payroll taxes,
- capital gains taxes,
- sales taxes,
- gross receipts taxes,
- value-added taxes,

- excise taxes,
- property taxes,
- tangible personal property taxes,
- estate and inheritance taxes,
- wealth taxes.

The US tax code is vast and complex, and tax professionals, companies, and individuals have to deal with federal tax laws, multiple state jurisdictions, and international taxes. Tracing the ever-changing tax rates can be overwhelming for companies. Data analytics is helping companies comply with their tax filing requirements, reduce tax errors, and find tax-saving opportunities.

Tax Filing and Compliance Analytics

Traditionally, tax filing and compliance uses data from the financial report system. However, general ledger accounting systems are meant to prepare companies' financial statements, not collect data for the tax calculation and compliance issues. Tax filing has been burdensome and time-consuming because of the lack of a separate system devoted to collecting data for tax purposes. It sometimes leads to tax calculation errors and omission that triggers an audit and exposes companies to potential non-compliance tax liability. Data analytics tools provide the tax department with an efficient way to organise and access tax data stored in multiple departments across the organisation. This process has helped tax professionals minimise tax errors and efficiently track tax rates and tax laws in numerous jurisdictions to calculate the tax due to these jurisdictions accurately. The increasing requirement for more details in tax filing by tax authorities has made data analytics usage in tax filing and compliance a basic need for companies.

Tax Planning Analytics

Constant changes in the tax laws make tax planning a fundamental concept for businesses, individuals, and tax professionals. **Tax planning analytics** is the process of putting together procedures that will reduce the amount of tax paid by a company or individual and minimise the potential for tax audit or exposure to tax liability. The process involves analysing the tax laws and a massive amount of the company's transactions to identify potential tax savings and reduce tax liability. Because of Big Data, tax professionals can efficiently analyse a vast amount of internal and external data and transactions to identify opportunities that will reduce the tax paid by a company. The following questions are considered in putting together a tax planning analytics procedure:

1 What will be the impact of a new tax rate on tax liability?
2 Are we minimising our tax burden by tracking all eligible deductible expenses and transactions that qualify for tax credits?

3 What is the tax exposure for owners in the case of a potential merger or significant change in ownership?

4 Does our transfer pricing contract on certain products put us at a higher risk of a tax audit because they have abnormal margins?

5 How are we addressing tax complexities resulting from online sales due to new sales tax legislation?

6 How would tax law changes affect pension or profit-sharing plans and top employee compensation packages (including stock options)?

7 How would the use of independent contractors affect payroll tax liabilities?

As tax laws increase in complexity, tax professionals use analytics tools to identify potentially questionable deductions and extract relevant tax laws to help keep them abreast of the ever-changing tax regulations. Advances in data analytics have broadened and enhanced the tax department's functions. It allows them to be more effective and add value to the organisation.

Key Term

Accounts Payable Analytics; Accounts Receivables Analytics; Auditing; Revenue Recognition; Delinquency Risk Analytics; Working Capital Management; Text Mining Analytics; Sentiment Analytics

Chapter Key Takeaways

- The accounting profession provides three primary services to businesses: financial statement reporting, auditing, and tax planning.
- Accounting helps companies maintain accurate records of their day-to-day business transactions. These business records are summarised into three main reports: Profit and Loss Statement or Income Statement, Balance Sheet, and the Cash Flow Statement.
- Big Data and data analytics tools have provided a platform for accountants to process and convert data into actionable insights to facilitate the decision-making process that adds value to the company.
- Data analytics has a significant impact on a company's cash flow and working capital management. For example, it can improve the cash collection process, reduce late payments, and better understand customers' creditworthiness and payment patterns.
- Four basic data analytics techniques are used to analyse financial statements: sentiment and text mining, horizontal, vertical, and ratio analysis.
- Financial statement analytics such as sentiment analytics, horizontal, vertical, and ratio analysis have become more efficient in predicting a company's future performance because of data analytics tools that can bring different data sources into one place.

- Data analytics has enabled auditors to detect fraud more efficiently at a low cost.
- The availability of Big Data and data analytics tools allows companies and organisation to identify or address potential compliance violations before they occur and meet the compliance requirement mandated by different agencies.
- Data analytics tools provide the tax department with an efficient way to organise and access tax data stored in multiple departments across the organisation. This process has helped tax professionals minimise tax errors and efficiently track tax rates and tax laws in numerous jurisdictions to accurately calculate the tax due to these jurisdictions.

Discussion Questions

1 List and explain the four basic financial statement analytics.
2 How has data analytics changed the way revenue is recognised?
3 List and explain the five-step process of how a business recognises revenue that involves a contract with a customer. Explain how data analytics has made the process efficient.
4 Explain how data analytics has made accounts receivable management efficient.
5 Identify how data analytics is making the accounts payable department very efficient.
6 Explain how accounts payable analytics is improving the cash projection of a company.
7 What is Sentiment and text mining analytics? How is it helping users of financial statements?
8 How has data analytics expanded the capabilities of auditors when they audit the financial statements of a company?
9 Explain what is compliance analytics?
10 Discuss how the tax department of a company is using data analytics for tax filing and compliance. Explain tax planning analytics.

References

1 Financial Reporting Center (2016). Financial reporting brief: Roadmap to understanding the new revenue recognition standards, https://www.aicpa. org/interestareas/frc/accountingfinancialreporting/revenuerecognition/ downloadabledocuments/frc_brief_revenue_recognition.pdf
2 Loughran, T. & McDonald, B. (2015). The use of word lists in textual analysis. *Journal of Behavioral Finance, 16*(1), 1–11.
3 Peirson, J.(2010). *Continuous monitoring and continuous auditing: From idea to implementation.* Technical report, Deloitte & Touche LLP, 2010.[cited at p. 13], https://www2.deloitte.com/content/dam/Deloitte/us/Documents/audit/ us-aers-continuous-monitoring-and-continuous-auditing-whitepaper-102910.pdf
4 PCAOB; Public Accounting Oversight Board: AS 2315: Audit Sampling, https://pcaobus.org/oversight/standards/auditing-standards/details/AS2315

5 United States of America Financial Crimes Enforcement Network Department of the Treasury against Capital One, National Association, McLean, Virginia. (Matter number 2021–01), https://www.fincen.gov/sites/default/files/enforcement_action/2021-01-15/Assessment_CONA%20508_0.pdf   https://www.fincen.gov/news-room/enforcement-actions
6 https://taxfoundation.org/the-three-basic-tax-types/

11 Data Analytics in the Medical Industry

From public health issues such as global epidemics to managed healthcare, data analytics, and Big Data is improving and transforming the medical industry. However, it faces many challenges such as preventing and effectively managing epidemics, making better clinical decisions, improving clinical effectiveness and patient satisfaction, enhancing patient safety, and reducing medical errors. The challenges also include: utilising better disease management, improving risk management and regulatory compliance, and developing financial and operational efficiency.

This chapter details how data analytics is used to address the challenges faced by the healthcare industry and how it has enhanced the clinical and business components of healthcare. As a result, data analytics in the healthcare industry helps deliver excellent results for both the patient and the financial bottomline of the industry.

LEARNING OBJECTIVES:

At the end of this chapter, you should be able to:

- Develop a general understanding of the healthcare industry
- Identify the different sectors within the healthcare industry
- Know the value of Big Data and data analytics in Public Health
- Assess the value of Big Data and data analytics in Patient Care
- Understand the importance of Big Data and data analytics in the financial health of healthcare providers
- Know the data analytics tools most often used in the healthcare industry

The Healthcare Industry

Healthcare is essential to people regardless of where on the planet they live. The industry consists of a range of businesses that facilitate the provision of healthcare to patients. It includes various players like doctors, hospitals, pharmacies, nursing homes, medical device manufacturers,

DOI: 10.4324/9781003129356-11

diagnostic laboratories, drug manufacturers, and many other healthcare ecosystem components. In the US, healthcare spending is 17 percent of gross domestic product (GDP), and these costs are increasing at twice the country's economic growth rate. In Europe, healthcare costs are also rising beyond national and regional growth rates. The Organisation for Economic Co-operation and Development (OECD) claims that healthcare spending represents an average of 9.5 percent of GDP for the 34 OECD countries in North and South America, Europe, and the Asia/Pacific areas. The average yearly growth rate in healthcare costs for the group is 4.9 percent. In China, where most people are not insured, healthcare spending is rising by16 percent annually. Regardless of the payment system, the global phenomenon is that the pool of available capital to pay for healthcare decreases or stays flat while costs increases. The pharmaceutical sector reflects this new reality, where overall revenue is expected to remain flat or decline over the next ten years.[1] With technological innovations, smart healthcare management, and patient-focused restructuring, the healthcare industry is transforming its operations.

Sectors Within the Healthcare Industry

The healthcare industry contains various sectors, with activities ranging from research and development to facility management.

Drugs

Drug manufacturers consist of biotechnology firms, pharmaceuticals companies, and makers of generic drugs. The biotech industry comprises companies that research and create new drugs, devices, and treatment methods.

Some of these companies are small and lack dependable sources of revenue. Large pharmaceuticals firms also engage in research and development but often focus on manufacturing and promoting an existing portfolio of drugs.

Medical Equipment

Medical equipment producers range from companies that manufacture standard and popular products such as scalpels, forceps, bandages, and gloves to those that carry out innovative research and produce hi-tech equipment. Medtronic PLC is an example of a specialised medical equipment manufacturer.

Managed Healthcare

Managed healthcare companies provide health insurance policies. Examples of these companies include UnitedHealth Group Inc., Anthem Inc., Aetna Inc., Molina., and Centene.

Healthcare Facilities

Healthcare facilities companies operate hospitals, clinics, labs, psychiatric facilities, and nursing homes. Examples of these types of firms include Laboratory Corp. of America Holdings. They control facilities that perform blood tests and other analyses, and HCA Healthcare Inc. operates hospitals and other healthcare facilities in the US and UK.

Big Data in Healthcare Industry

There are several key drivers of the digitisation of healthcare, which also leads to Big Data generation. These are:

- 5G network with performance advancements serves as the backbone of emerging technologies. Companies are using 5G technology to reinvent the healthcare world and drive improvements.
- Cloud Computing – In the US, the emergence of federal laws and regulations and the increase in telehealth services highlighted the lack of interoperability between payers and providers who could not easily and securely share patient data. Several solutions on the market can remove data exchange barriers and enable streamlined care. Still, ingrained data exchange practices, privacy concerns, and the persistently high number of COVID-19 cases hamper regulatory compliance efforts. Using cloud computing, healthcare providers are overcoming these interoperability issues.
- Wearables – Wearable technology in healthcare includes electronic devices consumers use to monitor their health, such as Fitbits and smartwatches. These devices can send user's real-time health information to a doctor or other healthcare professional.
- Digital Therapeutics (DTx) – DTx provides evidence-based therapies via software, such as mobile health apps that exchange or complement the current treatments. The increased prevalence of chronic illnesses fuels the growth of the global DTx market. In addition, as COVID pandemic anxiety and depression continue to rise, digital therapeutics (DTx) is more critical than ever. However, regulatory bodies must approve these treatments.
- Telehealth – Telehealth employs mobile technology, such as video doctor visits and remote patient monitoring tools, to foster a constant relationship between patients and caregivers. These services eradicate the need for unnecessary doctor visits and make it easier for patients living in rural areas or without easy transportation access, to see a doctor or other healthcare professional.

Digital healthcare improves the quality of care by ensuring medical compliance. It allows for better diagnostics, improved care quality, and reduced operational costs. Large-scale data analysis and the use of Big Data are also changing the value proposition of healthcare. Data analytics allow providers to determine the patients with severe conditions and facilitate real-time, real-world analysis regarding the effectiveness of certain medications on the patient populations.

From the patient point of view, the digitalisation of healthcare is powerful and empowering as it allows physicians and consumers to communicate with each other outside of doctors' offices. In addition, through social media platforms and rating sites, patients effectively will reduce costs by sharing experiences regarding prices and quality of physicians, hospitals, and procedures.[1] Furthermore, Healthcare data management employs smart technology that provides permission control, anonymity, and patient record confidentiality.

The healthcare industry is seeking to strike the perfect balance between value-based care and fee-for-service. However, it faces many challenges, such as the ever-changing healthcare policies, the pressure to increase revenue and profitability, and patient demand for the latest equipment and technology. Therefore, many players in the healthcare industry have deployed data analytics to enhance operational efficiency. Data analytics in the healthcare industry is taking a large amount of healthcare data such as patient procedures, diagnosis, medical claims, patient engagement, spending, and analysing them to have a holistic understanding of the patient and make strategic improvements to the healthcare operations. In addition, analytics help finds opportunities for improving healthcare management, patient care, and the financial bottomline by providing trends and revealing actionable insights. As a result, analytics enhance healthcare quality and operational efficiency.

Key Players in Healthcare Industry

There are four critical stakeholders in the healthcare industry who supply and extract information:[2]

1 **Policymakers.** Policymakers develop and establish the policies and procedures within which healthcare is provided to the consumers. They hold jurisdictional responsible for the health of the population. Policymakers are responsible for collecting and analysing data from patients, providers, and payors to develop population-level metrics that inform health and economic policies.
2 **Patients.** Patients are consumers or beneficiaries of healthcare treatments or products. These are typically residents of the country where treatment is carried out. However, medical tourism has gained popularity over the last few years. Policymakers have a fiduciary responsibility to establish policies and implement frameworks to benefit these consumers. Patients obtain care services from providers and are the beneficiaries of the payors. Patients now are also demoing access to their information via mobile devices and are more engaged with their care.

3 **Providers**. Providers execute the care delivery established within the policy framework. They offer health services to consumers and maintain relevant health records. In addition, healthcare providers coordinate with other stakeholders to provide the best possible patient care.
4 **Payors.** Payors are responsible for the financial components of the policy framework. Payors enrol patients as beneficiaries. They acquire care services from providers on behalf of their patient beneficiaries. Providers also ensure the financial sustainability of the care program. They report to policymakers.

The Value of Big Data and Data Analytics in Public Health

Public Health Analytics

Public health could be defined as the science of promoting and protecting the health of people and the communities where they live. This is done mainly through education, policymaking, research, and disease monitoring and prevention. In addition, public health officials perform various functions, such as developing policies that support community health efforts and enforce laws and regulations that protect community health initiatives.

Data analytics and Big Data are extremely valuable to public healthcare. COVID-19 has demonstrated that public health issues such as global epidemics, disease surveillance, efficiency in preventive measurement, management of outbreaks, and other disease are severe challenges to the healthcare industry. With its diagnostic and predictive power, data analytics has significantly enhanced how public health officers and healthcare researchers can collaborate and better manage the spread of disease and allocate resources accordingly. In addition, data analytics has improved the collaboration between universities, researchers worldwide, the World Health Organization (WHO), and healthcare workers to detect and prevent pandemics as quickly as possible. An example of Big Data and data analytics application in public healthcare is the collaboration between the WHO, researchers, individual nations, a not-for-profit organisation such as the Bill Gates Foundation, and pharmaceutical companies such as Moderna to combat the spread of COVID-19. For example, the WHO website was able to show in its descriptive analytics the percentage of people who have contracted COVID-19 and the confirmed death by countries. This dashboard is possible because of Big Data and data analytics and the collaboration of these entities to make data transparent and accessible.[3] Additionally, the WHO, John's Hopkins University, University of Washington, and other universities worldwide have used Big Data and data analytics to predict COVID-19 infection, recovery, mortality rate, and spread globally and domestically. The insights from these analytics have been beneficial to public health officials in helping them warn citizens about the infectious nature of the Coronavirus and how to allocate resources to their public healthcare facilities effectively.

Disease Monitoring and Surveillance Analytics. Predicting the spread accurately and the possible severity of a disease is very important to public health policymakers. Knowing the number of people exposed to the disease, the rate of those infected, and how many of those infected may need urgent medical attention will help policymakers plan accordingly and determine where and when intervention is required. However, public health data such as age, demographic, social habits, location, and other data are accessible because of Big Data. Data analytics can predict the likelihood of a particular individual or group of people contracting the disease. With such information, health officials can respond accordingly. The predictive power of data analytics is used to project the severity of infection not only for COVID-19 but also for other viruses such as the common cold.

Public health organisations may utilise analytics to monitor disease trends, determine patterns in specific populations, guide disease control programs, and set priorities for allocating health resources to people in need. In addition, social media aided tremendously in the circulation of health data throughout the world. As a result, this enables public health organisations and the WHO to monitor and detect early signs of disease trends and collaborate on prevention. Additionally, data analytics help public health officials answer the following questions:

1 What are the variations in health care costs geographically?
2 How are costs for various aspects of health care likely to rise in the future?
3 How are specific policy changes impacting cost and behaviour?

The Value of Big Data and Data Analytics in Patient Care

Patient Care Analytics

Patient care means different things to different people, but in its most basic form, it refers to the prevention, treatment, and management of ailments through services offered by healthcare professionals. Because of the vast amount of data generated in the healthcare ecosystem, data analytics presents many opportunities for healthcare institutions to provide efficient and quality care for patients. Data analytics, when used strategically, will not only improve the quality of patient care but also reduce error and provide cost-effective care.

The following are among the areas in which data analytics provide value in patient care:

• Eldercare
• Mental health
• Personalised and precision medicine

Data analytics allow doctors to make better decisions on patient care by analysing many historical medical patterns of patients' diseases across different scenarios.

Elder Care Analytics. Increasingly seniors opt for independent living rather than assisted-living lifestyles. For this to be possible, Big Data technologies have presented possible solutions, one of which is wearing sensors that continuously monitor the elderly and alert caregivers and emergency-care staff of a crisis. These wearable sensors provide essential information about the patient, and the data it collects is beneficial for analytics. However, some system poses challenges. One major challenge is that the sensor readings do not accurately correlate between observable human behaviours and health conditions. In other words, the sensors provide information about the symptoms and illnesses but not necessarily about the behaviours that lead to the diseases. Therefore, a wearable sensor system that provides intelligent data such as behaviour patterns is ideal for collecting all the necessary data for analysis. Data analytic model can then analyse the data and provide healthcare professionals with the insight needed without interrupting the patient's daily life.

Mental Health Analytics. The amount of people suffering from mental illnesses in recent years has increased significantly. According to the National Council for Mental Wellbeing, about 43.8 million people in the US experience some type of mental illness in any given one year.[4] That is about 5 percent of US adults. Furthermore, almost half of US adults would experience some mental illness during their lifetime. Mental illnesses come in various forms, such as anxiety, depression, schizophrenia, and addiction. Some of these illnesses are visible and recognisable immediately, but others are harder to see or diagnose.

Big Data and data analytics are becoming the key to creating personalised care for those facing mental illness challenges. By collecting large datasets, researchers and healthcare professionals can identify patterns that can help them diagnose mental illness more accurately and quickly. In addition, Big Data and data analytics can help reduce diagnostic errors, leading to fatal consequences for patients.

Big Data technologies are being used to gather large amounts of data on Alzheimer's disease. This information is necessary to advance the Central Nervous System (CNS) research and mental drug development. While the empirical data will provide valuable information, understanding the pathology for developing drugs has been challenging for drugmakers. Big Data, data-driven analytics, and pharmacology systems bring predictive, actionable drug discovery and development.[5] As a result of increasing clinical trial failure rates, new approaches are also being explored to gather Big Data to speed up the discovery process in global research studies of diseases and genetics. It's good that advanced deep analytical approaches have been developed and used in bioinformatics and pharmacology. However, these approaches are still limited in particular areas of medical research, such as brain diseases. Therefore, it has been suggested that combining these advanced approaches with predictive analytical models will turn "Big Data into smart data," thereby improving future clinical trials and research.

Personalise Medicine And Data Analytics. Due to advancements in treatment, Big Data, and data analytics tools personalised healthcare is becoming a reality. Customised service is already being used in other industries. Netflix, for example, uses predictive analytics tools to analyse customers' viewing habits and other activities in their platform to offer them personalised content. The healthcare industry is moving in the same direction to provide customised services to its patients. This is becoming increasingly possible because of real-time data, patient medical history, lifestyle information, and genetic sequencing. Combining this data and data analytics tools can predict disease occurrence and provide real-time guidance on curing the sickness. Big Data and data analytics tools are enhancing personalised medicine in the following way:

- **Predictive Analytics** enables healthcare professionals to facilitate targeted diagnostics based on demographic or pre-existing conditions or other metrics. In addition, prescriptive analytics empowers them to develop personalised treatment plans for patients.
- **Data Analytics Enhance Efficient Collaboration in Patient Care.** Data generated from different groups such as hospitals and insurance companies are primarily unstructured and deemed unusable. However, data analytics tools and analysis help provide insight into these data and allow these entities to collaborate and deliver a better healthcare system to their patients.
- **Big Data And Data Analytics Tools** allow healthcare professionals to use clustering techniques and segment patients with similar symptoms and care patterns over a long period to help doctors deliver much more data-driven healthcare to a cluster of patients. Data analytics also provide relevant information on past treatment options used in the routine care of a particular disease cluster. This allows healthcare workers to selectively determine the best course of action in the resurgence of such a disease.
- **Data Analytics** has enormous benefits for clinical practice. Big Data offers early disease detection, a more accurate prediction, diagnosis, and treatment. As a result, therapies are more targeted and cost-effective. In addition, it lends to precision medicine, actionable recommendations between physicians and patients, and solid decision-making support for clinicians.
- **Big Data And Data Analytics Help in Creating an Accurate and Effective Patient Journey.** Journey maps are used across many industries by marketers and advertisers to determine how the customer would identify with the product or service. For example, the patient journey map charts the patient's experience in the healthcare industry and provides the doctor with a more in-depth look into the patient health.

Patient journey mapping can be very detailed, from demographics and clinical data to the treatment and patient-care services. The mapping creates a patient-care funnel, and it channels the how, where, and why of the patient's healthcare. This information is available in a system, and it helps provide the healthcare provider with the necessary information needed to diagnose and appropriately treat patients accurately. As a result of these great benefits of journey mapping, it contributes favourably to patient success.

The Value of Big Data and Data Analytics in the Financial Health of Healthcare Providers

Data analytics not only improve patient care but also has an impact on the healthcare facility financial bottom line via:

1   market share growth that is achieved through target marketing
2   increased revenue occurs when market share increases, and
3   reduced cost through efficient hospital staffing and a decrease in patients skipping appointments.

Data analytics brings clinical, financial, and operational data together, paving the way for the data to be analysed in real time therefore providing better patient care at a lower cost. It is achieved in various ways.

- Healthcare facilities can use predictive analytics to identify the patients most likely to miss an appointment without advanced notice, improve provider satisfaction, reduce revenue losses, and allow organisations to offer open slots to other patients, increasing speedy access to care.
- **Healthcare Providers Analytics and Profit.** Big Data and data analytics provide practical ways to evaluate the performance and effectiveness of healthcare providers at the point of delivery. Using various health data related to patient care and wellness, data analytics can provide continuous feedback to health care administrators and providers. Additionally, Big Data and analytics can be an effective tool for The Ongoing Professional Practice Evaluation (OPPE).[6] For example, data analytics tools can continually evaluate healthcare practitioners' performance by aggregating data from patient outcomes, direct observation, complaints, practice patterns, peer reviews, and code of conduct breaches. The insight from the analytics can improve practitioners' effectiveness in healthcare delivery to improve patient care, which lowers cost and increases profit margin.
- **High-Cost Patient Analytics**. Treating chronic diseases is very costly in the healthcare industry. However, on a national level, predictive analytics can cut costs significantly by predicting which patients are at higher

risk for disease and arrange an early intervention before problems develop. This involves aggregating data related to various factors such as medical history, demographic or socioeconomic profile, and comorbidities.

- **Staffing healthcare facilities analytics**. One classic problem most healthcare shift managers face is the problem of over- or under-staffing. Managers must figure out the number of staff needed to run a shift smoothly and seamlessly. Understaffing leads to poor customer service and patient care, which can be fatal in the health industry. On the other hand, overstaffing can cause unnecessary labour costs and possible medical errors caused by overcrowding. Big Data has been instrumental in solving this problem in a few hospitals in Paris. Data analytics can predict the number of patients' visits to each hospital.[7] This data is also based on past hospital admission records to determine pattern rates. Data analytics will also help reduce patients' wait times and improve the quality of care.

Sources of Healthcare Data

Developing analytics models that support effective decision-making in the healthcare industry requires vast data across multiple areas of the healthcare ecosystem. Healthcare data is spread among different entities such as hospitals, health insurers, researchers, academics, government entities, not-for-profit foundations, and patient advocacy groups. Unfortunately, most of this data is unstructured or semi-structured data. However, healthcare professionals need organised data to make informed decisions. Having structured and usable data gives healthcare providers the necessary tools to help make life-saving decisions. The advent of wearable devices has increased the amount of data collected in the healthcare industry. It has made it easier than ever before to collect fitness data, geriatric care data, and others. Below are some of the sources of healthcare data.

- Electronic Medical Records (EMRs)
- Diagnostic data
- Biomarkers data
- Ancillary and Administrative data
- Medical Claims
- Prescription Claims
- Clinical Research
- Patient-generated Data
- Wearable and Sensors
- Biometric data
- Clinical data
- Omics data
- Data from social media
- Real-time location systems data

Popular Data Analytics Tools in the Healthcare Industry

Early developments in Big Data analytics tools like the Google File system allowed the processing of large-scale distributed data-intensive applications on inexpensive commodity hardware. In addition, it used a fault-tolerant mechanism that is the ability of a computer system or network to continue working without disruption when one or more of its components fail. This paved the way for further developments in distributed computing. Later, Google developed MapReduce, a programming model based on Java language, which is helpful for writing applications to process large volumes of data, in parallel, on clusters of commodity hardware. Recently, Hadoop and Spark are the latest buzzwords in the Big Data universe.

Big Data analytical tools and technologies have been helpful in the multi-dimensional healthcare data, especially in medical images (X-ray, MRI images), biomedical signals (EEG, ECG, EMG), audio transcripts, handwritten prescriptions, and structured images data from EMRs. Listed below are some general Big Data and data analytics tools commonly used for healthcare analytics.

1 Hadoop

Hadoop allows healthcare data to be stored naturally regardless of its original format and provides storage for billions of unstructured data.

- **Hadoop in Healthcare analytics**. Hadoop is one of the Big Data analytic tools used in many healthcare analytics platforms for various reasons and advantages. One of them is that Hadoop data storage is less expensive. The healthcare industry has one of the most complex and large amounts of data that needs large digital storage capacity. Data such as doctors' notes, lab results, X-rays, medical reports, and others primarily unstructured need ample storage space. Hadoop can store different types of data in various formats at a very low cost. Another essential attribute of Hadoop in healthcare is that it helps organise data simultaneously as an analytic tool. For example, it allows users to write program codes that can eliminate duplicate X-rays, MRI images from a database of millions of images. Hadoop's ability to remove identical pictures and medical reports enhance effective, accurate detection and cure of disease.
- **Hadoop in cancer treatment**. What most healthcare researchers and professionals have discovered is that bioinformatics data transfer very well to Hadoop. Such research is fundamental in cancer detection and treatment since it is estimated that at least 3 billion base pairs make up human DNA. Furthermore, cancer mutates differently based on the genetic makeup of an individual. Therefore, each patient may need to be given a personalised treatment based on their genetic makeup to cure cancer effectively. It is in such situations that data analytics and Hadoop technology have had the most significant impact. Therefore, it helps support the mapping of the 3 billion DNA base pairs in an individual. In addition, because of its ability to store large amounts of genomic data, Hadoop has given healthcare researchers

the tools needed to potentially identify the cancer gene in each individual, leading to the development of individualised cancer treatment.

2 MapReduce

MapReduce programs are typically written in the Java language. However, high-level languages like Hive and Pig Latin make it easier for people unfamiliar with Java to write MapReduce applications.

- **MapReduce in Healthcare analytics**. MapReduce can improve the performance of standard signal detection algorithms for pharmacovigilance at approximately linear speedup rates. Algorithms based on the Hadoop distributed platform can refine protein structure alignments more accurately than existing algorithms. In addition, MapReduce-based algorithms can improve the performance of neural signal processing. MapReduce framework has also been used to find optimal parameters for lung texture classification and increase the speed of medical image processing. Hadoop-based Big Data processing tools like Oozie and Pig are used for batch processing by the healthcare industry, and non-Hadoop processing tools like Storm, Spark, and Hive can stream data analysis and enable timely data processing. MapReduce performs reasonably for ad hoc data summarisation and querying.

Benefits and Challenges of Big Data in the Healthcare Industry

Big Data offers speed and opportunity for growth across all industries. It is promising for the healthcare industry because it plays a crucial role in patient data management, patient care, and predictive analysis. Technologies like Hadoop and Spark are providing solutions that are incrementally scalable and offer speed and advanced analytics. As shown in our example, healthcare facilities and the public sector use Big Data technologies to tap into the opportunities. On the other hand, there are challenges to data privacy and security, data restrictions, and limited accessibility; and therefore, Big Data cannot be fully utilised in healthcare facilities. In addition, regulatory policies and laws can pose a challenge to data accessibility. The procedures and regulations were put in place to protect patient privacy. While this may be so, Big Data in healthcare still provide efficiency in preventative and predictive analysis, which leads to practical processes and quality patient care.

APPLICATION CASE 11.1

St. Charles Health System: Looking Forward with Predictive Analytics

The tradition of medicine and healthcare is, by nature, predictive. Patient assessment leads to prescribed treatment and a prognosis for recovery. However, a web search on healthcare analytics yields dashboard

(Continued)

projects that focus on what happened yesterday or last week and shows very little work being done with predictive analytics. This underscores the innovative course charted by Rapid Insight customer, St. Charles Health System (SCHS).

Today, all healthcare organisations are pursuing the triple aim: a better patient experience, more robust population health, and cost containment. However, SCHS is raising the bar with the use of data and technology in pursuit of the triple aim by establishing a goal to use predictive modelling to manage their organisation better to pave new pathways in healthcare.

St. Charles is the largest provider of medical care and the largest employer in Central Oregon, with 4,200 caregivers at four hospitals, 350 active, and 200 visiting staff members. Actionable and effective information is vital to their decision-making process. With four major capital projects weighing in at 80 million dollars, optimising their resources is crucial.

Improve Healthcare With Predictive Analytics

To ensure this was happening, Dr Michael Johnson came on board as the Analytics Specialist for Decision Support at SCHS. As a result, several predictive models are now in place, and the team is seeing exciting signs of positive change. Dr Johnson had previous experience with predictive analytics and modelling. First, during his career in the army and, more recently, as Director of Institutional Research at Dickinson College. At Dickinson, he first began using Rapid Insight software and saw it as a natural fit to blend data and develop predictive models for SCHS.

"The Decision Support Team is a relatively new addition to the St. Charles IT department, and there is some very forward-thinking in the organisation," says Johnson. He's excited by what they have been able to accomplish in a relatively short amount of time. The flexibility of Construct, Rapid Insight's data blending software, allows the team to pull data from any source, including their electronic health record (EHR), and to incorporate pre-built SQL scripts provided by their data experts. The easy aggregation and transformation of this data let Johnson and his team deliver predictive models very quickly, and they have become essential to the hospital staff's daily routine.

The goal of the first model, analysing Length of Stay (LOS), is to improve patient care by optimising LOS based on the primary diagnosis. This particular model uses approximately 18 months of historical data to "score" current in-patients on their potential to exceed the recommended length of stay. Johnson has used Construct's scheduling tools to automate this process. Each night, the model runs, incorporates the latest data, and creates a report distributed to administrators and clinical managers at all four SCHS locations early each day. These emailed reports make a higher level of treatment and help caregivers to modify care plans, prioritise efforts, and provide care attuned to the potential needs of patients with higher LOS scores.

The second model is a project to address the potential for patient readmission. Again, the work proved remarkably effective. "It didn't take much work to tweak the Length of Stay Model for the readmission project," Johnson said. "The same Construct job could be used to pull the historical data."

These models were created with the intent of being able to score both pre-and post-discharge patients. The former goal is to improve patient care by minimising the number of current in-patients who have unscheduled readmission within 30 days of discharge. However, Dr Johnson and his team also found that the Rapid Insight readmission models that incorporated data from LACE assessments became significantly more accurate than the LACE scores on their own. The more accurate risk rating derived through predictive analytics is a vital tool for caregivers in treatment and aftercare who work to reduce readmission… a costly process to the organisation, and an unpleasant experience for the patient.

SCHS can predict whether or not a pre-discharge patient will have unscheduled readmission. All patients are scored every day like they are in the LOS model, and automated reports are sent each morning to the teams. The process for the post-discharge model is similar, but it scores patients who were discharged in the last five days and are no longer at the facility. As a result, caregivers and administrators get deeper insights into who could walk back through the door, allowing them to develop better protocols for these patients and tune resource planning.

Get Cozy with Predictive Analytics

A concern in healthcare is always how staff adapt to the use of predictive analytics. Caregivers at SCHS are receptive to the new insights that can help them improve patient care. To some, the reporting model functions as a task list for patient follow-up. The reporting also assists with staff time management and helps to allocate limited resources to those who are most at risk. Additionally, the unit staff uses the pre-discharge readmission list to assign a case manager to each patient. This ensures that high-risk readmission patients are closely monitored, and aftercare gets focused attention.

For SCHS, this is only the beginning, and plans for predictive analytics are evolving. Dr Johnson shares that they will begin to build models that

(Continued)

predict which individuals are prone to expensive high utilisation of services and a model to evaluate the potential for complication or improvement by primary diagnosis. Also in the line-up are two more readmission models. One model focuses on predicting readmit rates by a physician. Specifically, identifying over and underperformers based on their patient's acuity and the case mix index. The second is a readmit model for short-stay and observation patients. The Decision Support Team would also like to create an employee turnover model for human resources.

St. Charles has rejected the status quo of using retrospective, descriptive metrics, realising that management against what has already happened is simply not good enough. Instead, with Rapid Insight's Construct and Predict, SCHS has genuinely adopted a forward-looking analytic mindset that helps them change the course of costly outcomes and negative patient experiences. As a result, predictive modelling is driving exciting changes in their daily operations and inspiring an innovative future with predictive analytics.

Source: Rapid insight case studies, a data analytics company: *St. Charles Health System: Looking Forward with Predictive Analytics*, https://www.rapidinsight.com/why-rapid-insight/ case-studies/st-charles-health-system-looking-forward-predictive-analytics/?hsCtaTracking=085b190c-f90a-4f56-9ba6-650f4a5e9a77%7C8a920765-01a5-4d6a-9ee4-c0cb32dfaf20. Used by permission from Rapid Insight.

Key Term

Public Health; World Heal Organization (WHO); Public Health Analytics; Electronic Medical Records (EMRs); Biomarkers Data; Omics Data; Hadoop; MapReduce

Chapter Key Takeaways

- The healthcare industry is essential to people globally. The industry consists of a range of businesses that facilitate the provision of healthcare to patients.
- Public health could be defined as the science of promoting and protecting the health of people and the communities where they live.
- With its diagnostic and predictive power, data analytics has significantly enhanced how public health officers and healthcare researchers can collaborate and better manage the spread of disease and allocate resources accordingly.
- Public health organisations may utilise analytics to monitor disease trends, determine patterns in specific populations, guide disease control programs, and set priorities for allocating health resources to people in need.

- Data analytics, when used strategically, will not only improve the quality of patient care but also reduce error and provide cost-effective care.
- Big Data and data analytics are becoming the key to creating personalised care for those facing mental illness challenges.
- Big Data offers early disease detection, a more accurate prediction, diagnosis, and treatment.
- Data analytics brings clinical, financial, and operational data together, paving the way for the data to be analysed on all fronts in real time to provide better care at a lower cost.
- Healthcare data is spread among different entities such as hospitals, health insurers, researchers, academics, government entities, not-for-profit foundations, and patient advocacy groups.
- Big Data analytical tools and technologies have been helpful in the multi-dimensional healthcare data, especially in medical images (X-ray, MRI images), biomedical signals (EEG, ECG, EMG), audio transcripts, handwritten prescriptions, and structured images data from EMRs.

Discussion Questions

1 Explain the four P's in the healthcare industry.
2 What is the importance of Big Data and data analytics to public healthcare?
3 List and discuss three sectors in the healthcare industry.
4 How can you use data analytics to enhance public healthcare?
5 What is the value of data analytics in elder care?
6 How are data analytics and Big Data used in mental health care?
7 In what ways are Big Data and data analytics tools enhancing personalised medicine?
8 Please explain how data analytics is helping to improve the operational efficiency and profitability of healthcare providers.
9 What is the patient journey? How is it beneficial to the financial success of the healthcare industry?
10 List and explain five sources of healthcare data.
11 What is Hadoop Big Data analytic tool, and how is it used in the medical industry?
12 What are the challenges of using Big Data in the healthcare industry?

References

1 Bouwens, J. & Krueger, D.M. (N.D.) (2014). Embracing change: The healthcare industry focuses on new growth drivers and leadership requirements. Russell Reynolds Associates. http://www.russellreynolds.com/content/embracing-changehealthcare-industry-focuses-new-growth-drivers-and-leadership-requirements; https://1library.net/document/q07v25lz-healthcare-industry-focuses-new-growth-drivers-leadership-requirements.html
2 Ritz, D. Althauser, C., & Wilson, K. (2014) Connecting health information systems for better health. Joint Learning Network for Universal Health Coverage Publishers.

3 WHO Dashboard, https://covid19.who.int/
4 National Council for Mental Wellbeing, https://www.mentalhealthfirstaid. org/2019/02/5-surprising-mental-health-statistics/
5 Geerts, H., Dacks, P.A., Devanarayan, V., Haas, M., Khachaturian, Z.S., Gordon, M.F., and Brain Health Modeling Initiative. (2016). Big data to smart data in Alzheimer's disease: The brain health modelling initiative to foster actionable knowledge. *Alzheimer's & Dementia, 12*(9), 1014–1021.
6 The Joint Commission. OPPE, https://www.jointcommission.org/standards/ standard-faqs/critical-access-hospital/medical-staff-ms/000001500/
7 Durcevic, S. (2020). 18 Examples of Big Data Analytics in Healthcare That Can Save People **Business Intelligence,** https://www.datapine.com/blog/ big-data-examples-in-healthcare/

12 Data Analytics in the Manufacturing Industry

One of the most innovative and dynamic industries is the manufacturing industry. However, the ever-changing technological landscape and the demand for high-quality products by consumers have brought many challenges. This chapter details how the industry has embraced data analytics to address some of the most challenging issues, such as: maintaining quality across the entire product life cycle, identifying issues earlier, reducing scraps and increasing productivity, reducing maintenance cost, reducing warranty cost and warranty claim rate, and reducing the recall rate.

LEARNING OBJECTIVES:

At the end of this chapter, you should be able to:

- Define manufacturing and have a basic understanding of the manufacturing industry
- Access the importance of Big Data and data analytics in production planning and control
- Understand the value of Big Data and data analytics in quality management
- Identify the value of Big Data and data analytics in maintenance and diagnosis
- Analyse the value of Big Data and data analytics in product research and development

What Is Manufacturing?

Manufacturing is an important commercial activity conducted by businesses that sell products to customers and is accomplished by automated and computer-controlled machinery. It includes assembling multiple parts to make products and often involves a combination of machinery, tools, power, and labour. It is usually carried out as a sequence of operations or activities, with each adding value and bringing the material closer to the desired final state. In economic terms, manufacturing adds value to the material by changing its shape or form or combining it with other materials. Thus, the manufacturing

DOI: 10.4324/9781003129356-12

process makes the material more valuable. For example, value is added when iron ore is converted into steel, or when sand is transformed into glass. Manufacturing, therefore, is essentially a means by which a country creates material wealth.

Big Data and Data Analytics in the Manufacturing Industry

The manufacturing sector generates large volumes of data daily as multiple sensors, electronic devices, digital machines, cloud computing, and IIoT platforms are used in production lines, shop floors, and factories. Big Data analytics allow this industry to uncover patterns that help improve the efficiency of supply chain management. Big Data analytics in the manufacturing sector focus on high-performance operational data management systems, cloud-based data storage, and better decision-making.

Big Data analytics is crucial to real-time performance, supply chain and price optimisation, fault prediction, product development, and intelligent factory design. Instances of Big Data analytics in the manufacturing industry include:

- Merck, a pharmaceutical firm specialising in producing vaccines, uses Big Data analytics to optimise its manufacturing.
- Raytheon Corp. uses Big Data to enable smart factories based on the powerful capacity to manage information from numerous data sources such as CAD models, sensors, instruments, Internet transactions, simulations, and digital records in the company.
- Itron, a water meter manufacturer, uses Big Data analytics to provide "smart grid" solutions to consumers and manage its trailers' maintenance, cargo temperatures, and routes.
- GE uses Big Data analytics to improve its operational performance significantly.
- Siemens uses Big Data analytics to measure power plants worldwide built up remote diagnostic services (RDS) to analyse the operational behaviours.
- Rolls-Royce, the engine manufacturer, uses Big Data to improve product quality.
- Ramco Cements Limited (RCL), an Indian company, uses Big Data to manage its product development, operations, and logistics.

What Is Manufacturing Analytics?

Most industrial manufacturing companies have complex processes and relationships across the supply chain with vendors and sub-assembly suppliers. As a result, mistakes are expensive, and downtime is enormously costly. Data is an increasingly essential aspect of many of today's industrial products, and this is likely to increase as products become more integrated and intelligent. Many manufacturers include sensors in their products, allowing owners to use connective data technologies to monitor these items, creating new and enormous data streams relevant to predictive maintenance, predictive quality, and other supply chain applications. As seen in Figure 12.1, this data is then collected, processed, and aggregated to make decisions, control costs, optimise resource consumption and manage sustainability efforts amid changing regulations.

Big Data analytics is used to explore new potentials while focusing on production planning and control in the manufacturing industry. As manufacturing companies begin to widely use advanced information technology to carry out their general management, a large amount of multi-source, heterogeneous, and real-time data is generated during the R&D, manufacture, operation, and maintenance phases of production. Thus, the era of industrial or manufacturing Big Data has come. Consequently, Big Data analytics has gained extensive employment in the manufacturing industry due to its ability to integrate, process, and analyse dynamic and real-time data.

Manufacturing analytics using operations and events data and technologies in the manufacturing industry to ensure quality, increase performance and yield, reduce costs, and optimise supply chains. It seeks to move beyond a simple collection and display of data (descriptive) to leveraging that data in real-time (predictive). It is part of the Industry 4.0 revolution where factories employ smart technologies to achieve automation and data exchange. Traditional manufacturers were unable to harness and use all the data generated from the end-to-end manufacturing process. Instead, traditional manufacturers rely on complex and expensive tools that collect limited data from operators or machines. For example, waiting to identify why a manufacturing process was breaking down could take weeks.

Current manufacturing analytics relies upon predictive analytics, Big Data analytics, the Industrial Internet of Things (IIoT), machine learning, and edge computing to enable more innovative, scalable factory solutions. Manufacturing analytics collect and analyse large amounts of data from unlimited sources to identify areas for improvement. It provides actionable insights in real time or establishes automatic business processes to respond to in real time. Data-driven product optimisation that relies on IoT sensors and machine learning models can optimise production based on several factors. For example, companies can adjust the components that lead to higher usage rates by analysing product usage. With data collected from digital factories, manufacturers can also understand the process states that increase defect density.

Applications of Manufacturing Analytics

- Predictive maintenance is used to analyse performance data to identify when a component is likely to fail. For example, using time series data from IoT sensors (such as those for vibration or temperature) can predict

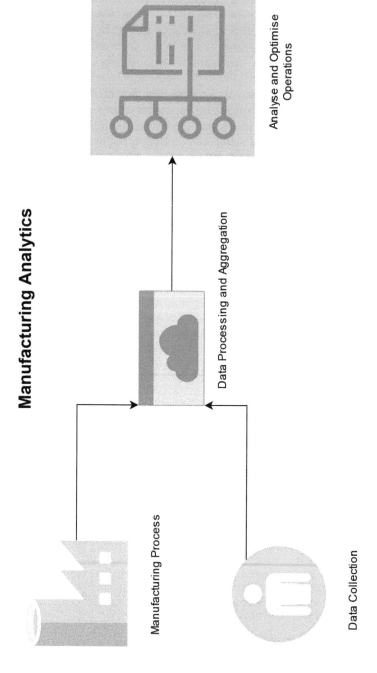

Figure 12.1 Manufacturing Analytics.

equipment failure. This helps limit systems interruption and stoppage by identifying the cause of the problem and allowing appropriate adjustments to avoid repeating it.

- Yield-energy throughput (YET) analytics guarantees that the different components and machines are utilised as efficiently as possible to help increase productivity and reduce energy consumption. YET works by real-time monitoring and optimising the parameters under which the devices operate.
- Profit-per-hour (PPH) maximisation analytics is employed to identify the optimal setup to impact the final profitability. These include conditions found in the supply chain and sales mix.
- Demand forecasting enables employees to respond quickly to any gaps or trends identified in the data. Manufacturing analytics allows manufacturers to combine existing data with predictive analytics to build a precise purchasing trends projection.
- Inventory management makes it easier to establish efficient arrangement structures, improve product flow management, make effective replenishment procedures, and improve profit margin.

Data Analytics in Production Planning and Control

Big Data in manufacturing is essential in achieving increased productivity and efficiency and uncovering new insights to promote creativity and innovation. With Big Data analytics, manufacturing companies can discover further information and identify patterns that allow for process improvement, increase supply chain efficiency, and isolate variables that affect production. Furthermore, to compete successfully in a data-driven economy, Big Data analytics helps companies achieve digital transformation and gain a competitive edge.

Asset Performance and Efficiency Gains

An increase in asset performance gains can result in substantial productivity improvements – even if asset performance is only improved on the margins. Likewise, a decrease in asset breakdowns can reduce inefficiencies and prevent losses. As a result, decision-makers in the manufacturing industry focus on maintenance and continuously optimise asset performance.

Machine logs contain data on asset performance. However, the IoT adds a new dimension with connected systems and sensors capable of measuring, recording, and transmitting performance in real time. The data from these systems are potentially crucial to manufacturers, and data analytics help capture, cleanse, and analyse machine data to expose information that can improve performance. In addition, predictive analytics can help manufacturers schedule maintenance, thus preventing costly system breakdowns and avoiding unexpected downtime.

Production Processes and Supply Chains

In the increasingly interconnected and integrated environment, supply chains are long and complex. Efforts to streamline processes and optimise supply chains must be supported by examining every process component and supply chain link in granular detail. Big Data analytics give manufacturers this capability. Manufacturers can explore the different production process segments using data analytics and inspect supply chains in minute detail. The ability to narrow the focus on individual activities and tasks allows manufacturers to identify bottlenecks and reveal underperforming processes and components. Big Data analytics also reveal dependencies, enabling manufacturers to enhance production processes and create alternative plans to address potential pitfalls.

Product Customisation

Big Data analytics allows manufacturers to predict the demand for customised products accurately. By detecting changes in customer behaviour, Big Data analytics provide manufacturers with the opportunity to produce customised products. Big Data analytics allows manufacturers to identify where they can profitably insert custom processes using in-house capabilities or postpone production before completing the manufacturing process. The ability to delay production provides new flexibility that allows manufacturers to take on tailor-made requests.

Data analytics helps manufacturers identify defects in processes, increase the rate of product development, improve (or maintain) product quality, and reduce variation in quality. For example:

- Process manufacturers use predictive analytics tools to assess the constitution of chemicals, minerals, and other raw materials to guarantee they meet production criteria.
- Biopharmaceutical manufacturers employ advanced data analytics to significantly increase biologics such as vaccines without incurring additional capital expenses.
- Chemical manufacturing companies use advanced data analytics to compare and measure the effect of several production inputs, like coolant pressure, temperature, or carbon dioxide flow, on yield.
- Companies gain insights from production data across various processes to discover correlations between specific variables' final output quality.
- Pharmaceutical manufacturers use data analytics to verify that processes observe the standards established to maintain quality.
- Big Data analytics assist manufacturers in managing the long-term operational health of production equipment, reduce unscheduled downtime, and prevent system failures using the "internet of things."

Big Data and Data Analytics in Quality Management

Increasing market demand and customer requirements towards better product and process quality and efficiency forces companies to develop innovative ways to optimise production. In addition, the growing importance of quality for competitive success is increasing. Based on these trends, manufacturing companies must rapidly optimise complexity within their manufacturing and business processes to meet the expected product quality.

The international standard ISO 9001, a body that specifies the criteria for a quality management system, requires that industrial products and manufacturing processes be designed to meet customer expectations through the specific engineering specifications of critical product characteristics. Therefore, controlling and managing these vital characteristics is a fundamental task of the quality management system. In addition, data accuracy, completeness, context richness, availability, and archival length are essential to provide data quality.

Manufacturing companies are making use of the IoT, which connects cyber-physical systems. Embedded sensors in machines and gadgets are used to collect large volumes of data to indicate the quality of products and processes, e.g., product features or machine parameters. As a result, companies can improve production yield while lowering maintenance costs. Data analytics tools allow manufacturers to monitor equipment and system performance automatically and gather all relevant operational data regardless of source system or format. Predictive modelling is used to uncover hidden patterns and correlations that may lead to failures. Using high-performance analytics, companies can reduce unplanned downtime and eliminate unnecessary maintenance by predicting the likelihood of a failure in advance to perform orderly, planned maintenance and avoid costly line stoppages.

Manufacturers can also reduce warranty costs and lessen their impact by developing an understanding of product performance. Developing products with high quality allows companies to detect potential issues and resolve issues quickly. Such practices keep product warranty costs to a minimum in terms of repair and replacement costs. Since fewer customers are affected, enterprise brand equity is protected and reputation maintained. Real-time customer feedback can provide design suggestions or early warning of warranty and recall concerns. Perceptual quality analysis can also identify issues that annoy customers but are not formally documented as complaints.

Using predictive analytics, manufacturers can identify problems in advance, prioritise, and implement quality standards. To achieve quality control in the production process, companies should perform the following:

1 *Collect the Right Quality Data*

All manufacturers collect data to check product quality, machine safety, personnel compliance, and inventory levels. Having access to this increased data collection will ensure that companies prepare for audits, prevent the release of sub-quality products, avoid injuries, increase efficiency, maintain adequate materials supplies, and deliver product orders.

2 **Predict the Best Opportunities for Improvement**

Applying this proactive, predictive strategy, manufacturers can examine poor performing areas or known facility shortcomings to obtain operational insight, identify areas for improvement and improve performance. As a result, such practices improve plant performance and quickly reduce costs, recalls, and defects.

3 **Apply Best Practices across the Enterprise**

Manufacturers can aggregate data across operations to make enterprise-wide adjustments to improve quality across multiple facilities.

4 **Improve ROI**

Manufacturers are interested in quality control and guarantee that the entire plant operates at an optimal level – uptime, staff efficiency, timely measurements, and the best product possible. Using predictive analytics, companies can improve manufacturing quality, increase equipment return on investment (ROI) and overall equipment effectiveness (OEE), anticipate needs across the enterprise, enhance brand reputation, develop a competitive advantage, and guarantee consumer safety.

Big Data and Data Analytics in Maintenance and Diagnosis

In the environment of Industry 4.0, maintenance is more than merely preventing downtimes of individual assets. Machines are increasingly interconnected along the production chain. As a result, one failing device can terminate the entire production process. Today, poor maintenance strategies can reduce the overall productive capacity of a factory by 5–20 percent. Thus, long and continuous runtimes of capital-intensive, highly-integrated assets can represent a significant competitive advantage for a company.

Predictive Maintenance Strategy and Big Data

Depending on assets, costs, and technical sophistication, several maintenance strategies can be applied. These strategies range from sheer reaction to failures to highly evolved systems optimising maintenance efforts for groups of assets. Figure 12.1 highlights four maintenance strategies by the level of sophistication.

- **Reactive Maintenance** involves responding when a failure has already occurred. It is the typical form of care, usually applied when the object is of low value, easy to replace, and does not severely impact the business process. Examples include replacing a broken light bulb or gear as well as fixing a ruptured tube.

- **Preventive Maintenance** attempts are made to prevent failure by maintaining machines at pre-scheduled time intervals. Preventive maintenance is usually employed when the maintenance cost is moderate and can be done outside of production hours. A typical example is the biannual checkups of wind turbines.
- **Condition Based Maintenance** considers the actual use of the object instead of relying on pre-scheduled intervals. It is usually done when maintenance costs are not very high and can be carried out conveniently. An example of this includes inspections for aeroplanes that have travelled a certain distance or hours (Figure 12.2).

Predictive Maintenance (PdM) utilises Big Data and advanced analytical techniques to determine equipment's health and predict failures. It reduces the uncertainty of maintenance activities and assists with identifying and solving problems before potential damage. With the implementation of Industry 4.0, additional process data is available to manufacturers, allowing for estimating the remaining runtime of assets with increasing accuracy. Predictive maintenance seeks to create transparency of the machine condition and utilise available information for maintenance decision-making. Using a Big Data platform in PdM allows for closer data acquisition and the maintenance decision support system (MDSS). These systems are used to highlight the data flow process in diagnostics and prognostics procedures. PdM analysis allows companies to identify machine or asset failure and provide accurate future breakdowns. The predictive maintenance module monitors the machine's condition and constantly aids the diagnosis and prognosis analytics

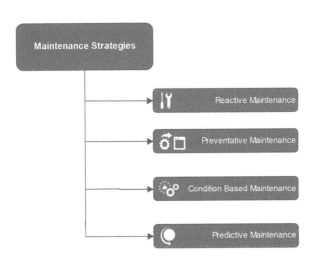

Figure 12.2 Maintenance Strategies.

process. A predictive maintenance approach is conducted when high costs are incurred due to downtimes or maintenance. Also, it can ease scheduling when maintenance activities are complex.

A Big Data platform allows for more precise sensory data acquisition and accurate maintenance decision-making to manage critical machines, with maintenance objectives in advanced or just-in-time (JIT) maintenance for supply chain management. It is practical for decision-makers to select appropriate analytic processes and recognise the functionalities of the suggested algorithms for maintenance planning. Therefore, a comprehensive discussion of algorithm design is necessary:

- Knowledge-Based System (KBS) – These analytics processes require logical deduction and cognitive reasoning to resolve complex problems and support decision-making. They attempt to extract rules for algorithm contexts by human intelligence and expert opinion, which are practical. The practical necessity of KBS is increased due to the advancement of sensor-based PdM. KBS offers a more flexible solution to improve quality in problem-solving and extract relevant data into knowledge for decision-making, like machine failure identification and taxonomy in maintenance policies. The rule-based and inference engine expert system can simulate a human expert to decrease Manufacturing Process Management (MPM) complexity and discovering hidden machine failures.
- Data Mining (DM) – The DM process seeks to develop a practical model of pattern recognition and feature analysis, which can classify data, detect irregular features, and measure data dependencies. Moving toward a total productive manufacturing system, DM is an instrument that can extract data from different types of manufacturing sources such as job shop scheduling, quality control, yield improvement, and even predictive maintenance strategy. In the DM technique, the accuracy of the information discovered increases proportionally as the amount of data from the sensors increases.

Machine Learning (ML) – ML is an online measurement tool to determine a system's health. It is used to reveal machine degradation and anomalies from the models. Self-learning and reinforcement in ML and expected degradation allow companies to predict machine failure effectively and efficiently to plan for the best before failure occurs. In ML projects, historical data helps companies to understand previous shortcomings.

Stages of Predictive Maintenance

Once system failure is identified, predictive maintenance, as seen in Figure 12.3, seeks to:

- Detect failures
- Predict outcomes

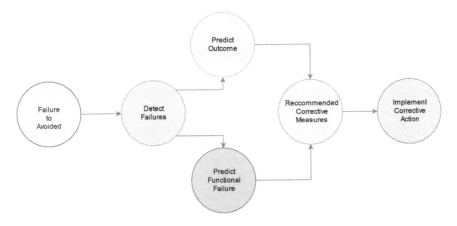

Figure 12.3 Predictive Maintenance.

- Predict functional failure
- Recommend corrective actions
- Implement corrective actions

Big Data and Data Analytics in Product Research and Development

Data analytics allows the research and development process to be more efficient by replacing instinct and guesswork with a base for decision-making. Therefore, the required resources are deployed to suitable projects and used optimally throughout the project life cycle. Companies can use data analytics to improve R&D effectiveness and efficiency by statistically modelling the complexity of tasks and identifying optimal staffing levels. It also plays an essential role in streamlining R&D processes, optimising product portfolios, and helping business leaders reduce costs.

Data analytics also improves many R&D processes, including some cumbersome, time-consuming, or error-prone tasks. For example, a large chip manufacturer wants to increase its market time by four months and stabilise development costs, growing at over 20 percent annually. However, problems often arose because the company did not automate the process for comparing the results of extensive simulations. It also faced problems assessing the quality of the test inputs. To address this, the manufacturer used advanced data analytics tools to automate its design verification process to reduce the number of regression testing and improve the test's quality. By using automation, the company was able to shorten the product development cycle to three months. Applying advanced data analytics and reducing the product development cycle leads to an additional $100 million in revenue. The manufacturers could also eliminate several development costs, resulting in over $3 million savings annually.[1]

Optimising Resources throughout the Project Life Cycle

Manufacturing enterprises can create predictive models for R&D projects by using proprietary advanced data analytics tools that employ chip- and block-level parameters (like node, power, transistor count, and memory) as proxies for design complexity. These models allow businesses to objectively view R&D performance compared with companies experiencing outstanding productivity levels. Implementing root-cause analyses can help decision-makers understand the gap between current and best-in-class performance and identify the specific drivers for productivity and increased performance. In addition, using predictive analysis R&D models provides companies with rapid insights into project performance, allowing for real-time adjustments, thus increasing the efficiency of R&D investments. For example, during a project, companies can use advanced analytics tools to simulate realistic scenarios – such as altering the number of sites or the size of teams – and predict the impact on time to market and other essential variables. Likewise, advanced data analytics tools help minimise risk, allowing companies to predict the potential consequences of new strategies before implementation.

Customer Preferences

Manufacturing companies can create products that connect with the consumer, provide increased product value, minimise the risks associated with new product development and launch, and allocate and coordinate the use of internal R&D resources efficiently. Through DM, companies can also identify customer's preferences that otherwise would not have been captured. By continuously developing products that fulfil consumer needs, manufactures can expand customer brand engagement and increase customer lifetime value.

Aggregating data and supplying it to product marketers at the idea generation stage can lead to new product ideas and concepts. In addition, companies can mine social networks, industry websites, and other online sources for relevant data about brand image and product ability to fulfil customer needs. They can also use this data to develop solutions to products currently on the market or build solutions into planned product extensions/next-generation products. Finally, through modelling and predictive analytics, companies can predict product performance pre- and post-launch in near-real-time, define the optimal distribution chains, and enhance marketing strategies to obtain the most significant number of customers at the lowest cost.

Industrial Upgrades

Big Data enables industries to harness the complexity of data interconnection and master uncertainties caused by redundancy and shortage of data. Companies can use data analytics to create models anticipating future developments, such as R&D bottlenecks that could interrupt production. With this information, manufacturers can direct the business towards increased productivity and improve many critical manufacturing dimensions, including yield, throughput, equipment availability, and operating costs. These upgrades result in production efficiency, which is essential in the manufacturing industry. The manufacturers' ability to sustain production and control schedules tightly and on track can differentiate between a good and a bad reputation. In addition, Big Data analytics lessens breakdowns and unscheduled downtime by about 25 percent.

APPLICATION CASE 12.1

Big Data Increase Manufacturing Operational Efficiency at Rolls-Royce

Rolls-Royce operates as an industrial and manufacturing company. Its headquarters is in London, United Kingdom, and was founded in 1884. The company has four primary segments: power systems, Civil Aerospace, ITP Aero (aeronautical and gas turbine manufacturer), and Defense. The company manufactures engines for commercial aircraft, business aviation markets, and regional jets. The defence unit manufactures engines for patrol aircraft, military transport planes, and submarine nuclear powers plants. Rolls-Royce also engages in research, development, design, and testing of aeronautical engines and gas turbines and provides repair and maintenance for regional airlines. Total revenue in 2020 was $11.8 billion, and in 2019 it was $16.6 billion.

The manufacturing industry requires perfection and accuracy in its operation – especially a high-tech company like Rolls-Royce that manufactures engines for large commercial aircraft. Errors may not only cost billions of dollars but human lives. Therefore perfection and error-free manufacturing process is a basic necessity in the industry. Like many other manufacturing companies, the manufacturing process of Rolls-Royce generates a massive amount of data that needs analysis to make sure that everything is going well. For example, in one of their factories in Singapore, they produce 6,000 fan blades and each fan blade produce half a terabyte of data. It is quite a lot of data that requires advanced analytic tools to make sense of. The company has various manufacturing centres worldwide, and data collected need

(Continued)

to be aggregated and analysed mainly for their jet engines' use in commercial flights flying around the world. Data on those engines needs to be collected, fed into a central system, and monitored to determine when maintenance is required or if there are possible defects on the horizon.

There is also the need of monitoring quality control for various components included in making one product or one engine. Additionally, their manufacturing systems are interconnected and have several manufacturing locations in different parts of the world. The sensors included in Rolls-Royce commercial aircraft engines gather massive amounts of data every time they are in air. This data need to be analysed in real time on the ground using advanced analytic tools to identify and correct any potential issues. The company also needs Big Data and analytical tools to analyse its design, engine simulations, and production design. Data collected by the sensors, such as temperature, vibration, and pressure on the engine, will give them an idea of whether the machines are operating at optimum capacity.

In 2013, the company fully embraced Big Data in most of its operations. They established a working partnership with the Nanyang Technology University in Singapore. The partnership focused on how Big Data can help them improve their computational engineering, manufacturing, repair technology, and control systems. They also build working relationships with other universities around the world.

Adopting Big Data and data analytics tools has immensely improved Rolls-Royce operations in many areas. For example, using Big Data analytics in diagnosing their engines and machines has significantly increased fault detection ahead of time. Detecting these faults way in advance and correcting them has reduced operation interruption and reduced the cost of repairs. The analytics has also helped them identify potential defects and eliminate them before the finished product is released for commercial use.

Adopting Big Data and predictive maintenance has helped Rolls-Royce determine when maintenance should be scheduled and predict the life cycle of most of its equipment. As a result, it helps reduce safety issues, costs and extend the life of the equipment. In addition, the analytics helps the company promptly identify potential maintenance issues, making their engines perform at their maximum level and saving on fuel and other operational costs for the airline.

A data-driven manufacturing process will minimise human error and help identify quality control issues very quickly. Big Data also improves the manufacturing process's supply chain by tracking inventories, parts, and tools in real time. The tracking and locating items needed in the manufacturing process reduce interruptions and delays, thereby increasing efficiency and optimising the manufacturing process.

Source: Yahoo Finance: https://finance.yahoo.com/quote/ RR.L/profile?p=RR.L

Source: Smart data collective: The Amazing Ways Big Data Drives Success at Rolls Royce. https://www.smartdatacollective. com/amazing-ways-big-data-drives-success-rolls-royce/

Source: Forbes: How Big Data Drives Success At Rolls-Royce: https://www.forbes.com/sites/bernardmarr/2015/06/01/ how-big-data-drives-success-at-rolls-royce/?sh=229437101d69

Key Terms

Manufacturing; Industrial Internet of Things (IIoT); Supply Chain; Quality Management; Maintenance; Manufacturing Analytics; Product Research and Development

Chapter Key Takeaways

- Manufacturing is a sequence of operations or activities that add value and bring the material closer to the desired final state. Thus, the manufacturing process makes the material more valuable.
- Data analytics allows manufacturers to monitor equipment and system performance and gather all relevant operational data regardless of source system or format.
- Predictive modelling is used to uncover hidden patterns and correlations that may lead to failures. Using high-performance analytics, companies can reduce unplanned downtime and eliminate unnecessary maintenance by predicting the likelihood of a failure in advance to perform orderly, planned maintenance, and avoid costly line stoppages.
- Predictive Maintenance (PdM) utilises Big Data and advanced analytical techniques to determine equipment's health and predict failures.
- Manufacturing analytics relies upon predictive analytics, Big Data analytics, the IIoT, machine learning, and edge computing to enable more innovative, scalable factory solutions.
- Data analytics allows the research and development process to be more efficient by replacing instinct and guesswork with a base for decision-making.
- Companies can use data analytics to improve R&D effectiveness and efficiency by statistically modelling the complexity of tasks and identifying optimal staffing levels.

Discussion Questions

1 What is your understanding of the manufacturing process?
2 What is manufacturing analytics?
3 How is Big Data used in production planning in the manufacturing industry?
4 How do chemical manufacturing companies use Big Data in their production process?
5 Quality management or control is critical in the manufacturing process; how do Big Data and data analytics add value to this process?
6 Explain what Predictive Maintenance is.
7 List and explain at least three types of maintenance discussed in this chapter.
8 What is Yield-energy throughput (YET) analytics?
9 Discuss what Profit-per-hour (PPH) maximisation analytics is.
10 How has data analytics improved research and development (R&D) in the manufacturing process?

Reference

1 Batra, G., Jacobson, Z., & Santhanam, N. (2016). Improving the semi-conductor industry through advanced analytics. McKinsey & Company, https://www.mckinsey.com/industries/semiconductors/our-insights/improving-the-semiconductor-industry-through-advanced-analytics

13 Data Analytics in the Marketing Industry

With the advent and popularity of free internet access, participating in social media and conducting transactions on the Internet has become a considerable portion of the daily routine of most individuals. As a result, all online activities contain user data that contributes to an increasingly large and varied dataset. Data analytics is used to transform this data deluge into valuable insights. Over the last decade, data analytics has revolutionised marketing, allowing brands to deliver more targeted messaging and measure their return on investment. Predictive analytics is increasingly employed to analyse the Big Data from social media and identify common behaviours between different customers. This chapter examines how companies use data analytics to personalise customer interactions, provide greater visibility, and determine which promotional campaign contributed significantly towards a purchase.

LEARNING OBJECTIVES:

At the end of this chapter, you should be able to:

- Identify what is marketing analytics and the various marketing analytics models
- Determine the value and role of Big Data and data analytics in observing customer behaviour
- Understand the value of Big Data and data analytics in market segmentation and targeted/personalised marketing
- Analyse the value and role of Big Data and data analytics in customer relationships and customer responsiveness

Introduction to the Marketing Industry

The goal of the marketing industry is to communicate companies' products and services to consumers, clients, and the general public. Thus, marketing professionals seek to bridge the gap between companies and their customers. The American Marketing Association (AMA) defines marketing as

DOI: 10.4324/9781003129356-13

"the activity, set of institutions, and processes for creating, communicating, delivering, and exchanging offerings that have value for customers, clients, partners, and society at large."[1] In other words, marketing is a combination of activities that explores and delivers an optimal mix of pricing, product development, distribution, and advertising for a company to achieve strategic goals and success. In 2021, there were over 232,482 marketing consultant companies in the United States.

Companies employ marketing consultants to advise businesses on improving their marketing tactics to understand what customers want, give them what they want, and increase profits. Companies hire marketing professionals for several reasons, including:

- to conduct marketing and sales research
- sales forecasting
- to create marketing objectives and policies
- to develop and price new products
- to improve and enhance business operations

Institutions and non-profit organisations hire marketing experts to manage products and services and promote their image and brand. Marketing companies may offer different types of services, including analytics. Marketing companies use analytics to study data upon the completion of an advertising campaign to identify where improvements are required and media research for traditional, digital, social media, and search engine marketing. These marketing companies may also offer public relations and social media research and strategy, production and creative services, consumer research, and brand development. All of these services improve connections with customers and boost sales.

Types of Marketing

The marketing industry began in the early 1900s when scholars started to study the relationship between sellers and buyers. By the 1950s, competition between companies was intense. Since then, the concept of marketing has evolved with the proliferation of ubiquitous technologies. It has also changed how companies target consumers. Consequently, there are different types of marketing[1]; these are:

1 **Influencer Marketing:** focuses on leveraging popular or famous individuals to influence potential buyers and orienting marketing activities around these individuals to drive a brand message to the broader target population.
2 **Relationship Marketing**: utilises database marketing, behavioural advertising, and analytics to target consumers specifically and create loyalty programs.

3 **Viral Marketing**: is often done using emails that facilitate and encourage individuals to pass along a marketing message.

4 **Green Marketing**: developing and marketing environmentally safe products.

5 **Keyword Marketing**: involves placing a specific ad when certain keywords and phrases are entered.

6 **Guerilla Marketing**: describes an unconventional and creative marketing strategy intended to get maximum results from minimal resources.

7 **Outbound Marketing**: is used to influence consumer awareness and preference for a brand.

8 **Inbound Marketing**: customers initiate contact with the marketer in response to various methods to gain their attention. These methods include email marketing, event marketing, content marketing, and web design.

9 **Search Engine Optimisation**: developing a marketing plan to improve visibility within search engines.

10 **Content Marketing**: creates and distributes valuable, relevant, and consistent content to attract and acquire a clearly defined audience.

Marketing and Big Data

The way marketing is conducted has changed dramatically over the years. Before the Internet and the digital age, marketing companies and the marketing department of companies relied heavily on television, radio, and print to reach their customers. In print advertising, the objective was to distribute as many print materials as possible to reach customers. In addition, the aim was to place as many ads as possible on every time slot available for television and radio. Therefore, the way ad effectiveness was measured was straightforward. If sales increase after a certain period of advertising, then the ad campaigns are effective. However, the emergence of the Internet, social media, and online shopping has changed the marketing approach. Today, consumers are spread all over the media landscape, including online, social media, radio, television, print, outdoors, Instagram, and other handheld devices that customers interact with every day. As a result, advertising is no longer as straightforward, and measuring ad effectiveness requires different methods. Because of the amount of data generated by these multiple interaction points between consumers and marketers, data analytics tools and marketing analytics have become necessary in marketing.

The main objective of marketers is to understand the customer's need, offer them a product or service they believe they need, and persuade them to buy the product. While the objective is straightforward, achieving this objective is very complex in today's digital age. Using Big Data in marketing is making it more effective. In terms of Big Data, marketers are typically interested in the customer, financial, and operational data. These are usually generated from several sources and stored in different locations.

- **Customer data** helps marketers understand their target market and generally includes names, email addresses, purchase histories, and web searches. However, customer attitude towards the brand is equally important and may be collected from social media activity, surveys, and online communities.
- **Financial data** helps businesses to measure performance and operate more efficiently. For example, the companies sales and marketing statistics, costs, and margins are all considered in this category. In addition, it can include competitors' financial data such as pricing.
- **Operational data** considers the business processes. For example, it may reflect shipping and logistics, customer relationship management systems, or feedback from hardware sensors and other sources. Data analysis of this data can lead to improved performance and reduced costs.

Marketing Analytics

Marketing analytics refers to the process of gathering marketing campaigns' data to gain insight into consumer behaviour, preferences, and what makes them buy a particular product or service. The main objective is to find patterns in the data that can be used to improve future campaigns.

Marketing analytics has the following advantages.

- It helps marketers understand what factors drive brand awareness.
- It ensures that the targeted customers see the ads that are specifically created for them. When this personalised campaign reaches the targeted audience, the potential to persuade them to buy the product or service is very high. This will lead to a higher return on investment.
- It enhances accurate prediction on where the consumer may be found so that the right ad will be presented to them at the right time for maximum effect. This avoids the random and mass communication used in the past when it was difficult to measure how effective it was to persuade consumers to buy a product or service.
- Analytics tools help marketers determine the best medium to display their ads. Consumers have many choices of media to obtain information. Therefore, marketers need to determine whether their targeted customers can be found on social media, television, print, and radio. Knowing which media customers interact with is essential in deciding which media space to buy to display an ad and achieve a successful campaign.
- It provides marketers and companies with an insight into what is trending in the market in real time. The analytics offers an idea of customer preferences, the products they are currently buying, and why they buy them. It also helps marketers identify a particular ad driving them to purchase the product or a specific product feature? Knowing this information is vital as this knowledge allows marketers to adjust their messaging to optimise future advertising.

- Marketing analytics provide real-time product intelligence to marketers and companies. The analytics provide how a company's product stacks up with a competitor's product on the market. By engaging consumers through surveys, feedback, reviews, pooling, and sentiment analysis, marketers can understand customers' perceptions of a particular product compared to similar items. Product intelligence helps marketers target customers interested in their goods to persuade them to buy the product.
- It helps the customer support team to do their job effectively. In addition, the analytics will provide insight into which area of the buying process customers are facing challenges. For example, are customers struggling with the online check-out process, payment with credit or debit cards, refunds, and delivery delays? Knowing the issues affecting the customer buying process will make the customer support team provide better services to the company's customers.
- It helps companies benchmark their marketing campaigns against competitors. Data analytics also allows marketers to see the effectiveness of each campaign and decide how to improve the messaging to persuade customers.
- It allows marketers and companies to quickly collect and analyse a vast amount of consumer data to make real-time and data-driven campaign decisions.
- Because of the speed at which data analytics tools can collect, organise, and process data, companies can adjust ad placement quickly to the targeted market before the campaign ends. Therefore, the analytics inform the marketers whether the targeted consumers engage with the product content on a particular media space in the morning, afternoon, or evening.
- Data analytics tools also offer insight into how consumers react to a particular advertisement; whether the messaging in the campaign promotes brand-building and brand awareness in the eyes of the consumers.

Marketing Analytics Methods

Each company or marketer tries to measure a different aspect of the consumer and their campaign. Depending on the Key Performance Index (KPI) a marketer is trying to achieve, there are various methods to analyse the data. For example, one marketer may want to measure conversion rate, and another brand awareness, and lead capture. Therefore, each of them may need to use different analytic methods. The analytics process can be complex and challenging because of the vast amount of data available to marketers. Big Data enables companies to collect customers' data every step on the Internet that engages with their product or brand, including clicks, views, and impressions. While the ability to gather a large amount of data is welcoming to marketers, it also comes with challenges such as the quality of data, the usefulness of data collected, and how best to organise it and select which one to use. Therefore, marketers need to decide which KPIs are essential and what metrics should be measured. For example, do they want to increase brand loyalty, brand awareness, conversion rate, and clicks? The answer to these questions will help to determine the type of data to collect and analyse. Therefore, knowing the objective of the campaign help determines the kind of analytic method to deploy. The most basic and popular analytics methods are:

- Media Mix Models (MMM) Analytics
- Multi-Touch Attribution (MTA) Analytics
- Unified Marketing Measurement (UMM) Analytics

Media Mix Models (MMM) Analytics

Media Mix modelling is a marketing analytics approach that uses aggregate data to measure the effect of a marketing campaign. The model allows marketers to identify which variables contribute the most to the campaign's success. This is possible because MMM uses both non-linear and multiple-linear regression to analyse the data. That is, it examines the relationships between various variables that make up a particular campaign. For example, a marketer will like to know which media space (outdoor, digital, radio, or TV) increase of ad spending will increase the sales of a particular product. A marketer may also like to know the effectiveness of marketing in different parts of a country using several radio stations and television networks at other times of the day. The result of the analytics will show companies the effectiveness of the campaign across media channels. With such insight, marketers can adjust the variables least impactful to optimise their ads as quickly as possible. MMM analytics provides high-level insights into marketing effectiveness and allows marketers to forecast sales accurately and allocate future ad spending effectively. MMM looks at aggregate data over two to three years, and it provides a holistic view of the marketing campaign. It provides insights into how variables such as holidays, weather, and seasons affect sales and advertising. It offers a historical perspective, patterns, and trends of sales and campaign effectiveness over many years. Marketers can use MMM analytics in long-range planning and forecasting of sales and campaign deployments.

The challenge of MMM is that it uses aggregate data and does not analyse user-level brand and product interactions and engagement on variables such as clicks. As a result, MMM does not track the customer's journey to a buying decision. The model is very good at measuring the effectiveness of marketing campaigns and provides high-level insights. However, today's media space is fragmented. Customers are dispersed over the media eco-system that aggregated analytics may not be instrumental in some instances where marketers want to personalise their campaign to individual customers. Therefore, some of the MMM analytics do not provide insight into the customer experience and brand perception.

Multi-Touch Attribution (MTA) Analytics

The MTA model is a marketing analytics method that measures and evaluates the effect of each touchpoint on customers buying journey that leads to purchasing a product or services. Touchpoints are engagements and interactions between a company's product or services and a customer that occur along their journey until they buy the product. For example, when customers consider purchasing a product, they conduct some research on the item. During and after the research on the Internet, they will be targeted by various ads, emails, discounts, product reviews, and promotional materials to influence them to buy the product. Each of these attempts to influence the customer represents a touchpoint. MTA weighs and evaluates the impact of each of these touchpoints on a sale.

Touchpoint plays a significant role in marketing analytics and provides valuable data to measure the effectiveness of a campaign through MTA analytics. Examples of commonly use touchpoints in marketing analytics are:

- Social Media
- Customer Loyalty Programs
- Online Advertisement
- Television advertising
- Radio advertising
- Outdoor advertising
- Digital Marketing Content
- Product Reviews
- Point of Sale
- E-commerce
- Product Feedback Surveys
- Emails

Each touchpoint could be the significant moment that influences the customer to buy the product or have a favourable perception about the brand or product. Marketing analytics use each of these touchpoints to determine the most significant customer buying journey.

MTA analytics allows marketers to determine the impact of each of these touchpoints on a sale. This is significant as it enables marketers to focus on those touchpoints that impact a sale and allocate their ad spending effectively. Knowing which touchpoint influences a customer's purchase allows marketers to customise and personalise their advertisement. There are different types of MTA analytics models.

- First-Touch Attribution
- Last-Touch Attribution
- Linear Multi-touch Attribution Model
- U-Shaped Multi-Touch Attribution Model

- Time Decay Multi-Touch Attribution
- W-shaped Multi-Touch Attribution Model
- Full Path Multi-Touch Attribution Model
- Custom Multi-Touch Attribution Model

First-Touch Attribution Analytics. These analytics emphasise the first interaction customers have with a product or service. This model gives the credit for a sale to the first touchpoint a customer comes into contact with a product. It ignores any other touchpoints along the customer buying journey. The model considers the first interaction to be the most significant, especially in niche situations. In this model, the first interaction is the most important as it drives the customer to do something about the product.

   Last-Touch Attribution Analytics. This analytical model considers the last marketing interaction, leading to a sale as the most significant. Therefore, the Last-Touch Attribution analytical model gives all of the credit to the last touchpoint. The rationale for assigning full credit to the last interaction is that this model proposes that the other touchpoints on the customer's buying journey increase awareness of the product and focus on the one that drove conversion. Of course, many will disagree that the other touchpoints on the customer buying journey are relevant.

   Linear Multi-Touch Attribution Analytics. This analytical model considers that each interaction a customer makes with a product along the customer journey is equally important. Therefore, the model gives each touchpoint equal credit for a sale. Of course, it can be argued that not all touchpoints have equal significance in influencing a customer to buy a product. Still, the Linear multi-Touch Attribution analytics model considers that every interaction with a customer is essential. Therefore, it does not ignore any touchpoint.

   U-shaped Multi-Touch Attribution Analytics. This analytical model considers the first and the last interaction customers have with a product before buying the product to be the most important. This analytic model gives 40 percent credit to the first touch and 40% credit to the last touchpoint that leads to a sale. The remaining touchpoints along the customer buying journey are allocated the remaining 20 percent. The 20 percent is equally divided into the other touchpoints along the way. This model emphasises the importance of the first and last touchpoints, which seems logical to most marketing analysts and executives that the initial and final interactions are critical.

   Time Decay Multi-Touch Attribution Analytics. This analytic model considers the interactions customers have with a product closer to the time of purchase to be the most important. Therefore, the model assigns higher weights to the touchpoints closest to a sale than the first and the preceding touchpoints along the customer journey. For example, the Time Decay Multi-Touch model gives 50 percent to the last touchpoint, 25 percent to the touchpoint before the last touchpoint, 20 percent to those before, and 5 percent to the first touchpoint. The model considers the other touchpoints as awareness interaction and should have lesser weights in persuading customers to purchase a product or service.

W-Shaped Multi-Touch Attribution Analytics. This analytic model considers three interactions between the customer and product to be significant. These interactions are the first touchpoints, the lead creation touchpoint, and the opportunity creation touchpoints. The model assigned 30 percent credit to each interaction with the customer and allocated 10 percent to the other touchpoints along the customer buying journey. A lead creation in this model occurs when a customer signs up for more information and receives updates on the product. The opportunity creation represents the last touchpoint that persuades the customer to buy the product. Even though it is challenging to categorise customers buying journeys perfectly, the model has been helpful in the instance wherein the buying stages can be easily identifiable.

Full Path Multi-Touch Attribution Analytics. This analytic model considers four interactions between the customer and product to be very significant. In addition to the three touchpoints considered by the W-Shaped model, the Full Path model considers the final touchpoint equally important. Therefore, the model gives 22.5 percent credit to the first touchpoint, 22.5 percent to the lead creation touchpoint, 22.5 percent to the opportunity creation touchpoint, and 22.5 percent to the final touchpoint. The other touchpoints along the customer buying journey are allocated 10 percent of the credit. The full path analytic model is standard in business to business (B2B), and other interactions wherein the buying journey could easily be identified and categorised. For example, when buying a custom-made luxury car.

Custom Multi-Touch Attribution Analytics. This analytical model gives the marketer the power to determine which interaction is essential along the customer buying journey. The Custom Multi-touch model allows marketers to develop weighing attributes as to which touchpoint is more significant and contributes the most to persuade customers to buy the product. The flexibility of this model makes it attractive to most marketers, but it requires advanced analytical tools to determine which touchpoint weighs better than the other.

Benefits of Multi-touch Attribution Analytics

MTA is essential for determining the impact of digital campaigns because it provides user-level data that can accurately track a customer's buying journey. MTA provides a clear view of the entire customer buying journey across several touchpoints the customer engages with along the way to a buying decision. As a result, MTA is valuable to marketers because it allows them to target the specific touchpoint that has the most impact on a customer's buying journey, increasing return on investment on ad spending.

Unified Marketing Measurement (UMM) Analytics

Unified Marketing Measurement is a marketing analytics method that brings together the MTA Analytics Model and the Marketing Mix Analytic Model to provide a cohesive and comprehensive view of the marketing performance of a campaign. Also known as Unified Marketing Impact Analytics (UMIA), UMM uses both aggregate and user-level data to measure marketing effectiveness and provide marketers actionable insight into optimising marketing spend.

Measuring the effectiveness of a marketing campaign is crucial as it helps marketers reduce ad spend waste and increase ROI. Since it combines both the top-down approach of the Media Mix model and the bottom-up approach of the Multi-touch approach, it is considered the most advanced analytic approach. This analytical model can use offline and online marketing data and non-marketing data, such as the weather, to develop accurate measurements. Unified marketing analytics combines broader marketing data, external data, and user-level data from all marketing mediums in its analytics. Since it is difficult to determine which marketing medium (offline or online) the user will interact with, the unified approach covers all touchpoints a customer may interact with a product or brand.

Benefits and Challenges of Marketing Analytic Models

Marketers and companies have the choice of numerous marketing analytics models. The choice of a model may depend on several factors. First, the marketers must consider that today's customers' buying journey may involve multiple touchpoints in different media platforms and use various devices before finally deciding to buy a product. To choose a model, marketers also need to consider the life cycle of a sale, if the touchpoints can be easily identified, and the type of KPIs to be achieved. Finally, decision-makers need to consider: are they trying to improve user experience, increase sales, or improve ROI? Answering these questions will help marketers determine the analytical model to choose. For example, most of the MTA analytics work well in measuring digital advertising effectiveness because it is easier to track down customer buying journeys on a digital media platform than on non-digital platforms. However, tracking offline touchpoints such as TV ads or outdoor advertising on a billboard is challenging.

Marketing Analytics Tools Are Effective When

- Providing real-time analytics insights
- Integrating offline and online data
- analysing in-depth personal-level data
- Measuring brand and ad effectiveness
- Providing insight into media planning and buying for effective ad placement on all the media eco-system.

The Value and Role of Big Data and Data Analytics in Observing Customer Behaviour

Once marketers understand customer behaviour and needs, the sales team can sell the product and offer more efficient services. Big Data and data analytics have given marketers various options to observe and understand how customers behave. As customers interact with the marketers and retailers through multiple channels, data is collected, aggregated, and analysed to help marketers position spending patterns in a more targeted and effective way. This section details various data sources such as social media, location data, web traffic, and product usage data. These sources provide marketers with the ability to observe customers' behaviours.

Data from Shoppers

The Internet offers a vast wealth of information on consumer behaviour and product trend. The data is not just retrieved from site browsing and viewing. It is also gathered from online shopping, brand comparisons, and reading product or service reviews. This kind of data is most valuable. It leads marketers to what consumers are seeking, allows marketers to know if consumers are willing to pay the current price, and provides the percentage of those visitors to the site who will not make a purchase. Automation in online shopping makes all this data possible, and marketers have come to rely heavily on this kind of analytics. Now in the age of COVID-19, where more people are shopping online, it's increasingly essential for companies to take advantage of the click-stream data (the detailed log of the consumer's online interaction) to understand the buying psychology of their target market.

Data from the Purchase Basket

While shopping data provide insight into consumer behaviour, purchase data give even more details about the customer. For instance, in a single purchase, details such as location, amount, type of loan merchant (credit cards), type of purchase, type of shipment, the destination address, and purchase frequency are gathered for data analysis.

Data from Product Usage

Product usage data yields insights into factors such as channel-surfing, device and application platform access, device data usage, and content viewing. Marketers surmise that if they know the viewing habits of consumers and the kind of devices they stream on, then advertising can be more targeted. However, further research into this indicates that product usage data cannot fully ascertain consumer behaviour because discrepancies can cause an error in analysis. For example, the truth in product usage data may be difficult to determine without real-time observation. In addition, using a device or an application/platform does not necessarily mean that the consumer is actively engaging with it. It could simply mean the application or the device has been left running while the user is involved in another activity. Finding a way around this issue is relevant for marketers, as this kind of data can reveal valuable information if accurate data is harnessed.

Data from Purchaser Location

Location data refers to the collection of mobility data, and this includes location analytics. Nowadays, marketers find it helpful to combine social media data with mobility data to get valuable access to consumer profiles, behaviours, and travel patterns. These, in combination, can yield information about an individual's preferences, lifestyle, daily and monthly routines. With this kind of detailed data, marketers can conduct more targeted campaigns.

Sentiment Analytics from Social Media Data

Social media data gathered from public websites and online social platforms play a crucial role in public sentiment analytics. Many marketers now find this data type valuable because it can predict trends, a valuable sales and market forecasting tool.

Data from Customer Conversation

Customer communication with customer services, such as web chats, call centres' interactions, and emails, captures essential data that peeks into the consumer's intention. This data also fills the gap and answers questions marketers ask – Why was the purchase not made? Such insight can help marketers address the issues that caused the sale to be unsuccessful. It also allows companies to pinpoint or identify gaps within the buying process.

APPLICATION CASE 13.1

How Big Data Helps Pepsi Target Its Customer and Increase Sales

Pepsi is a worldwide food and beverage corporation that has operations in almost every country in the world. Its leading brands include Frito-Lay, Quaker Foods, Cheetos, Doritos, PepsiCo Beverages, Lipton, Gatorade, Tropicana, and Aquafina. Its products include branded dips, cheese-flavoured snacks, tortillas, corn, potato, chips, rice, cereals, pasta, granola bars, Oatmeal, grits, cakes, fountain syrups, tea, coffee, ready-to-drink tea, juices, and dairy products. The company serves and distributes its products to food service customers, drug stores, grocery stores, convenience stores, membership stores, discounters, e-commerce retailers, discount/dollar stores, and authorised independent bottlers. Pepsi corporation was founded in 1898. The company is headquartered in Purchase, New York. It recorded a total revenue of $70.3 billion in 2020 and a market value of over $214 billion in September 2021.

For many years the company has been trying to find a way of using the vast amount of data it collects every day, both in-store and online business. Therefore, to understand its customers and make its supply chain more efficient in over 200 countries, it created its own in-house data analytic platform called Pep Worx.

The Pep Worx analytic platform has ten variables ranging from the most valuable shopper to the most beneficial store. Pep Worx is a cloud-based platform that is helping the company and its affiliates make a data-driven decision of product assortments and identifying shoppers by shipping habit and location. Jeff Swearingen, Senior Vice President of Marketing at PepsiCo, said, "Pep Worx is an analytics capability that allows us to hopefully create a more personal experience for consumers and be a better partner to our retailers."

The company is leveraging the power of Big Data to make its operations more efficient. Therefore, it uses this data analytics platform to determine what kind of promotions to offer and which items are to be stocked in the stores. The platform also helped them identify who their customers are and where they are located. In addition, PepsiCo uses the data to map out customers' shopping places and shopping habits for in-store and online purchases. They also use it for targeted media campaigns for specific products.

For example, in 2017, the company launched Quaker Overnight Oats. This is a single-serve cup of dry oats soaked overnight in milk or yoghurt in the refrigerator for on-the-go breakfast. The company uses its data analytic platform Pep Worx for a targeted marketing campaign. Out of the 110 million US households in its database, the analytical platform was able to identify 24 million that are a good fit for the product. The analytics was able to locate these customers by location and shopping preference. The targeted marketing campaign was highly successful. This is what Jeff Swearingen, Senior Vice President of Marketing at PepsiCo, said:

> We were able to launch the product using very targeted media, all the way through targeted in-store support, to engage those most valuable shoppers and bring the product to life at retail in a unique way. These priority customers drove 80% of the product's sales growth in the first 12 weeks after launch,

The Big Data analytics platform helps them identify their customers' brand, product, and location preferences. Even though PepsiCo brands

(Continued)

are popular, the company wants to make sure that customers have access to their favourite brands and products in the store or online at all times. In other words, they want to match their customers and the product choice at the most convenient location possible. The platform has helped with in-store product placement, inventory selection, promotion, and advertising strategies. Big Data analytics has also helped them bringing new products into the market based on customer analytics trends. It has also helped them determine store format, store location, and getting the right products in the right stores at the right time.

Source: PepsiCo 2020 SEC Annual Report. https://www. pepsico.com/docs/album/annual-reports/pepsico-inc-2020-annual-report.pdf?sfvrsn=d25439e4_4: *Source*: Supermarket News: *Using data to help retailers get closer to customers*: https:// www.supermarketnews.com/marketing/using-data-help-retailers-get-closer-customers: *Source*: *How PepsiCo is leveraging digital with its big data platform.* https://techhq.com/2018/10/ how-pepsico-is-leveraging-digital-with-its-big-data-platform/ : *Source*: Built-in Beta: PepsiCo embraces big data with new Pep Worx platform https://builtin.com/big-data/ pepsico-embraces-big-data-platform-pep-worx

The Value and Role of Big Data and Data Analytics in Market Segmentation and Targeted/Personalised Marketing

Market segmentation has been the focus of marketing for many years, but the availability of Big Data and data analytics makes this process more efficient and effective. For example, marketers can use data analytics to group customers by geography, ethnicity, religion, preferences, and social class. In this case, the marketing campaign can be targeted or personalised to the different buckets of market segmentation. Therefore, analytics can reduce the marketing cost and increase sales because the campaigns are not random but are targeted to a specific group based on predictive models. This section covers how Big Data plays a fundamental role in a more targeted and personalised marketing campaign.

Customer Profile Analytics

The customer profile is one of the most analytical artefacts marketers can use to gain information and evaluate the target market. It provides detailed information to help marketers segment the market based on needs, buying preferences, personality traits, and lifestyles. Big Data contains many different forms of data gathered on a single customer. However, in most cases, this data is scattered in various departments, but data analytic tools can integrate the information easily into a Master Data Management (MDA) system. The customer MDA system aggregates all the customer data into one unified database. As the number of new transactions increases, the database is updated so marketers can accurately predict customers' buying preferences, payment methods, vacation destinations, travel habits, and other information that will help them personalise the marketing campaign.

Social Media Review Analytics

Big Data and customer analytics have led to the collaboration of social media and customer reviews and have revolutionised marketing and the customer's buying experience. Social media has provided marketers with a platform to communicate and understand customer's opinions about products and services. It offers marketing companies a first-hand look at what customers think via reviews and ratings. Reviews are vital as they allow companies to take note of trends and improve their products and services. Realising how powerful reviews are, Amazon encourages buyers to provide feedback about their purchasing and product experience. The social media platform offers a unique service for marketers, grouping buyers according to their interests. This allows marketers to provide targeted campaigns to a more specific group of buyers, otherwise known as micro-segments. Customer review analytics have been effective in market segmentations.

Big Data and Pricing

Pricing, like the rest of marketing and sales, has been affected dynamically by Big Data. The ability to find price deals online has created a new marketplace with new types of buyers. Now that consumers are armed with platforms like Bing, Travelocity, and Priceline, where they can search and compare prices against each other, more and more buyers search for deals and low prices. One advantage of this is real-time data that allow prices to be updated in real-time. Therefore, companies and marketers can interact simultaneously and offer more deals to customers while shopping. A second advantage is that companies can now keep up with their competitors by analysing the data for faster price optimisation. Data analytics has made online shopping a more active marketplace. Today's marketers and customers are brought close together in a virtual world negotiation, even though they may be miles and miles apart.

Marketing Metrics and Big Data

Knowing the company's marketing metrics is essential for marketers to evaluate and measure marketing campaigns and advertising effectiveness. The marketing metrics yield valuable information such as conversion rates, cost per lead, and click and indicate the campaign's success. With Big Data, Google analytics, social media analytics, and personalised marketing, companies can now effectively measure and monitor most of these metrics, such as customer acquisition cost (CAC), customer attrition, and customer retention.

Customer Attrition Analytics. Attrition refers to customers whose membership, subscription, and/or auto-ship payments are delinquent or in arrears. Attrition, also referred to as churn, is another concept that must be monitored and tracked. Analytics has helped tremendously in this area, allowing companies to keep more abreast of delinquent customers. Customer service can begin reaching out to the customer (by their preferred mode of contact) to remedy the issue with an automatic prompt.

Customer Retention Analytics. While customer acquisition is vital for the success of a company, customer retention is equally important. Customer satisfaction plays a crucial role in keeping the customer loyal to the company, brand, and product. Good customer service, a strong brand, and a rewarding purchase experience can inspire customer loyalty or retention. Data analytics helps companies to determine the most critical factors that contribute to customer retention.

The Value of Big Data and Data Analytics in Customer Relationships and Customer Responsiveness

Responding to customer demands promptly is the path to customer satisfaction. Also, improving customer satisfaction is a core aspect of marketing. Customer responsiveness is a big focus to many successful companies, but this can only be achieved if there is real-time feedback. Using Big Data, mainly social media data, companies can have a conversation with customers, allowing them to adjust quickly to the campaign, product, price, and even product design. The CRM system is possible because of Big Data.

Customer Relationship Analytics

A company's relationship with its customers needs to be carefully managed and nurtured. Data analytics tools are making this process very effective. For example, the Customer Relationship Management (CRM) analytic tool helps businesses gain new customers and keep existing ones by creating a line of communication between customers and marketers. The analytical tool collects and organises data, such as website visits, browsing and buying history, tracks customers' buying habits, and records of complaints.[2] This analytic tool is viable for a marketing company for the following reasons.

- It provides an overall picture of the customers' profile and behaviour. As a result, when looking at complaints, it helps companies prioritise complaints.

- Customers are categorised according to the details from the profile data. For example, they are organised by shopping patterns and order history.
- The data collected is valuable and extensive and can be used to push marketing campaigns and targeted advertising.
- Marketers will be able to communicate more efficiently with customers as they become more aware of their needs.

Key Term

Marketing Analytics; Key Performance Index (KPI); Media Mix Models (MMM) Analytics; Multi-Touch Attribution (MTA) Analytics; Unified Marketing Measurement (UMM); First-Touch Attribution; Last-Touch Attribution; Linear Multi-Touch Attribution Model; U-Shaped Multi-Touch Attribution Model; Time Decay Multi-Touch Attribution; W-Shaped Multi-Touch Attribution Model; Full Path Multi-Touch Attribution Model; Custom Multi-Touch Attribution Model; Customer Attrition Analytics; Customer Retention Analytics; Customer Relationship Analytics

Chapter Key Takeaways

- The main objective of marketers is to understand the customer's need, offer them a product or service you believe they need, and persuade them to buy the product.
- Marketing analytics enhance accurate prediction on where the consumer may be found so that the right ad will be presented to them at the right time for maximum effect.
- Data analytics provide marketers and companies with an insight into what is trending in the market in real-time. The analytics give them an idea of customer preferences, the product they are currently buying, and why they buy it.
- The marketing analytic tools allow marketers and companies to quickly collect and analyse a vast amount of consumer data to make real-time and data-driven campaign decisions.
- Depending on the Key Performance Index (KPI) a marketer is trying to achieve, there are various methods to analyse the data. For example, one marketer may want to measure brand awareness, lead capture, and others to measure conversion rate; each of them may need to use different analytic methods.
- Media-Mix Model analytics provides high-level insights into marketing effectiveness and allows marketers to forecast sales accurately and allocate future ad spending effectively.
- The Multi-Touch Attribution model is a marketing analytics method that measures and evaluates the effect of each touchpoint on customers' buying journey that leads to purchasing a product or service.

- Multi-Touch Attribution analytics allows marketers to determine the impact of each touchpoint on a sale.
- Because it combines both the top-down approach of the Media Mix model and the bottom-up approach of the Multi-touch approach, Unified Marketing Measurement is considered the most advanced analytic approach.
- Product usage data yields insights into factors such as channel-surfing, device and application platform access, device data usage, and content viewing.
- The marketing metrics yield valuable information such as conversion rates, cost per lead, and click and indicate the campaign's success.

Discussion Questions

1 Before the digital age, what was the traditional marketing medium advertisers used to reach their customers?
2 What is one of the main objectives of marketing?
3 What do you understand by marketing analytics?
4 List and explain four benefits of marketing analytics.
5 Explain what Media-Mix model marketing analytics is.
6 How is Media-Mix marketing analytics beneficial to marketers?
7 What are the challenges of Media-mix model analytics?
8 Explain what Multi-Touch Attribution analytics is.
9 What is the significant difference between Media-Mix and Multi-Touch Attribution analytics?
10 Explain what touchpoints are and give at least six examples of touchpoints.
11 Explain what Linear Multi-touch Attribution Model is.
12 What is a W-shaped Multi-Touch Attribution Model?
13 What is a Custom Multi-Touch Attribution Model?
14 What are the challenges of marketing analytics models?
15 What is the value of Big Data and data analytics in observing the behaviours of customers?
16 How has data analytics made marketing segmentation easier?

References

1 https://www.ama.org/the-definition-of-marketing-what-is-marketing/
2 https://www.vault.com/industries-professions/industries/marketing/industry-outlook

14 Data Analytics in the Transportation Industry

The movement of goods from one location to another is increasingly complex. Some call it supply chain logistics. The need to meet customers' demands to receive products on time and for travellers to reach their destination on time has put pressure on the transportation industry. The transportation industry is a blend of the networks, infrastructure, equipment, information technology, and employees necessary to transport various products and people safely and efficiently throughout the nation and worldwide. As a result, the transportation industry produces vast amounts of diverse and complex data. Data collected from the transportation industry can predict traffic flow in real time and predict commuters' journey patterns (rail, bus, air), leading to better public transportation service planning. This chapter details how data analytics is used to predict traffic accidents, provide real-time response to emergencies, assist with maintenance decisions, improve customer experience, reduce environmental impact, and increase safety.

LEARNING OBJECTIVES:

At the end of this chapter, you should be able to:

- Define and identify the primary modes of transportation
- Understand the value of Big Data and data analytics in traffic management and efficiency
- Recognise the importance of Big Data and data analytics in road safety and real-time response to emergencies
- Understand the value of Big Data and data analytics in logistic and supply chain management
- Assess how Big Data and data analytics is used to reduce environmental impact

What Is Transportation?

Transportation involves moving goods and people from one place to another. It is a basic human need and has played a significant role in the development

DOI: 10.4324/9781003129356-14

of human civilisation. Moreover, it is among the more vital economic activities for a business. Moving goods from locations where they are sourced to areas where they are demanded, transportation provides the essential service of linking suppliers and customers. However, at times there are barriers to the efficient exchange of goods and services.

The solution to transportation problems must be analytically based, economically sound, socially credible, environmentally sensitive, and practically acceptable and sustainable. Additionally, the transportation solution should be safe, rapid, comfortable, convenient, economical, and eco-friendly for both men and material.

The ease or difficulty with which a business can transport goods within a country can affect its competitiveness in global trade. Suppliers can efficiently ship their goods to end-users when transporting merchandise is easy and costs are relatively low. The demand for transportation depends on the need for other goods and services in the economy. When a company seeks supplies from distant locations, there is a demand for transportation. Likewise, when consumers have demand for goods produced elsewhere, transportation is demanded. So the need for transportation tends to follow the economic activity in an area. Therefore transportation shipment data present an accurate, timely picture of economic vitality for a region or country.

Transportation also plays a crucial role in emergencies and humanitarian relief. Transportation is vital to supporting lifesaving missions. Relief companies use advanced transportation methods to help deploy essential resources to those in need whenever and wherever there is a humanitarian crisis.

Core Components of Transportation

There are four essential components of transportation[1]:

1 **Modes.** These are primarily a form of vehicle that is used to support people's mobility or goods. Some methods are designed to carry only passengers or merchandise, while others can take both. However, transportation is multi-modal and considers travel by air, land, and sea.
2 **Infrastructures.** These are the physical support of the different transport modes via rail tracks, canals, highways, and terminals like ports or airports. Infrastructures also include superstructures. These are movable assets with a shorter lifespan. The infrastructure would be assets such as the runways for an airport, while the superstructure would be the terminals and control equipment. The infrastructure would include piers and navigation channels for a port, while the superstructure would be cranes and yard equipment. Transportation infrastructure plays a critical role in the production and generation of wealth. Transport infrastructure is necessary to support the market exchange of final goods and inputs. Investments in transportation infrastructure are essential to improve

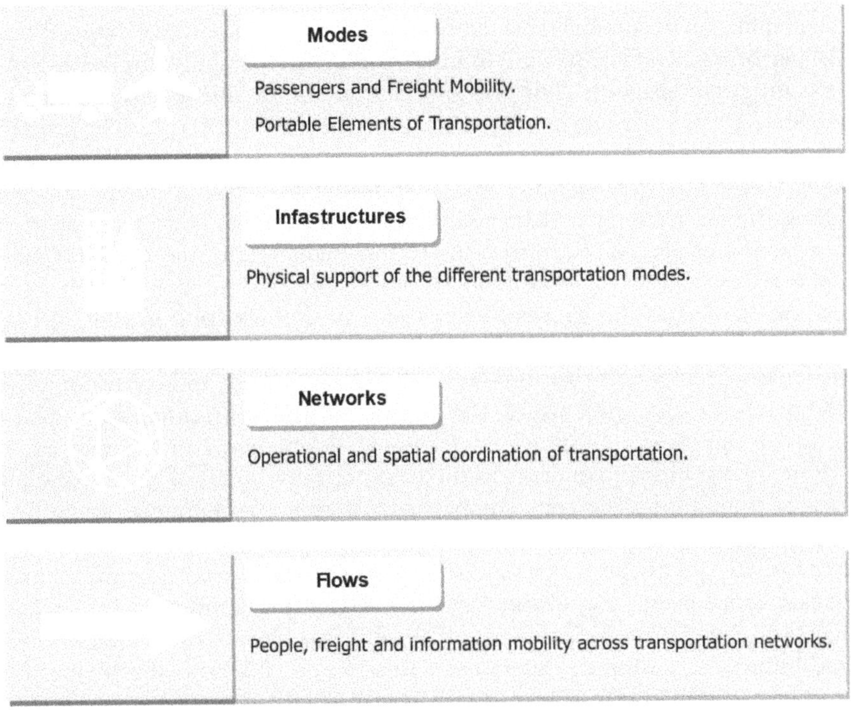

Modes

Passengers and Freight Mobility.

Portable Elements of Transportation.

Infastructures

Physical support of the different transportation modes.

Networks

Operational and spatial coordination of transportation.

Flows

People, freight and information mobility across transportation networks.

Figure 14.1 Components of Transportation.

connectivity as this is most effective at delivering long-term growth and increase productivity. It is often referred to as the backbone of a modern economy (Figure 14.1).

3 **Networks.** This refers to the framework of routes within a system of locations identified as nodes. A route is a single association between two nodes that are part of a more extensive network. They can refer to tangible routes such as roads and rails or less tangible routes such as air and sea corridors – a system of linked locations used to represent the functional and spatial organisation of the transportation system. Transportation networks are used to indicate which areas are connected and how they are serviced. Some sites within a network have greater access (more connections) than others (fewer connections).

4 **Flows.** These refer to the movements of people, goods, and information over their respective networks. Flows have origins, intermediary locations, and destinations. The sources, destinations, and intermediate points are collectively called network nodes, and the transportation links connecting nodes are called arcs. An intermediary location is often required to move from an origin to a destination. For instance, flying from one airport to another may require transit at the hub airport.

Big Data in the Transportation Sector

The rapid growth of cities and their population has made travel demand and the performance of transportation infrastructure a critical task for transportation and urban planners. The fast-growing rate of urbanisation is placing increasing stress on already burdened transportation infrastructure. The growth of ubiquitous mobile computing presents new opportunities to measure the demand for this infrastructure, diagnose problems, and plan for the future. Using Big Data resources that capture the movement of vehicles and users in real time provides solutions to some of the challenges of the transportation industry. However, these new opportunities are associated with new estimation challenges, integration, and validation with existing models. While these data are readily available at low cost, they often lack essential contextual, demographic information owing to privacy reasons and consist of noise and biases. Despite these issues, Big Data for urban and transportation planning can significantly improve the transportation network in urban areas.

One of the biggest concerns in the transportation industry is the constant lack of time. Using Big Data comprises collecting relevant electronic information from various sources in a brief period. The gathered data is then analysed to identify patterns that can help the company to predict future events. This practice brings many advantages to the transportation industry, such as increasing operational efficiency and flexibility, reducing fuel consumption, and improving customer experiences. In addition, Big Data also helps with improving safety in the transportation sector.

Data sensors provide real-time information regarding vehicle performance. For example, they provide accurate data regarding travel speeds, transit, and length of idleness. Sensors also monitor the condition of the equipment and the entire engine. This allows for the prediction of errors and timely preparations for maintenance. In addition, Big Data can be used to provide real-time information such as traffic jams and weather and road conditions to help companies and travellers maintain high safety levels.

Transportation and Big Data Analytics

Public transportation organisations generate vast volumes of data as part of their daily operations. For example, Automatic Vehicle Location (AVL) systems track the location of buses and trains and collect a constant stream of information. Passenger counting systems record the number of passengers getting on and off each stop, fare collection systems and smart cards record trips, transfers, and travel patterns among passengers. Other data sources include time tracking, absenteeism data, safety incidents, and other employment data sources. Transportation agencies are using these data sources to provide valuable insights and improve public transportation service and efficiency. Emerging technologies and services are facilitating transformative data analysis. For example, cloud computing permits data sharing across an entire organisation, allowing convenient access for different departments. Transportation organisations have traditionally been impeded in planning, managing, and evaluating their services by relying heavily on costly and unreliable manual data collection systems. However, information and telecommunications technology development has changed the amount, type, and quality of data available to planners and decision-makers. Transport agencies can estimate and predict travel demand by utilising multiple automatic data sources, such as smart cards, GPS vehicle locations, cell phone records, and mobility tracking apps. These data can also estimate and predict travel demand, explore behavioural regularities, quantify service reliabilities, and evaluate demand programs. Advanced analytics can help managers identify traffic problems and answer questions about the optimal time to start bus lanes and the best place to add more bus lanes.

The Value of Big Data and Data Analytics in Traffic Management

As one essential element of human life, transportation also confronts the promises and challenges brought about by Big Data. Big Data in the transportation arena comes from several different sources and over vast geographic regions. Currently, the most widely used data sources are traffic surveillance systems. Data sources used in the transportation sector include:

- in-roadway detectors
- over-roadway detectors and off-roadway technologies
- demographic data
- weather reporting system
- mobile devices
- social media data geometric characteristics
- crash data extensively used in traffic operation, safety management, and research

This data contains pictures and video and is sometimes stored in different divisions, which can be very difficult to use. Moreover, traffic management facilities, equipment, and application systems often operate in silos and need to be integrated. Finally, as cities continue to develop, the scale of traffic monitoring operations has also increased.

Big Data in the transportation sector is enabled by the rapid growth of the Intelligent Transportation System (ITS). Operational efficiency and traffic safety are priorities among highway system performance measurements. While efficiency can be evaluated in terms of traffic congestion, safety is measured through crash analysis. With the spread of Big Data, monitoring and improving both operation and safety proactively in real time have become significant. Effective strategies to improve traffic operation and safety simultaneously require a deep understanding of their characteristics and relationship. Using Big Data applications, decision-makers can efficiently achieve both priorities.

The demand and growth in vehicular traffic have caused problems for most major cities and developed countries. For example, in 2018, traffic problems cost $ 461billion in Britain, Germany, and the US, equivalent to $ 975 per person.[2] The annual financial cost of traffic congestion has risen to 97 billion, and each day Germans burn approximately 300 million litres of fuel while idling in heavy traffic. High demand periods during peak hours can result in recurrent congestion while incidents, such as crashes, reducing roadway capacity can temporarily lead to non-recurrent congestion. Data generated from the ITS detection system provide congestion measurement in real time. Likewise, a crash occurrence is affected by human behaviour, road-way design, traffic flow, and weather conditions. Big Data applications also introduce new perspectives in safety analysis as researchers can analyse crash case data and draw general conclusions. Consequently, Big Data applications focus on developing congestion measurement and uncovering the relation-ship between safety and congestion in real time.

Big Data technologies have both direct and indirect applications. Direct applications include congestion reduction, incident prediction, and travel time estimation. Indirect applications are derived by enhancing traffic mod-elling during the development, calibration, and validation processes. Traffic simulation is also improved based on the actual data collected from the field.

Applications of Data Analytics

Here are some examples of uses of Data analytics applications in numerous cities around the world:

- **Real-time vehicles monitoring in India**
  The project focuses on deploying modern technologies like Big Data analytics and Hadoop to improve operational efficiency for logistics and transportation firms.[3] These technologies are used to assist managers in making informed business decisions. The researchers collected data from vehicles about fuel, speed, acceleration, GPS location coordinates using vehicle sensors and GPS devices and analysed it with data such as date, time, driver's ID. Packets sent this information over wireless communi-cation (GPRS) to clustered servers running Hadoop. The results could monitor driving behaviour and answer the following questions: Which vehicles are wasting fuels? Which drivers have the highest risks?
- **City of Dublin, Public Transit System**
  As part of a smart city project, IBM's Big Data analytics helped the city of Dublin to improve its public bus transportation network and reduce the increasing traffic congestion problem. The project aims to reduce Dublin's traffic congestion in its public bus transport network without significantly modifying its historic infrastructure. The data was collected from numer-ous sources, including bus GPS devices that send data from 1,000 buses

every 20 seconds, bus timetables, cameras, and traffic sensors in roads, tramways, and bus lanes. Collecting such large volumes of multiple and fast data was made possible by using clustered servers running IBM Big Data analytics to build a real-time digital map of the city's transportation network.[4]

- **City of Da Nang, Vietnam, Traffic Management System**
  Da Nang is the fourth-largest city in Vietnam, with one of the highest population growth rates in the country. Consequently, because of the demand for resources, government officials use technology to increase the manageability and efficiency of the city's systems. It was developed by IBM smart city technologies to reduce traffic congestion and pollution. This project aimed to build a water and transportation traffic management system capable of coping with the city's fast-growing population. Sensors on Da Nang's buses, roads, and highways collect data for the management system that uses the collected data to optimise traffic lights' synchronisation and reduce traffic congestion.[5]

Data Used for Maintenance and Operations

Big Data analytics is used in the transportation sector to improve and optimise operations and maintenance. Predictive modelling allows decision-makers to assess asset conditions and performance. Companies can predict breakdowns and remove vehicles for maintenance before they break down in the field. Using predictive analytics enables significant cost savings for companies resulting from improved efficiencies and reduced costs. Big Data sources such as on-time performance and vehicle location can be matched with schedules to measure how employees perform compared to peers. Based on this data, these agencies can understand what type of situations require additional training for operators. Companies are also applying Big Data analysis for safety and security purposes. Hacking in the transportation industry is becoming more advanced, and using Big Data tools for cybersecurity initiatives is increasing to protect against attacks. Machine learning tools analyse the different dimensions of the data environment and network users to identify abnormalities. The data collected can also improve the safety of public transit operations for passengers and people in the outside environment. Data is also collected from systems on the vehicle, such as collision avoidance sensors and onboard cameras that monitor the roads and intersections used by the transit vehicles. By merging this data with vehicle tracking information, transportation agencies can locate problematic streets and intersections where transit vehicles face the most challenges.

Data Used for Service and Planning

Transport agencies can use mobile devices and applications to improve service planning decisions. The data collected from these devices and apps can determine route patterns of public transit customers to help identify potential transfer and connection points between fixed routes. The addition of smart card systems allows transport agencies to collect information with the potential to alert individual transit passengers about impacts to their trip and provide alerts about potential delays to their usual journey and suggest alternative routes to avoid interruptions. The partnership between public transit agencies and private companies to analyse travel data generated by users and external data sources presents new opportunities. It allows planners and decision-makers to conduct a financial and economic appraisal, demand forecasting, service planning and coordination, operational and business-case analysis, network connectivity, interchange design, route selection, network optimisation, and travel planning.

Transportation System Monitoring and Management

The application of Big Data analytics to the transportation sector can improve transportation system monitoring, thus enhancing the effectiveness of management strategies. Using mobile devices to capture data from connected vehicles and travellers presents transportation agencies with a veritable pool of new data for transportation operators. The data from these devices include a wide range of vehicle and traveller data for essential locations throughout the multi-modal transportation systems, such as freeways, arterial streets, buses, trains, sidewalks, parking lots, and border crossings. In addition, new streams of real-time data from non-transportation sources supply further enrichment and create a holistic viewpoint for planners. Advanced data analytics can also be used to track bus and train schedules, breakdowns, and eliminate signal or network issues by determining alternative options and mitigating their impact. By applying Big Data analytical approaches, decision-makers can enhanced methods or generate new techniques for incident detection in the transportation system.

Traveller-Centred Transportation Management

In addition to enabling more decadent and more effective monitoring and management, smartphones coupled with Big Data techniques allow a different relationship between transportation agencies, public or private entities, and transportation system users. The change in the relationship could manifest in two ways: (1) personalised transportation services and (2) targeted incentives to influence users' travelling behaviour.

Targeted transportation services are becoming increasingly prevalent. The growth of personal and on-demand mobility providers such as Uber and Lyft and corporate car-sharing services such as Zipcar have contributed to this increase. Service providers of targeted transportation are likely to see this continued growth in market share based on:

- increase use of smartphones and mobile devices for transportation purposes

- consumer acceptance of mobile applications
- olicies concerning insurance, industry regulation and taxation, and parking

Users' transportation decisions and preferences are subject to external influence. Mobile applications can be employed in the transportation industry to track when, where, and how people use the transportation system. When linked with other variables, these software applications should predict future travel choices and potentially influence them. By applying data analytics to the transportation sector, decision-makers and planners can understand and treat users more as customers, which allows for increased engagement and influence on their behaviour. Transportation agencies can use predictive analytics to improve public transport across the globe by analysing people's movement between and within different cities. Predictive data analytics helps determine the schedules of public transport services such as buses and trains, forecasting weather conditions, and analysing the effect of both on commuters.

The Value of Big Data and Data Analytics in Road Safety and Real-Time Response to Emergencies

Due to the complexity and pervasiveness of transportation in everyday life, the use and combination of Big Datasets and datastreams promise smarter roads and a better understanding of our transportation needs and environment. Affordable computing and sensor technology are transforming current practices and methods for traffic data collection, monitoring, and analysis. Big Data is changing how organisations and individuals interact with the environment and approach problem-solving tasks in transportation. Consequently, mobile and/or fixed video sensors for traffic monitoring and data collection are becoming popular for freeways and urban streets. The availability of such large datasets allows for more dynamic traffic load balancing and easing congestion of road networks.

Traffic Safety

As cities become more crowded, the number of automobiles and demands on public transit are increasing rapidly. Consequently, traffic problems have become a significant source of concern, as it wastes resources and time and causes severe losses to the economy. Therefore, traffic safety is of paramount significance in the transportation industry. Accident occurrences cause immense losses and has human, economic, and social implications, especially in cases of injury and fatalities. Among the different aspects of the traffic safety investigation, crash injury severity analysis is a vital component. It reveals the relationships between crash injury severity and various explanatory variables (including driver behaviour, environmental conditions, traffic flow, and geometry characteristics). Such studies provide vital information for planners and decision-makers in roadway design, freeway management, public health, enforcement, emergency and trauma, policy, education, and awareness. Advanced parametric models such as random parameter logit model, Markov switching multinomial logit model, and emerging data mining techniques such as neural network models and support vector machine models can be employed to address the crash injury severity issues.

Real-Time Crash Prediction

Existing traffic safety analysis can be grouped into two main categories: aggregate analysis dealing with crash frequency and disaggregate analysis examining each crash case. The development of the ITS detection system supplies Big Data, which allows decision-makers to retrieve real-time traffic information from each collision case. The evaluation of this data provides real-time traffic safety information with increased accuracy and relevance. Real-time crash prediction is based on disaggregate analysis, classifying crash and non-crash incidents based on real-time traffic information before the crashes. There are two general approaches used to evaluate real-time safety, statistical methods and data mining methods. These approaches require detailed information over a short time interval which is generally unavailable in aggregate analysis. Statistical methods such as simple/matched-case logistic regression and Bayesian statistics present the effects of candidate variables in a more interpretable way. Data mining techniques include neural networks, random forests, and support vector machines. These techniques have high prediction accuracy but are criticised for the black-box-like process. Predictive data analytics tools can also determine the impact of traffic congestion and ongoing maintenance projects on public transit networks thereby devising alternative transit schedules and message strategies. In addition, transportation data analytics can predict the impact of unplanned events such as traffic accidents, vehicle breakdown, transport labour strike, and their impact on the local economy.

Rear-End Crash

It has been widely accepted that traffic conditions can directly impact traffic safety regarding crash type and severity. Single-vehicle crashes frequently occur from driving errors under free-flow conditions, while sideswipe crashes are likely to arise from inappropriate lane-change behaviours and speed variation between lanes. Rear-end crashes often involve multiple vehicles, with the leading vehicle suddenly decelerating. Rear-end crashes are correlated with congestion, mainly when there are speed variations. Big Data enables the restoration of traffic for each crash case. Data mining and Bayesian statistics techniques were adopted to identify the leading contributing factors of crashes in real-time.

APPLICATION CASE 14.1

Big Data and Alaska Transportation Network

The Alaska Department of Transportation and Public Facilities (AD-OT&PF) has one of the most challenging jobs in the US to keep its transportation network moving smoothly. The state has 836 bridges, about 5,600 miles of roads, 242 airports, 21 harbours, 300 aviation facilities, and ten vessels. They have to keep this network of roads, airports, and vehicles moving in an area with severe and unpredictable weather conditions. For example, certain areas of the state could be in deep freezing and snow conditions, while just a few miles away, there is average sunny weather.

The transportation network and traffic are affected mainly by weather conditions that are very severe and unpredictable in most cases. For example, in the winter of 2010, within 24 hours, the temperature goes from 25 degrees Fahrenheit below zero to 45 degrees above zero. This is a logistical challenge for the department of transportation that has to make sure that commuters, commercial trucking fleets, airports, harbours, and vessels that are the lifeline of the Alaskan economy are moving and operating efficiently. At times, the temperate can go 85 degrees below zero.

They needed a more predictable and accurate weather forecast system locally to be well prepared. In addition, the ADOT&PF needs a ground-level temperate reading system on the roads to analyse the impact of the sudden weather change on the road network and when to schedule maintenance and road crew to clear the ice. The solution to the problem was a Big Data platform that consolidates the road and traffic network with the weather data to manage the transportation system in Alaska.

So in 2013, they decided to invest in a Big Data platform. More specifically, in a Road Weather Information System (RWIS), a WeatherCloud solution, and Microsoft Azure, a Platform as a Services (PaaS) analytic tool. These data analytics tools track and consolidate air temperature data, surface temperature data, dew point temperature, wind speed, wind direction, relative humidity, and precipitation. The data is collected through a cellular network and aggregated to the Maintenance Decision Support system (MDSS) cloud-based database. Their cloud-based database also includes weather data from NOAA, the US's National Oceanic and Atmospheric Administration. The ADOT&PF wanted to know the impact of ice and rain on the paved network of roads. Consequently, they installed mobile sensors on trucks and other vehicles to track weather conditions on the road, such as humidity, precipitation, and road temperature, to accurately predict weather locally

(Continued)

and determine when and where to send road crew for road maintenance or finding traffic solutions.

The data collected and analysed help them determine road conditions such as precipitation on paved streets and accurately predict local weather conditions and their impact on the road. The real-time data analytics results from the Big Data platform are helping them to be proactive in sending emergency weather and traffic crew to areas that might be affected soon. In this way, road traffic is reduced or eliminated even before it happens. The data-driven approach they have taken increases road safety and allows traffic on both land and sea to run smoothly, with reduced cost of maintenance and repairs.

Source: Alaska Department of Transportation & Public Facilities (ADOT&PF) https://dot.alaska.gov/index. shtml; *Source:* Microsoft: *How Alaska outsmarts Mother Nature in the cloud.* https://customers.microsoft.com/en-us/story/ alaskadotpf-government-azure-iot:

The Value of Big Data and Data Analytics in Logistics and Supply Chain Management

Social networks, mobile e-commerce devices, and many other devices and sources generate large quantities of unstructured and complex data. Big Data provides unique insights into market trends, customer buying patterns, and maintenance cycles, furthering insights into lowering costs and enabling more targeted business decisions. Therefore, the use of Big Data analytic tools has become an obligation for most companies. Much has been done recently to integrate Big Data analytics in the logistics industry. Logistics is part of supply chain management that plans, implements, controls forward, reverse flow, storage of goods, services, and associated information from the source to the destination or point of consumption to meet customers' requirements. Transportation provides the flow of inventory from the source in the supply chain to destinations or points of use and consumption. Most companies manage both inbound and outbound logistics. Inbound logistics deals with the procurement of materials and goods from supplier locations, whereas outbound logistics considers distributing materials and goods to customer locations. Therefore, transportation is essential on the inbound and outbound sides of the business. Big Data analytics have focused on road and vehicle sensors, GPS devices, customer applications, and websites for the logistics and transportation industry.

A supply chain consists of companies that work together to provide goods or services for customers. Most businesses operate within supply chains. Supply chain management is the planning and management of all sourcing, procurement, conversion, and logistics management activities. It also consists of coordinating and collaborating suppliers, intermediaries, third-party service providers, or customers. Transportation in supply chain management represents the physical connection among the companies in the supply chain. For example, when a supplier sells a product to another entity, transportation provides the delivery. When there is delay and problem in the supply chain, it has repercussions for the downstream members of the supply chain and their ability to serve their customers. As the central component of supply chain analytics, advanced analytics techniques form the basis for implementing supply chain strategies and daily operations. It helps organisations measure the performance of the different areas in logistics, supply chain management and provide them with the ability to establish a benchmark to determine value-added operations. In addition, supply chain analytics allow companies to monitor these metrics regularly, troubleshoot poor performance, identify a root cause, enable better business decisions, and provide tremendous benefits through the improvement of business processes.

The Value of Big Data and Data Analytics in Reducing Environmental Impact

Climate change has been of interest to individuals and corporations. Climate change and environmental conditions impact transportation systems regarding operating conditions and infrastructure requirements such as construction and maintenance. Total emissions are generally a function of the emission factor of each transport mode rather than the level of activity. Road transportation is considered one of the largest producers of carbon emission pollutants.

Concerns about air quality and global warming have led to several initiatives on how to reduce emissions. In general, carbon emissions are directly related to the amount of fuel consumed. Fuel consumption is a function of speed, distance, acceleration, and weight of the vehicle. As a significant source of carbon dioxide emissions, transportation has been a substantial factor in focus. Consequently, cities such as Amsterdam and London have introduced low-emission zones that restrict truck traffic near city centres. There is a high volume of emissions in urban areas due to congestion and vehicle traffic speed variations. At different times of day, the observations of speeds on an arc will display significant variability. Given the fact that emissions curves are nonlinear, optimising emissions in an urban area requires careful consideration of the variability in traffic speed in the network.

Humanitarian Operations

Transporting and delivering humanitarian services, especially in disasters, can affect the well-being of vulnerable citizens and society. Providing such services requires performing several activities: material flow, information exchange, and synchronised resource transfer. The synchronisation of such efforts is often managed by a focal non-governmental organisation (NGO) that marshals the necessary resources, identifies needs, and has the receptive infrastructure and human resources required to deliver the humanitarian services.

Big Data analytics in humanitarian operations are used to provide rapid response. For example, Google developed analytics to predict the occurrence of the H1N1 flu outbreaks on a spatial basis. At the same time, Walmart analysed POS data to lower logistical costs and improve the flow of supplies to stores. In addition, humanitarian organisations need access to real-time information to determine the position and availability of resources. Big Data analytics assist these organisations with decision-making while operating in complex and dynamic environments, visibility of mission-critical assets, and allocating and coordinating resources.

Sustainability

Due to the advancements in the use of technology like cloud computing and smart mobile devices, large volumes of data, mainly unstructured, have been accumulated. Big Data can transform business processes like finance or manufacturing and service operations, but it is applicable in all areas of life. In improving sustainability and developing resilient disaster infrastructure and capabilities, Big Data can assists scientists, policymakers, and city planners create and implement policies, strategies, procedures, and practices that will benefit the environment and human health. These advancements will help governments and organisations to make more effective local, regional, national, and global progress toward truly sustainable societies.

Big Data can assist policymakers to:

- develop and implement policies and approaches that protect and manage natural resources in an eco-friendly manner
- prevent wastage of resources and degradation of capacities that can provide vital services for the healthy and sustainable development of society
- limit the production of pollutants by transforming them into products
- develop appropriate environmental protection policies and frameworks
- focus on disaster management and analyse responses to disasters to take proper actions and devise policies that will enable recovery and restore normality for communities.

Big Data can help both lessen and recover from the negative consequences of disasters, build social and natural capital, and enhance the adaptive capacity to cope in the future.

Big Data is receiving increasing societal usage at the macroeconomic level, especially regarding resource consumption or pollution measurements. For example, Big Data analytics encourages and sustains smart city development, sustainable mobility, and policies. In addition, Big Data can be employed to make greener decisions leading to environmental improvement, energy efficiency, and management for ecological improvement. It can also be used to monitor air pollution by measuring air quality in real-time.

Optimising Resource Usage

Another significant contribution of Big Data analytics is to provide transportation companies with the ability to optimise resource usage. The ability to use resources efficiently and minimising waste is fundamental to the sustainability and profitability of many businesses. For example, Big Data generated by smart meters and sensors can track energy consumption and other resources in real time, transmit various kinds of information, and manage two-way communication with central systems. In addition, such data can identify sources of waste that would otherwise be invisible or require costly observation by employees.

Key Term

Intelligent Transportation Systems; Transportation Traffic Management; Traffic Safety; Sustainability Supply Chain Analytics; Logistics; Operations; Real Time Responses Procurement

Chapter Key Takeaways

- Transportation involves moving goods and people from one place to another.
- Transportation plays a crucial role in emergencies and humanitarian relief. Relief organisations use advanced transportation methods to support the deployment of essential resources to those in need whenever and wherever there is a humanitarian crisis.
- There are four essential components of transportation:
  - Modes
  - Infrastructures
  - Networks
  - Flows
- Using Big Data comprises collecting relevant electronic information from various sources. This practice brings many advantages to the transportation industry, such as increasing operational efficiency and flexibility, reducing fuel consumption, and improving customer experience. It also helps with improving safety in the transportation sector.
- Data sensors provide real-time information regarding vehicle performance. For example, they provide accurate data regarding travel speeds, transit, and length of idleness and monitor the equipment's condition and engine. In addition, it allows for the prediction of errors and timely preparations for maintenance.

- Big Data technologies have both direct and indirect applications. Direct applications include congestion reduction, incident prediction, and travel time estimation. Indirect applications are derived by enhancing traffic modelling during the development, calibration, and validation processes. Traffic simulation is also improved based on the actual data collected from the field.
- Big Data analytics is used in the transportation sector for:
  - Maintenance and operations
  - Service and planning
  - System monitoring and management
  - Traveller-centred transportation management
- Big Data is changing how organisations and individuals interact with the environment and approach problem-solving tasks in transportation.
- ITS detection system supplies Big Data, allowing decision-makers to retrieve real-time traffic information from each collision case.
- Big Data and data analytics is used in road safety and real-time response to emergencies.
- There are two general approaches used to evaluate real-time safety, i.e., statistical methods and data mining methods.
- Big Data provides unique insights into market trends, customer buying patterns, and maintenance cycles, and further insights into lowering costs and enabling more targeted business decisions.
- Big Data analytics in humanitarian operations are used to provide rapid response. It assists humanitarian operations with decision-making while operating in complex and dynamic environments, visibility of mission-critical assets, and allocating and coordinating resources.
- Big Data analytics allows companies to use resources efficiently, and minimising waste is fundamental to the sustainability and profitability of many businesses.

Discussion Question

1 Define transportation and explain how it has helped the development of modern society.
2 Discuss the core components of transportation. Discuss which of these, if any, is most significant.
3 Identify and discuss the different modes of transportation.
4 How is Big Data used in the transportation sector to improve operational efficiency?
5 Identify how Big Data analytics assist with Maintenance and Operations in transportation?
6 How are companies using Big Data analytics to prevent traffic congestion and rear-end accidents?
7 Describe how data analytics is applied in logistics and supply chain strategy.

8 Transportation and procurement can consume a tremendous amount of business resources. Explain how data analytics is helping companies to save resources.

9 Explain the impact of the transportation industry on the environment. What can be done to reduce emissions?

10 Describe how the ITS detection system is helping transport managers to retrieve real-time traffic information from each collision case.

11 Road transportation is one of the largest producers of carbon emission pollutants. So what can firms do to reduce the effects of carbon emissions?

12 Describe how Big Data analytics can help companies develop sustainable transportation modes that have little or no impact on the environment.

13 Identify how the transportation sector can employ Big Data analytics to optimise the usage of resources.

References

1 Rodrigue, J.P., Comtois, C., & Slack, B. (2016). *The geography of transport systems*. Routledge, https://transportgeography.org/contents/chapter1/what-is-transport-geography/core-components-transportation/

2 The Economist: Feb (2018). The hidden cost of congestion, https://www.economist.com/graphic-detail/2018/02/28/the-hidden-cost-of-congestion

3 Spec India: Vehicle Tracking System (VTS), https://www.spec-india.com/business-solutions/vehicle-tracking-system

4 IBM Newsroom (2013). Big data helps city of Dublin improve its public bus transportation network and reduce congestion, https://newsroom.ibm.com/2013-05-17-Big-Data-Helps-City-of-Dublin-Improve-its-Public-Bus-Transportation-Network-and-Reduce-Congestion

5 Armonk, N.Y. & Nang, D.A. (2013) Da Nang, Vietnam turn to IBM to transform city systems. IBM Newsroom, https://newsroom.ibm.com/2013-08-15-Da-Nang-Vietnam-Turns-to-IBM-to-Transform-City-Systems

15 Data Analytics in Education

Data analytics has shown its usefulness in many different industries. In education, these increasingly large datasets are used to access the learner's performance and progress. It assists instructors with developing an adaptive teaching policy, improves teaching and learning outcomes, increases student enrolment, improves student retention and completion rates, increases faculty productivity and research, and develops sophisticated predictive models for the future. Data analytics in education generate reports, thus satisfying operational, regulatory, or statutory compliance and supporting strategic, data-driven decision-making. Data analytics helps support a flexible decision-making process in which instructors need to increase the quality of the learning experience and the learning process. This chapter discusses using data analytics and predictive modelling to improve enrolment, retention, graduation rate, supporting students, and the institution's financial viability.

LEARNING OBJECTIVES:

At the end of this chapter, students should be able to:

- Identify the challenges of higher education
- Understand the value of Big Data and data analytics in admission and enrolment
- Identify the value of Big Data and data analytics in student retention rate
- Analyse the value of Big Data and data analytics in advisement and student success
- Recognise the importance of Big Data and data analytics in the financial success of the institution and operational efficiency

Higher Education Industry

Higher education or territory education is any schooling beyond high school that may lead to a bachelor's degree or a more advanced degree. A higher education degree is considered a requirement to be successful and remain

DOI: 10.4324/9781003129356-15

competitive in the marketplace. The higher education industry is complex and diverse. It combines a dominant public sector of state universities and community colleges that educate most students and the private sector encompassing some of the world's most elite research universities. Regardless of the institution, the higher education industry competes for outstanding students and funding sources such as government research grants and corporate research support.[1]

Educational institutions are seeing improving enrolment rates in both traditional and online formats. Traditional schooling is tailored towards younger students recently graduating from high school. Online instruction is tailored to working adults who prefer to attend classes in the evening or weekends. In addition, the rapid increase in online learning platforms is changing how the higher education sector does business. In addition, online courses typically carry higher margins than traditional courses since there are no direct brick-and-mortar costs.

Therefore, universities and colleges worldwide now have a broad reach of students globally at a fraction of the cost of travelling to campus. For example, as the US continues to transition from a manufacturing-based economy to a service sector dominant one, for-profit educational institutions are likely to gain from offering courses in information systems, healthcare, and business management. Again, middle-income countries produce the bulk of this growth.

Based on geography, the Global Higher Education Market is categorised into North America, Europe, Asia Pacific, and the rest of the world. The US ranks number one for people seeking to attain advanced educational qualifications. The country is home to some of the oldest and most renowned universities globally that are especially popular for graduate and doctoral degrees programs. In Europe, countries such as UK, Germany, France, and the Netherlands are aiding the regional market growth from equally prestigious universities.

Higher Education Challenges

The Higher education (HE) industry faces both internal and external pressure to meet and maintain specific standards and metrics for its survival. Internally, colleges and universities need to maintain a certain enrolment level and provide quality education to stay financially viable. Externally, they face pressures from different government-mandated retention levels, graduation rates, and other metrics to qualify for specific funding from the government. As a result, competition among higher education institutions for prospective students is intensifying. Also, the financial constraints can limit an institution's ability to expand its offerings.

Higher education campuses are places where students live and study close to each other. Unfortunately, with the outbreak of COVID-19, this ecosystem was severely impacted and has created uncertainty regarding the implications for higher education. Consequently, one of the biggest concerns for the sector is low enrolment and class cancellations. In addition, the number of international students has declined. This has severe repercussions on local economies. For example, Chinese students make up 33.7 percent of the international student population in the US, while Indian students comprise 18.4 percent.[2] Some universities like Georgia Tech have also cut their tuition rates to increase student enrolment. Others have engaged in debt forgiveness. Likewise, universities play a significant role in the economic recovery of a country, as governments and world leaders launch plans to stimulate and reopen economies.

While the HE industry has made several strides towards achieving equality, there are still some areas where there are inconsistencies. Examples[3] of these include:

- Globally, increasingly more young people between 20 and 24 are enrolling in tertiary education. However, in countries in sub-Saharan Africa, this figure remains below 10 percent.
- While technology is seen as the great equaliser, the digital divide in tertiary education remains stagnant owing to limited connectivity and access to devices. Often individuals from a poorer background are most impacted.
- Most middle-income countries struggle to produce high-quality education with significant resources devoted to tertiary education, without visible quality increases and persistent skills mismatches.
- Internationalisation can help countries, institutions, and individuals to connect to global developments and benefit from cross-country cooperation. However, besides its enormous potential, this remains the privilege of a small elite.
- In high-income countries, universities are changing their operations to become key lifelong learning players. However, HE institutions in middle-income countries find it challenging to evolve from traditional rote learning.
- While most countries recognise the crucial role the importance of HE in their advancement, they lack governance, financing, and quality assurance. Without strategic reforms, this industry will remain isolated and lack sustainability.

Data Analytics in the Education Sector

The HE sector produces enormous volumes of data from hundreds of thousands of adults each year. Big Data and data analytics provides these institutions with the predictive tools they need to improve the efficiency of the university's vast operations. As a result, Big Data and data analytics tools are helping universities and colleges improve their operational efficiencies, financial bottomline, and address the changing global demand imposed on them to produce the best students at the lowest cost.

Data analytics is used in the HE industry for the following purposes:

- **Intervention –** Intervention is an essential function in the education process. At a macro level, it identifies potential dropouts. These institutions can then direct resources for tutoring, financial aid, and even counselling toward at-risk students.
- **Forecasting –** HE institutions can use data analytics to predict students' grades based on demographics, curricula, institutions, and other factors. Interventions can be made for issues such as budgeting, teacher allocation, and deploying resources.
- **Teaching Styles –** Data analytics can identify and track the most talented instructors or the worst ones. Interventions can be done during their time in universities and during teacher training to adapt their skills to what works.

The Value of Big Data and Data Analytics in Admission and Enrolment

In most colleges and universities, the enrolment management department includes recruitment and admission, among other functions. Big Data and data analytics can make this process more efficient and cost-effective for colleges. For example, the admission process involves different students, including newcomers, transfer students, international students, veterans, nondegree students, and graduate students. All these groups come with varying datasets that can be analysed to decide which student to admit and the student's potential retention until graduation.

Recruitment Analytics. Colleges and universities spend a considerable amount of money and resources on recruiting students. The recruitment process includes visiting high schools, conducting college fairs and open houses, and hosting events on campus and in other cities. In addition, HE institutions send admission counsellors overseas and attend community meetings. Also, universities are involved in intense marketing, advertising on the internet, radio, TV, emails, sending postcards, brochures, and other marketing material. Finally, these institutions use Facebook and other social media to reach potential students. Even though this method has been used over the years, data analytics can streamline the process, thus determining more efficient and cost-effective.

Predictive analytics moves colleges away from a "best guest" outcome to a more precise targeted recruitment process. Colleges and universities can better target their recruitment process using predictive analytics to build a data-driven recruitment model with various access and contact points such as student demographics, location, ethnicity, expected concentration, and other data. Predictive analytics can help universities decide whom they recruit and how to recruit them. With an excellent predictive recruitment model, universities will not spend a significant amount of money and time on the wrong student population but instead on the students who are likely to accept and attend their university. Predictive analytics in higher education, especially recruitment, is not different from what is used in other industries. The main objective is to concentrate effort on those individuals who are more likely to purchase a product or attend an institution. Recruitment analytics is the process of using various data to target and recruit students.

Admission Analytics. The data collected in the admission process are high school diploma, high school GPA, standardised test scores (SAT/ACT), demographic, ethnicity, home address, high school activities, native language, and other specialised data. With the help of data analytics, colleges can accurately predict whether or not a given student will enrol in the college, succeed in classes, be involved in students' organisations, stay on or off-campus, and any likely support the student will need. With such a profile on an applicant, universities are better positioned to admit students who are likely to succeed and stay at the university until graduation.

Enrolment Analytics. Predictive analytics allow institutions to plan better by anticipating future enrolment. Accurately predicting enrolment enhances the university's operational efficiency and survival. Over-enrolment can lead to stress in the university facilities, and under-enrolment can lead to financial strains. As the student begins class and more data is collected, the university will have a better idea of the student performance and what kind of support the student will need to complete their education. By year two, with the combination of admission data and college grades and activities, the university will be better positioned to accurately predict course enrolment for each student. Big Data allows HE institutions to develop a real-time profile of each student.

Collecting data based on FAFSA filings and the number of credits will indicate attrition and which admitted student is less likely to attend. In addition, such data analytics helps the college develop a more precise enrolment forecast that allows the university to schedule classes appropriately. The accuracy of enrolment projections is essential since, with that information, the institution will know how many courses to offer each semester and what other students support services are needed.

APPLICATION CASE 15.1 (ENROLMENT ANALYTICS)

Predictive Modeling for Enrolment Management – Dickinson College

A Data-Driven Campus Culture

Data analysis and predictive modelling had been a part of the culture at Dickinson College long before Dr Mike Johnson came on as Director of Institutional Research. Dickinson found that predictive modelling allowed them to plan better by anticipating the future and has embraced the process, especially in enrolment. As the institution found more and more uses for predictive modelling to guide data-driven decisions, they realised that bringing it in-house would be the most efficient and cost-effective way to do so.

Bringing Predictive Modelling In-house

Initially, Dr Johnson wasn't sure which tools would be best to bring predictive modelling in-house, so he started looking at software packages and asking other people how they were doing it. He wanted a solution that could be used in near "real-time" and was flexible enough to have his hand in the modelling but didn't want to spend his time programming. Dr Johnson also knew he needed to defend the resulting models and predictions to campus leaders and decision-makers. This ruled out "black box" software programs that produce models that can be difficult to explain. He compared Rapid Insight's Predict to some sophisticated modelling packages and decided on it for its ease of use, transparency, and because he could produce results quickly.

Enrolment Cycle Modelling

Dr Johnson focused his initial predictive modelling efforts on the end of the admissions cycle; specifically, he was interested in enrolment modelling for the accepted applicant pool. He built individual models for each of three subpopulations within the applicant pool (early decision, early action, and regular admit) after finding that each subpopulation behaved quite differently.

The models make yield, quality, and financial aid projections for the accepted applicant pool or specific subgroups. Then, as each mailing date deadline approaches, his team uses the models to walk through simulations based on various scenarios to check things like diversity in the incoming class, projected quality of students, and projected gender mix. This allows for an interactive discussion between admissions, institutional research, and financial aid to make collective decisions about the class composition. Additionally, it enables them to fine-tune the prospective type before sending out mailings.

Outcomes

After several years of predictive modelling, Dr Johnson has been pleased with the results. The models have given them reasonable projections of what their incoming class will look like. This accuracy is important because

(Continued)

missing a class size by just a couple of percentage points can significantly impact financial aid, housing, and even the number of sections in a first-year seminar. As Dr Johnson observes, "You can never be too accurate."

Next Project: GPA Analytics

Dickinson has also built a separate model to predict the end-of-first-semester GPA for each student. They use this during the enrolment cycle as a litmus test to ensure that the incoming class has the potential to succeed – and again when enrolled students finish their first semester to identify underperformance. Dr Johnson's next project is to implement a new proactive retention strategy using this model. His team will be comparing predicted GPA with actual first semester GPA to find students who have underperformed within their cohort but are still in good academic standing. He's already found that the bottom 10 percent of underperforming students in actual vs predicted GPA are 1.7 to 2.3 times less likely to be retained. By targeting these students with resources and programs designed to improve their second-semester performance, Dr Johnson is excited about the process and thinks it can make an impact. "This is a new area of predictive modelling for us. We've been growing into it for two years, but now we're at the point where we can act on it."

About Dickinson College

Dickinson College, founded in 1773, is a highly selective, private residential liberal-arts college known for its innovative curriculum. Its mission is to offer students a proper education in the arts and sciences to prepare them for their lives as engaged citizens and leaders. The 180-acre campus of Dickinson College is located in the heart of historic Carlisle, PA. The college offers 42 majors with an emphasis on international studies, has more than 40 study-abroad programs in 24 countries on six continents, and offers 13 modern languages.

Source: Rapid Insight case studies, a data analytics company: *Predictive Modeling for Enrollment Management – Dickinson College*, https://www.rapidinsight.com/why-rapid-insight/case-studies/ predictive-modeling-for-enrollment-management-dickinson-college/. Used by permission from Rapid Insight.

The Value of Big Data and Data Analytics in Student Retention Rate

Even though some colleges have successfully recruited students, most cannot retain these students until graduation. Retention rate, defined as students who return for sophomore year, is very low in most colleges and universities. Nationwide, according to College Transition, the average retention rate is 78 percent for Fall 2018, that is, students who register in Fall 2018 and return in Fall 2019.[4] Some colleges and universities' retention rates are as low as 66 percent. As a result, many students start college and never complete their degrees. This affects the university bottomline and the individual student's unrealised dreams of a college degree. Improving retention rates even slightly has a positive effect on the university's financial health. For example, if the retention rate of an institution is 70 percent, it means that for every ten students that the institution recruits and enrols, they will lose three students. That is, an institution that enrols 1,000 first-year students will lose 300 of those students. If the median recruitment and enrolment cost is $100 per student, the university loses $3,000. This does not include the loss of tuition these students will have brought in. The price of poor retention is very high for the university.

Therefore, most colleges and universities are moving to Big Data and data analytics to make data-driven decisions on addressing the poor retention rate they are experiencing. Even though multiple non-measurable factors may contribute to a student dropping out of college (e.g., homesickness, emotionally unprepared for living away from home), predictable factors may indicate the possibility of a student leaving or staying in college till graduation. For example, distance between home and campus, financial, expected family contribution to finance education, social, declaration of concentration later, and time management may contribute to students dropping out of college.

Retention Rate Analytics. Universities and colleges collect a large amount of data from each student. These data include test scores, homework, class attendance, class participation, course assessments, and discussion board responses. Combined with the admission data collected when the student was first admitted, these data can be used to build a predictive analytic profile for each student. The university can use this report to intervene when needed. This model can generate correlations and patterns that can be used to intervene immediately. For example, the analysis may show a correlation between attendance, class participation, course load, financial aid, tuition payment patterns, on-campus living, off-campus living, campus employment, student activities, and final grade. The analytic profile will be able to identify students at risk of failing or dropping out of college. This profile can be updated frequently and provide trend analysis for each student over time. Colleges and universities can use this predictive analytic result to address the issues that might make the students drop out of college.

The university can also use this data to adjust the curriculum and course offerings to accommodate students with unique problems identified by the correlation. Additionally, the analytics will help universities and colleges determine which academic majors hold the highest retention rate. Data analytics help determine the long-term viability of specific majors. It links financial aid award to the student most likely to stay till graduation and determine what kind of capital improvement the university needs to engage in to support the factors that will enhance student retention. For example, should the college or university build a new student union building instead of a new science building? The analytics will also show whether the students leave the college because of course offerings, curriculum, college activities, or teaching methods.

The Value of Big Data and Data Analytics in Advisement and Student Success

Another aspect in higher education that data analytics could be beneficial is student advisement. Academic advisors are individuals responsible for helping students choose a major, minor, or class and ensure that they register for the required classes each semester and meet all the requirements to graduate with a degree in that field. Unfortunately, most colleges and universities cannot give individual students the personalised attention they may need during advisement because of inadequate student advisors. Therefore, student success is more than achieving good grades. Big Data and predictive analytics can help streamline this process by identifying students most in need of individual attention.

One way predictive analytics can help make this process effective is through the Early-Alert system. This predictive model uses student data such as GPA, class attendance, demographics, and other data collected during the admission process to predict and identify students needing personalised attention and advisement. In this way, the university or college can allocate its resources more efficiently without neglecting struggling students. In addition, good and personalised advisement will also help keep students in the university hence increasing the retention rate. In other words, predictive analytics will improve academic advising and communication between students, advisors, and university administrators through an early alert or early warning system.

The Value of Big Data and Data Analytics in the Financial, Sustainable, and Operational Efficiency of Colleges and Universities

Colleges and universities are confronted with considerable financial challenges due to various reasons: low enrolment, low retention rate, performance base funding from the federal government and states, and global trends affecting the institutions higher education. Changing international trends in education such as flexible classroom design, open-access online classes, and free online certificates are taking away the potential source of revenue in the form of tuition from universities and colleges. Other global issues such as recruiting international students and the inward-looking immigration policies pursued by governments worldwide have increased the competition to recruit international students. Some institution has responded by opening campuses overseas. In short, colleges and universities operate in a complex and competitive environment. They react to constant national, global, political, and social changes and try to ensure that their academic programs are nationally and globally relevant in the workplace. Data analytics and Big Data are playing a significant role in addressing these complex issues. Data analytics is helping colleges and universities improve their financial situation by providing real-time data that enhance evidence-based decision-making and operational efficiency to respond to the changing global education landscape.

Financial Sustainability in Higher Education

Alumni and Donor Analytics. One of the ways data analytics and Big Data are helping to improve colleges and universities' financial position is fostering a stronger relationship between the university and potential donors and alumni. With the availability of Big Data such as income, location, ethnicity, donation amount, education, religion, and various other available data, predictive analytics will identify which alumni and donors will most likely donate to the university. This allows the university or college to build a good relationship with individuals instead of spreading their resources to potential donors or alumni.

Performance-based Funding Analytics. Data analytics will also improve the university's access to more funding through newly adopted performance-based financing. Historically, state funding to universities and colleges is based on full-time student enrolment. However, many states are now adopting a performance-based funding criterion. For example, states base their budget on outcomes such as graduation rates, retention rates, credit hours earned, time to degree completion, course completion, number of minority and low-income student graduation, number of degrees conferred, transfer rate from two to four-year colleges, and job placement rates. New policies implemented by many states across the US use these criteria and metrics to fund public colleges and universities.[5] Big Data and data analytics are well placed to track these metrics and identify challenges and opportunities that colleges and universities can address to improve their financial sustainability objective.

Operational Efficiency in Higher Education

Colleges and universities are operating in a complex and competitive environment. They have to respond to national, global, and social changes and ensure that their academic programs are nationally and globally relevant in the workplace. To meet these challenges, colleges and universities need to operate in a highly efficient manner. Daniel (2015) proposed a four-step analytic process of looking at universities and colleges – Institutional analytics, information technology (IT) analytics, Academic/program analytics, and learning analytics.[6]

Institutional Analytics involves analysing various institutional policies and departments by using the data generated by these departments. Data such as reports, budgets, personnel, and operational data in one platform provide analytics that will allow management to make data-driven decisions across all departments in the university or college. In addition, gathering these data can help universities assess performance and prescribe operational efficiency for the university in all its departments.

IT Analytics in higher education should include collecting and integrating data from different systems used by the college or university. Most universities and colleges store student information, alumni information, classes, and curriculum in other networks. IT analytics aims to collect and aggregate data from the various systems to develop data collection standards across the university and look for duplications in data collection and synergies. These analytics help the university or college to detect obstacles and deficiencies in its operations. It enables data-driven decisions to eliminate these obstacles and weaknesses. This makes the institution operate efficiently, and students develop easy access to the university programs and class registrations. It also helps the university know whether certain critical data is needed to be collected or unnecessary data is collected.

Academic Analytics. Performance analytics in educational programs, research, and resource allocation is essential. By using the data available within the institution and other sources of academic program data, academic analytics can identify problems in a specific educational program and address the weakness in that program to help the university achieve its academic objectives. The analytics also measure the outcome of a program compared with other institutions.

Learning Analytics. Many universities and colleges use both face-to-face, online classes, and a combination of both. It means having access to many data sources that are used to collect and determine the effectiveness of the learning process for an institution. Data such as course evaluation, online discussion board posting, grades, and other data can be used in the analysis. Learning analytics looks at the relationship and interaction between learner, content, institution, and educator. Learning analytics aims to understand the students' learning process and the institutional environment and identify the best possible teaching method to administer in each class. For example, will a particular class be a face-to-face class, online, or hybrid? The ultimate goal is to improve the delivery of education to the students. As new learning technologies emerge, universities and colleges need to adapt and adjust their curriculum to respond to the demands of employers and other stakeholders.

With the large volume of data available to universities and colleges, Big Data and data analytics provide colleges and universities with the predictive tools required to improve the efficiency of the university's vast operations. When embraced and adequately implemented, data analytics will help the university enhance its admission process, enrolment management system, retention rate, advisement, learning, and student needs. Big Data and data analytics will also help the university improve its operational efficiencies, financial bottomline, and address the changing global, employer, and other stakeholder demands imposed on universities to produce the best students at the lowest cost.

APPLICATION CASE 15.2

Southern Adventist University Creates Advanced Revenue Attribution Report Using Rapid Insight (Revenue and Financial sustainability Analytics)

In this study, learn how Southern Adventist University implemented a revenue attribution report identifying which degrees, departments, and faculty members generate revenue. The report will enable Department Chairs and other college Administrators to gain a nuanced, cross-cutting understanding of where to make adjustments and streamline the college's offerings to serve its financial, educational, and mission-based goals.

The Benefits of Revenue Attribution Reporting

Southern Adventist University (SAU) is a co-educational institution located in Collegedale, TN. With a student population greater than 2,500, 171 faculty members, 64 majors, nine graduate degrees, and various unique programs, SAU constantly evaluates which programs achieve the institution's mission and priorities most effectively.

Like all universities, revenue is a persistent concern. SAU knew that improving their understanding of which programs and degrees generate positive revenue would be immense. This information would help them to prioritise funding and attention to efforts that lead to results. In addition, it would equip them to make informed changes to departments and degrees that did not provide as much value. For several years, the university saw revenue attribution reporting as a priority. In 2019, thanks to the work of Doug Frood and Ryan Harrell, that work truly got underway.

Launching the Initiative

Doug Frood, the Executive Director of Budgeting and Data Analysis, handles the Cabinet's budget and performs analysis for the CFO and Academic Vice President. Primarily, he ensures that stakeholders receive reliable, actionable information on which to base decisions. In addition, SAU hired Ryan Harrell in 2019 as a full-time data analyst for Enrollment Management. Frood and Harrell partnered to find a solution to provide Chairs and Deans with the information needed to

(Continued)

understand revenue attribution at the university. In June 2019, Frood and Harrell attended an Academic Impressions conference session focused on Academic Cost Models to learn more about structuring their revenue attribution report. Harrel was so inspired by what he knew that he sketched out the model while still at the conference.

Rapid Insight's products were already in use at Southern Adventist. For example, the school used Construct, Rapid Insight's data preparation tool, to organise and clean data from its many sources. SAU also used Predict, Rapid Insight's predictive modelling tool, for enrolment and retention modelling. Since the tool was already part of SAU's arsenal and worked well for those applications, Harrell considered it a perfect fit for building the new revenue attribution model.

Developing the Report

Harrell's first step was to allocate student income to credit hours and aggregate the information in various ways. The goal was to get the data to a granular format, to the level of individual instructors and students, so as many variables as possible be assessed. Next, Harrell worked with Frood to incorporate cost assessment into the report. Using Construct to connect to their Student Information and Finance systems, they attributed costs to individual instructors and courses. Construct allowed them to calculate cost and revenue in two separate workflows, then merge them into a single complete dataset with the necessary levels of granularity.

The result was a detailed net revenue analysis incorporating over 7,000 lines of data. The report can be used to view revenue by course, department, and degree programs. From there, it can be aggregated to highlight the impact that each program has on *other* programs. For example, the courses a typical student in the Music program takes outside their major might be key to a separate program's revenue generation. In this way, the report allows SAU to see the interactions and influence programs have on one another. The granularity of the report enables Harrell and Frood to drill down into complex factors. It will allow Chairs and Deans to make decisions with a complete understanding of potential ramifications in mind.

Informing a Mission with Data

As a faith-based institution, all decisions at SAU serve a greater mission. Thus, SAU embodies a data-informed (rather than data-driven) approach to decision-making. The data provide valuable information on which to base decisions, but the more significant priority is serving the mission. Ultimately, Harrell notes that this is no different from how a liberal arts school prioritises its literature programs, even if those programs were not its most significant revenue generators.

This is where the model's capacity to cross-reference variables truly pays off. As an example: perhaps the Religious Education program itself may not generate significant revenue on its own. Still, students within it frequently take courses key to support the Psychology department that does contribute to the University's bottomline. That knowledge is critical to making a truly informed decision about the value that students who major in Religious Education bring to the school. Beyond that, the school sees intrinsic value in its Religious Education program, so there are two reasons to ensure that it remains an option for students.

However, perhaps individual line items can be assessed with the analysis to make prudent fiscal decisions. For example, does it make sense for the Music department to have different focuses for piano and organ, or might they be combined? The revenue attribution model is flexible enough to allow for these data-informed but mission-driven decisions.

The Advantages of an In-house Analytic Model

Frood notes that the cost savings attributed to the approach they took are substantial. "There are outside consulting firms that could do this, but they cost 40 to 50,000 dollars, and we would have had to clean the data for them anyways." Beyond the strict cost savings, the real value of an in-house solution is in what they've learned through the process of working so extensively with their data. They're able to see connections and relationships in their data that would not have been apparent had they outsourced the project. This prompts questions Frood and Harrell may not have known to ask had they worked with a consultant to investigate a narrow range of specific inquiries.

"Consultants can never understand your institution as well as you do yourself," said Harrell.

> Their models may be effective, but they won't be as precise to the institution as a model you build yourself. By nature, consultants' models must apply to a wide swath of users and institutions. Our model is tailored to our specific needs.

Harrell and Frood note that the increased accessibility of their data created a culture shift at SAU. The level of data access increased exponentially over the past few years. Rapid Insight developed templates and analyses that allowed a data-informed methodology for decision-making to spread in finance and enrolment management departments. As a result, SAU now works with data comprehensively and robustly, rather than only consulting data to answer individual questions.

(Continued)

Looking to the Future

In the future, Harrell and Frood plan to share dashboards with the Chairs of multiple departments to help them rapidly make decisions based on up-to-date data. The academic cost model will also be improved as time goes on to serve the Chairs and Deans who use it.

Source: Rapid Insight case studies, a data analytics company: *Southern Adventist University Creates Advanced Revenue Attribution Report Using Rapid Insight,* https://www.rapidinsight.com/why-rapid-insight/case-studies/southern-adventist-university-creates-advanced-revenue-attribution-report-using-rapid-insight/. Used by permission from Rapid Insight.

The Value of Big Data and Data Analytics in Evaluating Physical Space Usage

Maintaining a physical space costs universities money as institutions must consider classrooms, energy consumption, security, water usage, and other resources required to operate. However, HE institutions can employ Big Data and data analytics to optimise the efficient use of every square inch of the campus. It does so in two ways:

1 **Tracking Resources** – Data analytics helps administrators track where students are at specific times of the day and days of the week. As a result, resources can be restricted or scaled back during low seasons and increased to match demand during peaks. It also helps with planning activities around students' preferences, which could also help increase enrolment.
2 **Section Fill Rates** – It helps to answer the following questions:
   a Which sections of courses are frequently cancelled?
   b What time of the day or weekdays do students prefer for periods?
   c How many sections of a class has a long waitlist?
   d Which modality is most popular with certain age groups?

These questions allow users to dive deeper into the data, thus opening up more possibilities to save additional resources.

Key Term

Graduation Rate; Retention Rate; Enrolment Analytics; Advisement; Academic Analytics; Institutional Analytics; Recruitment Analytics; Learning Analytics; Academic Analytics

Chapter Key Takeaways

- This chapter discusses using data analytics and predictive modelling to improve enrolment, retention, graduation rate, supporting students, and the institution's financial viability.
- Higher education is any schooling beyond high school that may lead to a bachelor's degree or higher. There are different kinds of institutions that offer higher education.
- By building a data-driven recruitment model with various access and contact points such as student demographic, location, ethnicity, expected concentration, and other data, colleges and universities can better target their recruitment process using predictive analytics.
- Even though some colleges have successfully recruited students, most cannot retain these students until graduation. As a result, the retention rate, defined as students who return for sophomore year, is very low in most colleges and universities.
- Data analytics will help the university improve its admission process, enrolment management system, retention rate, advisement, learning, and student needs.
- Big Data and data analytics will also help the university improve its operational efficiencies, financial bottomline, and address the changing global, employer, and other stakeholder demands imposed on universities to produce the best students at the lowest cost.
- Predictive analytics moves colleges away from a "best guest" outcome to a more precise targeted recruitment process.
- Predicting enrolment accurately enhances the university's operational efficiency and survival. Conversely, over-enrolment can lead to stress on the university's facilities, and under-enrolment can lead to financial strains.

Discussion Questions

1 Do you support the concept that education is a human right? If so, explain why everyone must be educated. If not, please explain your reasons.
2 Explain some of the challenges faced by HE institutions?
3 What impact COVID-19 has had on the education industry? Do you think these changes will be temporary and are they for the better?
4 Discuss the growth of HE on a global scale. What are some of the reasons for this development?
5 What are the internal challenges higher education faces? Please explain.
6 What do you think are the external factors higher education faces?
7 Explain what recruitment analytics is.
8 What do you think should be included in admission analytics?
9 What is the value of enrolment analytics to a college or university?

10 Do you think retention rate is a good measure of the quality of an institution?

11 What is performance-based funding? Is it a fair system?

12 Explain what donor and alumni analytics is.

13 Does learning analytics help students or the college and university?

14 What is the four-step analytics process to look at for higher education operational efficiency? Please explain each of them.

References

1 Weisbrod, B.A., Ballou, J.P., & Asch, E.D. (2008). An introduction to the higher education industry. Asch (Eds.), *Mission and money: Understanding the university*, pp.1–10. Cambridge University Press.

2 The World University Ranking (2021). The impact of coronavirus on higher education, https://www.timeshighereducation.com/hub/keystone-academic-solutions/p/impact-coronavirus-higher-education

3 World Bank (2021). Higher education, https://www.worldbank.org/en/topic/tertiaryeducation

4 College Transition, https://www.collegetransitions.com/dataverse/retention-and-graduation-rates. Also see National Center for Education Statistics, https://nces.ed.gov/fastfacts/index.asp?faq=FFOption5#faqFFOption5

5 Alshehri, Y.M. (2016). Performance-based funding: History, origins, outcomes, and obstacles. *Journal of Higher Education Theory & Practice, 16*(4), 33–42.

6 Daniel, B. (2015). Big data and analytics in higher education: Opportunities and challenges. *British Journal of Educational Technology, 46*(5), 904–920.

Index

Note: **Bold** page numbers refer to tables and *italic* page numbers refer to figures.